THE DAY BEFORE YESTERDAY

RECONSIDERING AMERICA'S PAST,
REDISCOVERING THE PRESENT

MICHAEL ELLIOT

Simon & Schuster

SIMON & SCHUSTER
Rockefeller Center
1230 Avenue of the Americas
New York, NY 10020

Copyright © 1996 by Michael Elliott
All rights reserved, including the right of reproduction
in whole or in part in any form.

Simon & Schuster and colophon are registered trademarks
of Simon & Schuster Inc.

Designed by Jeanette Olender
Manufactured in the United States of America

1   3   5   7   9   10   8   6   4   2

Library of Congress Cataloging-in-Publication Data
Elliott, Michael.
The day before yesterday: reconsidering America's past,
rediscovering the present/Michael Elliott.
p. cm.   (hc: alk. paper)
1. United States—History—1945–
2. United States—Civilization—1945–
I. Title.
E839.4.E45 1996 973.92—dc20
96-12090 CIP
ISBN 0-684-80991-5

ACKNOWLEDGMENTS

This book would not have appeared without the help of many people. My principal debt is to my wife, Emma Oxford. She was a researcher, a reader of countless drafts, and an honest critic. But she was far more than that. Books put a terrible strain on the writer's family. Emma tolerated my frequent absence from outings, put up with endless weekends wrecked by work, and generally kept my spirits up. For better or worse, there wouldn't have been a book (or much else that I manage to do) without her.

My second debt is just as easy to identify. From 1986 to 1993, Rupert Pennant-Rea was editor of *The Economist*—a period in which a fine magazine became one of the world's great publications. Working for him was a constant delight. He twice sent me to cover America for the paper, never accepted anything but the best, and allowed me astonishing freedom to wander around the country writing whatever took my fancy. And in 1993, he gave me three months' sabbatical to start work on the book. I cannot thank him enough.

In October 1991, I wrote a long "survey" for *The Economist* called "The Old Country." Although this book differs more than I had originally anticipated from that piece, and although since 1991 I have changed my ideas more than I expected, that survey remains the template for the book—the central idea of both is the same, and attentive readers of both will find plenty of common ground. I owe a debt to ex-colleagues at *The Economist* who helped with both the survey and the book: to Anthony Gottlieb, who edited the survey, and to John Grimond, Matt Ridley, and Ann Wroe, who were my London-based editors during my time in Washington. My colleagues in the Washington office, especially John Peet and Dominic Ziegler, were a constant source of ideas and fun, and I learned much in many discussions of economics with Clive Crook, now *The Economist*'s deputy editor. *The Economist*'s American friends were always hospitable and helpful: special thanks go to Tom Fiedler, Larry Mosher, Ferrel Guillory, Dan Gillmor, and Greg Bailey. Two ex-colleagues deserve a particular mention. Avril Riddell kept me almost organized (no easy task) for years. John Heilemann, now of *Wired* magazine and *The New Yorker*, read every word of the survey and most of the book, and engaged in line-by-line combat with me for hours and hours, to my great benefit. This is not the first book on modern America that he has improved; it's time he wrote his own.

On leaving *The Economist* in 1993, I was lucky enough to join another team of outstanding writers and editors at *Newsweek*. My thanks go to Joe Klein, whose idea the move to *Newsweek* was, and with whom I have discussed this book in late-night sessions everywhere from Manchester, New Hampshire, to Moscow. Thanks also to Maynard Parker, *Newsweek*'s editor, who got me on board and gave me some time off to finish the book; to Mark Whitaker, Nancy Cooper, and Ken Auchincloss, who have been my main editors at *Newsweek*; and to Evan Thomas, who has made *Newsweek*'s Washington bureau such a happy and productive place to work. My colleague Martha Brant gave me some unpublished reporting of hers, and David Gordon proofread and fact-checked the final version with consummate skill.

Other journalists offered up their brains to be picked, sometimes without knowing that they were doing so. In fact, so many did that this is bound to be a partial list—apologies to those I have inadvertently left off. Thanks, then, to Lionel Barber, Michael Barone, Alex Beam, Ron Brownstein, E. J. Dionne, Tom Edsall, Charles Eisendrath, Dan Goodgame, Mickey Kaus, Joel Kotkin, Sergio Munoz, Jonathan Rauch, Julia Reed (who put me straight on anything to do with the South), Neal Shine, Martin Walker, David Warsh (who told me where to find good economic historians), and Curtis Wilkie. To everyone of my generation in journalism, the work of Michael Kinsley is the standard against which we measure ourselves; he, too, has been a fount of ideas, as well as an unfailing friend.

This book is not an academic tome and does not pretend to be. But I was an academic long before I was a journalist, and I know that, in an enterprise like this, inky-fingered scribblers sit on giants' shoulders. I should like to thank (this is a partial list, too) Carl Abbott, David Ayon, Alan Brinkley, Robert Crandall, Rodolfo de la Garza, William Ferris, Todd Gitlin, the late Howard Higman, Christopher Jencks, Dale Jorgenson, John Kasarda (whose demographic data were truly invaluable), Clark Kerr, Steven McLaughlin, Michael Mandelbaum, Charles Moskos, Charles Murray, the brothers Dan and Nelson Polsby, John Reed, Robert Reich, Freya Sonenstein, Ben Wattenberg, and William Julius Wilson, all of whom I consulted on one matter or another. David Hale was the source of many of the book's economic themes, which I often discussed with Norman Robertson. To all of them, apologies if the subtlety of their ideas has been lost in the translation.

Some friends fall into a special category—those who suffered the company of both me and the book during what were meant to be vacations. For their forbearance, thanks to Lionel Barber (again) and Victoria Greenwood, Wendell and Carlotta Willkie, Pamela Davis and Gary Schpero (who proofread the galleys), and Dick and Pamela Sauber. A special thanks to David and Gail Ifshin.

My agent, Rafe Sagalyn, was wonderfully patient and supportive. In very large measure, the book was his idea, and he read successive drafts with an attentive eye for what worked. At Simon & Schuster, Alice Mayhew edited what was a sprawling manuscript (at one time twice the size of the finished product) with her customary boldness and sure touch. Her associate, Elizabeth Stein, is (as many others have said) simply a joy to work with. Fred Chase copyedited the book smoothly. Mac Nachlas helped me out with computer problems.

I'm sorry that two mentors of mine did not live to see the book. Robert Childres was a colleague at Northwestern University more than twenty years ago. He was a brilliant lawyer and teacher, and the first man ever to get me thinking about what made America tick; he died tragically young. Peter Goldman was one of the great (but unsung) Britons of the post-1945 generation. The best lunch partner in London, in 1986 he persuaded me, over a meal at Tante Claire, to go to Washington for *The Economist* when I was tempted to do something else. He paid for the lunch; I like to think he never regretted it.

Finally, there are my two beautiful daughters. For all the times when I should have been with them but wasn't, for all the joy and pride that they have given me, and because my work has been about their country (though the elder one, proudly British-born, has something to say about that), this book is dedicated to them, with love.

Bethesda, Maryland, 1996

For Roxana and Gina

CONTENTS

Prologue

In August 1974, a few days after Richard Nixon had resigned as president, I left Britain to take up a post at Northwestern University School of Law, in Chicago. In those
days the only way you could fly cheaply from Europe to
America was on a "charter flight." You had to pretend that
you were a member of a student club, or attending a tulip
growers' convention: something of that sort. That summer,
for some reason now long forgotten, the cheapest charters
were from Paris, not London. So on an August evening I
lugged my suitcase onto the boat-train at Victoria Station,
took a night ferry from Dover, watched the white cliffs
grow ghostly in the moonlight, and duly made my way to
Orly airport.

There we were told that the flight was to leave twelve
hours late. This was commonplace for charters (perhaps it
still is), but for me it was little short of calamitous. Instead of
arriving in Kennedy Airport at two o'clock in the afternoon,
to be met (I hoped) by an American friend, I would arrive at
two in the morning. Transatlantic calls were way beyond my

budget. I had no idea what to do when I got to New York, and remember feeling, as it were, lost in advance.

Eight hours after takeoff (we had refueled at Shannon Airport in Ireland—another of those details of international travel now long lost) we flew over what I was told was Cape Cod. And then it was Long Island, with lights showing that the streets were laid out at right angles. A surprise: European streets appear from the air to wander aimlessly.

On arrival at JFK I was out of my depth: I had only flown a handful of times, so had little idea of how to handle big airports. Sensing my unease, a student who had been on the flight approached me. He had just spent his junior college year in Paris, and invited me home for the night. It was now three o'clock in the morning; a friend had come to meet him, and so we piled into the car and headed off into the Long Island darkness.

I had no idea where we were going, but half an hour later we arrived at a big house: at least, it looked big to me. My new friend's mother welcomed her unexpected guest, and showed me to a spare room. I woke about five hours later, and, following the sound of chatter, walked downstairs, through a kitchen, and out onto a patio where the family were having breakfast. I gulped; and I mean, literally, I gulped.

Anyone who grew up in Europe would know why. Though Europe—Britain especially—has weather of seeming infinite variety, there are limits. Europe doesn't have the hot, still day dripping with humidity; even on the Mediterranean coast, heat is moderated by dryness or sea breezes. But this was mid-August, and this was Long Island, and that was how it was. And so I stood on the patio, and, looking over the heads of my hosts, saw a long, perfect lawn swoop down to a pool, and then to a dock, beyond which, shimmering in a heat haze,

I could make out a blue-gray expanse of water: Long Island Sound.

We were in Great Neck. I knew about Great Neck. I knew *The Great Gatsby* almost by heart, and I knew that I was now—as Fitzgerald put it—on a "fresh, green breast of the world," looking at "the most domesticated body of saltwater in the western hemisphere." The house was owned by a liberal, Jewish labor lawyer from New York. I sat down and was offered breakfast. I hate breakfasts, and mumble through them to the discomfort of anyone sharing a table with me. This was the only one in my life whose details I can remember: and I can, like it happened yesterday.

Coffee of a freshness and flavor unlike anything I had ever known was poured from huge pots. Orange juice came in massive jugs. This was new to me. In Britain, in 1974, frozen orange juice was a rare luxury; it came in cans not much bigger than a roll of quarters. I was shown how to eat lox and bagels; I knew about cream cheese, just about, but I didn't know you ate it with fish. Scrambled eggs, sausages: the food and the drink kept coming as if someone had tipped a giant horn of plenty in my lap.

Later, in the kitchen, I marveled not just at the gadgetry, but at the sheer, numbing size of everything. Refrigerators big enough to stand in; dishwashers, a television (in the kitchen!). There seemed to be telephones everywhere; at Oxford, I had friends whose families didn't have phones at all. I had to find a flight to Chicago: a choice of three or four airlines flew there. Very confusing.

For years, the house in Great Neck epitomized for me two things. The first was America's generosity of spirit. My hosts displayed a neighborliness toward me, despite the fact that I was not a neighbor at all. Nothing I have experienced in the intervening years has led me to believe that this instinct to be a "good neighbor" has atrophied in America; neighborliness remains one of the cornerstones upon which the American dream will be rebuilt.

Second, the house symbolized what it meant to be "modern." Everything in it was new, or seemed so. Everything was light; there was no stained brown furniture, no heavy curtains. Everything was big. A day later, in Chicago, the sense of wonderment continued. Most Americans grow up blasé about skyscrapers. But in Chicago the Sears Tower and the John Hancock Building were newly finished: as I drove in from O'Hare they loomed on the hazy skyline like fat giraffes.

Yet *my* sense of American modernity, I was later to find out, was a function of time and place; others would not experience it to the same extent. By the 1990s, Alan Riding once wrote in the *New York Times*, Italians were saying *"America è qui"*—as if the modernity for which they had once crossed an ocean was freely available in Milan or Turin. Indeed, some foreigners came to think that America was mired in ways that were "premodern"—for example, an attachment to capital punishment, almost unknown in modern Europe.

I came to realize that in a few pieces I had written, more or less by accident, I had been nibbling at something whose flavor I could not fully taste. I had arrived in America just at the end of a remarkable period. Between 1945 and the early 1970s, America enjoyed an unparalleled period of power and prosperity. When the war in Europe started in 1939, America was struggling, battered and bruised, from an economic recession that was far deeper and more wounding than anything known in Europe; its armed forces, small and ill-equipped, were capable only of a few police actions in the Caribbean. At the end of World War II, by contrast, America bestrode the narrow world like a colossus. Its military machine, enjoying scientific and technological advances far beyond those available to any other fighting men, had won two wars, each a wide ocean away from home.

On the twin rocks of its economic and military might, America then built a society which was the envy of the world—a society in which ordinary working people could enjoy a standard of living, with spacious homes and modern appliances, beyond the dreams of those in other nations. The outside world was kept at bay, like children pressing their noses to the panes of a party to which they have not been invited. Immigration was insignificant. America was essentially self-sufficient and scarely bothered with the business of exporting.

This was the America that I saw in 1974, and the America which, then and now, Americans think is the way things should be, the acid test against which everything should be measured. But this is an illusion. The America of the postwar years was a freak. It took its ineffable shape only because of a conjunction of circumstances which combined to form a society whose strength, inside and outside its borders, had not been seen anywhere in modern times. Postwar America was unique not only by comparison with every other nation at the time, but by comparison with every other period of America's past. The sort of life I saw at Great Neck was a shock not just to foreigners like me, but (if they dared to admit it) to the American grandparents of my friends. Those older Americans had lived in a country far less economically secure, far more messy and unstable. The older America did not speak only English; it was lapped by successive waves of immigrants; it did not have a monopoly of either military power or modernity.

For there's the rub: the Golden Age after 1945 ended. The period of American prosperity took shape in the shadow of World War II, in which the United States led the forces arrayed against ineffable evil. Later, there would come other wars; one in Korea, which was unpopular, and then one in Vietnam, which was catastrophic, and which for many Americans marked the end of the Golden Age. Twenty years after arriving in Chicago, I realized that there were some who had seen this at the time—as I had not. One night in 1994, I was listening to Bob Dylan's album *Blood on the Tracks*, recorded twenty years earlier, and which had once been a backing track for the time, long distant, when I had taught law by day and acted in theaters on the North Side by night. Listlessly, I started reading Pete Hamill's liner notes to the record, a cry of pain for what Vietnam had done to his country. "In the end, the plague touched us all," wrote Hamill. "It was not confined to the Oran of Camus. No. It turned up again in America, breeding in a compost of greed and uselessness and murder, in those places where statesmen and generals stash the bodies of the forever young. The plague ran in the blood of men in sharkskin suits, who ran for President promising life and delivering death. . . . And here at home, something died. The bacillus moved among us, slaying that old America where the immigrants lit a million dreams in the shadow of the bridges, killing the great brawling country of barnstormers and wobblies and home-run hitters, the place of Betty Grable and Carl Furillo and heavyweight champions of the world. . . . Poor America. Tossed on a pilgrim tide. Land where the poets died."

Something of Hamill's pain is with us still; a sense of loss, a sullen misery at our state that can turn murderous. My aim is not to anatomize that loss, but to make a rather different point. I argue that at the end of the Golden Age, America more resembled older patterns of itself. The Golden Age has had a complex effect on modern America. Many of its achievements were real and concrete. At the same time, the period after 1945 has become the great, defining American myth, as if it determined what we must aspire to be. In the years that have followed the Golden Age, this has placed unbearable demands on Americans great or small, leaders or followers. The strength of the memory of the Golden Age has made it painfully difficult for Americans to get an adequate fix on the times in which they now live.

This book attempts to explain how the Golden Age came about and how it ended, and asks Americans to understand that while today's nation has its problems, it is further (and needlessly) troubled by comparison with the years after 1945. We cannot, or at least should not, blame ourselves for the impermanence of a Golden Age. We have to get over it; to define our present condition, with all its difficulties, in its own terms, not those of a generation ago. That is what this book tries to do. It should be plain that a work this size cannot pretend to be a history of post-1945 America, were such a task possible. It is, rather, a series of linked, thematic essays, in which I explore postwar America, its roots, and how it ended. Only if we do that, I think, can we start to understand a curious, salient fact of the life of modern Americans. They are miserable.

CHAPTER ONE

Why Americans Whine

Americans whine. They live in the most prosperous society that the world has ever seen. They have a greater level of creature comfort than any nation has ever known before. They enjoy great personal freedom, and their government is systematically constrained in the ways in which it can intervene in their private lives. And yet they are convinced that their life is miserable. More than 60 percent of Americans routinely tell pollsters that their country is "on the wrong track." A whole new academic sub-discipline—the anatomy of American decline—has come into being. A best-seller of the early 1990s had the simple and arresting title *America: What Went Wrong?*

This national "funk"—as, in an unguarded moment, Bill Clinton once called it—has many manifestations. Sometimes, it is said that members of the thirteenth generation since independence will be the first unable to anticipate a life better than that of their parents. Sometimes it is said that the economy has been overtaken by those of other nations. In the 1992 presidential election, more than 60 percent of votes were won by two candidates—Bill Clinton and Ross Perot—who campaigned on the premise that America was in deep, deep trouble. Both men looked back to a small-town America, secure, prosperous, cohesive, whose values had died. Clinton—the man from Hope, Arkansas—made a soft-focus film full of misty stills of his happily named birthplace; Perot, from Texarkana, Texas, forty miles away, spun happy tales of his days as Boy Scout and newspaper delivery boy. From both men, there was the sense that something had been lost, as if Americans had let a great treasure dribble through their fingers.

At first blush, this mood of national angst is hard to fathom. America is far and away the largest and richest economy on the earth. It is one of the great "supernations"—those which cover a great landmass. But of this small group, India and China are too crowded for comfort; Russia and Canada are too cold, Australia too hot, Brazil too covered by jungle. And at least some of these other great nations are too divided between rich and poor in a way that Americans, with a quiet commitment to equality, have long dreaded. The United States is the only great nation blessed with a uniformly benign climate; there isn't a single state in the lower forty-eight where it is anything but easy to grow that staple of civilization, the humble potato. America is blissfully empty. Fly from Chicago to San Francisco, and great spaces of unpeopled land stretch out below—emptinesses of a kind that are simply unknown elsewhere in the developed world. In the Rocky Mountain states, at the end of a tumultuous period of population growth, a little more than 20 million people live on a slice of land about the size of Western Europe—more than 300 million Europeans are packed into the same space. In most of the key technologies of tomorrow—computing, telecommunications, advanced materials—American firms are world-beaters. In a growth industry like entertainment, American products are so dominant that there is a genuine risk of backlash against Yankee neocolonialism.

Almost alone among all the developed nations, the United States is insulated by two great oceans from the world's trouble spots. Squashed between a benign Canada to the north and a historically backward Mexico to the south, it has avoided any invasion of its mainland by a foreign power for nearly two centuries. And were some power foolish enough to try, it would find that the United States could swat away its efforts like an irritating fly. True, one other country—Russia—has enough nuclear weapons to threaten anyone it chooses. But only America has a monopoly of the really useful hardware: the spy satellites that can peek into the bedrooms of dictators thousands of miles away, the huge airplanes and ships that can project power to the far side of the world, the technological base which gives humble GIs the kind of equipment recently the staple of science fiction. In all the ways that count, Americans are, as the sociologist David Potter wrote in 1954, a "people of plenty." So what makes them so miserable?

It isn't simply that there is much about their country that is indeed depressing. More to the point, Americans have lost the ability to accurately assess their present condition. They constantly compare America to a world that we have lost. A billboard once seen on the road from the airport into Tulsa, Oklahoma, captures the mood of America in the 1990s. "Tulsa," read the sign. "America the way you remember it." That sad little phrase holds the key to understanding why America is an unhappy place. It isn't simply that the nation has problems: it is that Americans compare their present lot to another time—to a Golden Age that followed World War II. But that period of America's history was a massive freak. It is a false yardstick with which to measure the scale of our present discontent. Our obsession with those years is like the ultimately hopeless task of trying to recapture a dreamtime. We will only be able to view life today with clear eyes if we can reconnect with an America that predates the years after 1945.

When Americans assume that the years after World War II were "normal," any deviation from them is rendered somehow peculiar. But there was nothing normal about the world that America inherited in 1945. It was a world in ruins. It was only "normal" if "normality" means a state where every country except America is knee-deep in rubble. Alone among the belligerents of World War II, America avoided the physical devastation which shattered every other nation. No Stalingrad, no Caen, no Coventry; no Monte Cassino, no Dresden, no Hiroshima. War turned the world upside down. Britain and France, Japan and Germany, were not preordained by some celestial master plan to be in ruins, tired and hungry, empty of ideas—but in 1946, that was how they were. At the war's end, America accounted for more than 40 percent of the world's output, a higher proportion than one nation had ever had before. And so it was very largely America, not its allies, that remade Germany and Japan, and America that protected them and the older democracies from external threat.

In the years that followed victory, American society was more cohesive than it had ever been before. An external threat from Soviet communism provided an important unifying force. The population was spread more evenly across the whole continent, yet at the same time increasingly concentrated in suburbs whose essential characteristics were the same from coast to coast. The vagaries of climate were smoothed over by air-conditioning. There was little immigration to threaten a stable ethnic mix. In the South, blacks led a peaceful revolution which ameliorated the most bitter divisions between the races. Legally protected racial discrimination was ended. The period was the heyday of the nuclear family, when a husband could earn enough to support a household, a wife could afford to stay at home and raise a few kids, and when divorce was still stigmatized and—at least by comparison with what came later—quite rare. For a quarter of a century, economic growth kept this America broadly content, and broadly happy. It was indeed a Golden Age.

One way to capture just how golden were the years after World War II is to play a little thought experiment. Think what one word—"Detroit"—meant in 1945, and what it represents fifty years later. In the 1940s, Detroit was at the center of the greatest concentration of applied science and technology that the world had ever seen. The crown jewel of that brilliance was a bomber plant built by the Ford Motor Company at Willow Run, twenty-seven miles from Detroit along a new expressway which ran westward from the city across the bumpy glaciated land that envelops the Great Lakes. The plant was almost on the edge of the town of Ann Arbor, home of the University of Michigan. Ground was broken in April 1941, and the enormous factory, more than a mile long, was finished by June 1942.

In its first year of operation Willow Run was beset by difficulties. Though many of its workers were local, demand for wartime labor in Michigan was so great that thousands more had to be recruited in the South and Appalachia; locals still sometimes refer to Ypsilanti, the closest town, as "Ypsitucky." Some of the hillbillies couldn't adapt to assembly line work;

others, housed in spartan conditions in a makeshift village built on the edge of the plant, gambled, drank, and whored their time away. Mosquitoes swarmed through the works until Ford imported a bug-eating fish which Mussolini had found useful in the Pontine marshes of Italy. Slowly the kinks were ironed out; by the summer of 1943, at its peak, Willow Run was employing 42,000 people; by 1944 those workers were turning out a B-24 an hour. By the time production ceased in 1945, when a bomber rolled off the line each fifty-five minutes, Willow Run had become an authentic American success. All told, it produced nearly 9,000 B-24s.

Willow Run demonstrated the enormous innate strength of the American economy, a strength submerged during the Great Depression. The plant was just the most visible manifestation of a wartime transformation of Michigan's automotive industry—a transformation which saved the world, as Detroit and its environs became the arsenal of democracy. In 1942 General Motors took just two months to turn its Cadillac assembly line into one that turned out tanks. According to one estimate, by the end of the war, two-thirds of GM's output consisted of products it had never made before, from bazookas to ID bracelets. The University of Michigan played its part, too. Ann Arbor's researchers worked on scores of government contracts; the labs hummed with work on advanced materials, on homing devices that shot down kamikaze airplanes, and a system for targeting bomb sites. In fact, when the war was done, GIs from Michigan returned from Europe to tell their families that the Germans had never heard of Ypsilanti—but they knew all about Willow Run and its bombers. According to local folklore, when Stalin met Franklin Roosevelt at the Teheran conference in 1943, the Soviet leader told the American president that Germany was being buried in Detroit's steel. He had good reason to think so; many of the engines in the Red Army's tanks were made in Michigan.

Local people were intensely proud of the region's accomplishments. In 1946, Malcolm W. Bingay, a veteran editor of the *Detroit Free Press*, wrote that "For years Detroit has been the talk of the world. European writers on our civilization have even coined the term 'Detroitism,' meaning the industrial age. From all parts of the globe, men have come to our doors to gain knowledge and inspiration. Detroit has been hailed as Detroit the Dynamic; Detroit the Wonder City." And the hyperbole was justified. A European visiting Michigan in 1945 would have stood amazed. In Europe, for example, university education had always been reserved for an elite; no European country had anything like a system of "mass" higher education. But in 1948, after servicemen had cashed in their right to higher education under the GI Bill, the University of Michigan had no fewer than 21,000 students. One university, in one medium-sized state, had an enrollment equal to a fifth of the total number of students at every university in France. And a European visitor might have noticed the cars on the Willow Run Expressway itself—and who was in them. When Willow Run was planned it was assumed that new bus lines from Detroit to the plant would be needed; it was wartime, and both tires and gasoline were rationed. But the Detroit Street Railways Company soon realized that the buses were uneconomical. A newspaper report in 1945 said they never carried "even a sizeable fraction" of Willow Run's workers, because the workers were prosperous enough to use their own cars. In the mid-1940s there was nowhere in Europe where this would have been conceivable.

All this—the energy, the marriage of a university's brain

27

with a car company's brawn, the prosperity, the self-confidence—was what "Detroit" meant in 1945. The next year, Malcolm Bingay ended his memoirs by saying, "What the Detroit of fifty years from now will be we do not know. But one thing is certain: it will be dynamic. It is a destiny we cannot escape."

Fifty years later, the condition of his hometown would break Bingay's heart. By 1995, "Detroit" meant something quite different. In the intervening years, the car industry's workers and management alike got fat, happy, and lazy, thinking that they could keep their markets until doomsday, unwilling to invest in the sort of models and production processes that rivals made their own. Race relations, never great, soured in the 1960s. After the awful riots of 1967, white flight to the suburbs left a hollowed-out core of a city, bereft of the middle-class incomes that would sustain and grow its white-collar employment. Suburban—and white—Detroit perhaps was less willing to accept that its fate was bound to a majority-black inner city than other places (though only to a degree). As jobs left the city, so a range of pathologies gripped those who were left there, trapped in a declining economy—drugs, crime, out-of-wedlock births.

And so decline took root. In 1950, Detroit had nearly 2 million people. In 1995 it had barely 1 million; but though the population has halved in forty years, the number of murders has increased sixfold. In 1995 there were 475 homicides in Detroit. A city's "crumbling infrastructure" has become one of the journalistic clichés of the age; but the concrete of Detroit deserves the adjective. A drive along one of the city's bumpy, wide boulevards—dodging the whores who stand in the streets at all hours, in all weathers—is like negotiating a minefield. Off the main roads, fine nineteenth-century homes, now worthless, are boarded up, half-burned (on the night before Halloween each year, fires are set all over town). In the summer the inner-city housing reeks of decay and urine; in the winter damp the city almost visibly, drippingly, corrodes. American writers like to say that the frontier between San Diego, California, and Tijuana, Mexico, is a unique meeting place between wealth and poverty, between the developed and the developing world. That is too hard on Tijuana. For mindboggling contrasts in the quality of life, the Mexican-American border is rivaled by the line that separates the horror of Detroit from a suburb like Grosse Pointe, with its faux châteaus and its country clubs.

Willow Run provides, in microcosm, a sense of how far the economy of Detroit has fallen. When bomber production ceased there, the plant was sold to Henry Kaiser, who had made a fortune from the war and wanted to rival the Big Three auto manufacturers. In 1947 Kaiser-Frazer employed 15,000 at Willow Run, but by 1953 just 3,000 remained. That year the site was sold to General Motors, which used the old plant (and still does) to build transmissions. Later, GM built a car assembly line next to the transmission plant, and at various times Ypsilanti township gave GM tax breaks of $13.5 million to safeguard local employment. To no avail; in 1993 GM closed the assembly line and shipped the few remaining jobs to Texas. The Big Three car companies have shed scores of thousands of workers from their Detroit plants. By the early 1990s, the companies had become national jokes. In a moment of horrible aptness in January 1992, George Bush took Detroit executives with him to Japan—the land that in 1945 was shattered and hungry. The trip was laced with dread symbolism; the president collapsed at an official dinner. The friends from Detroit who surrounded him

later looked like patients in a nursing home where the termi-
nally ill drag the merely infirm down to their level. When
people ask of America "What went wrong?" a decent answer
is: Detroit did.

All of this is familiar, depressingly so. What is perhaps less
familiar—at least, less often remarked—is the psychological
damage that was wrought by the recent memory of Detroit
as a "wonder city." In all truth, it is hardly surprising that
those who live there—and who have a memory of the way
the city had once been—should conclude that America is on
the wrong track.

In short, in Detroit, and countless other places, the Golden
Age is over. In fact, it has been over a long time, and it is a
testament to the wonders of the Golden Age that it should
continue to hold such powerful sway over the American
imagination. America is the way that it has often been before. It is a messy, fragmented society, ragged at the edges. It
has serious cleavages within its midst, between races and ethnic groups, between social classes. But it has, at the same time
(and as it has always had), enormous cultural and economic
dynamism, together with a confidence in the future that enables it to transcend the temporary and partial difficulties
that it faces. At least, America *would* have such confidence if
it could get honest with itself. Americans have always been
tempted by exceptionalism; they have always wanted to see
themselves as the blessed inhabitants of a city on a hill,
uniquely deserving of the beneficence of Providence. But for
most of their history, Americans have tempered that sense of
God-given greatness with a healthy dose of pragmatism.
When faced with problems they have rolled up their sleeves
and gotten to work. Immigration, for example, has often
been unpopular in the United States; yet successive waves of

immigrants have eventually been healthily assimilated into American society. Class divisions have, in the past, been much sharper than they are today; racial animosity much more vitriolic than we can imagine. Yet at least since the Civil War, Americans have been able to transcend those divisions and build a society which offers a pretty good life to all. But we have lost touch with that past. An older America has been obscured by the sheer brilliance of the postwar years; understanding it is like trying to make out the shape of a distant shore through the haze of bright sunshine.

Outside fairy tales, Golden Ages always end; they are rarely repeated. But for the men and women who now run America—children or young adults when the nation was at its zenith—the memories of the years after 1945 are extraordinarily powerful. Their brilliance makes it all but impossible to find a realistic assessment of the current strengths of America and its future potential. Those years after World War II were indeed spectacular; but we fall into a fatal error if we elevate them into a corrosive national myth. We need to know the precise and unrepeatable conjunction of events that made the Golden Age golden. But we also need to look at what preceded the Golden Age. If we do that, we may understand both what led to the prosperity of the years after 1945 and—no less important—what we have to do now. We need to rediscover the America of the day before yesterday.

CHAPTER TWO

The Way We Once Were: America Before the Golden Age

What made America? What motivated those who settled on the forests and plains of the newfound continent? How do the traces of an old America make their presence felt today?

There are two things we know. We know that from almost the first moment that Europeans established their beachhead on American shores, they have staggered visitors with their energy and their self-confidence. And we know that America has rarely been a rational, ordered society, where every man knew his place. On the contrary, it has been a society riven by deep ethnic and cultural conflicts, one of which exploded into the first truly "modern" war—a civil war in which whole populations mobilized, and in which the level of casualties prefigured the charnelhouses of our own century. America's population has never been stable; rather, it has restlessly re-settled itself across a great landmass, and been periodically replenished by great waves of immigrants from the far side of the world. America isn't neat.

In other words, the muscular bravura of America in 1945 had deep roots in a society which, since its founding, had been both aspirational and entrepreneurial. Americans wanted to "better themselves"; they cleared forests, planted crops, started print shops and small factories. Take, as but one example, a small town in Kansas, almost dead on the ninety-ninth meridian. Settled in 1873 by a bunch of ne'er-do-well young Englishmen who wanted to hunt foxes among the cottonwoods (and who predictably named their town Victoria), it was saved by a hardier bunch entirely. In 1876 Volga Germans arrived from Russia. A square-built, determined lot they must have been, if the statue commemorating them in Victoria is accurate. And they rolled up their sleeves and got to work. Devoutly Roman Catholic, the Volga Germans erected a cross in the center of the village, and then built a simple frame church. When they outgrew that first church, they built another one, this time of stone. When they outgrew that, they built yet another, which could seat 600 people. And in 1908, when only a couple of thousand people lived in Victoria, they started work on their communal masterpiece, the magnificent Romanesque church of St. Fidelis. Granite was brought from Vermont, glass from Germany; Carrara marble was shipped from Italy. Each family had to cut a set amount of stone from local quarries. In just three years the church was finished. It was 220 feet long; its twin towers soared 141 feet above the plain. William Jennings Bryan, the great populist, stopped in the town in 1912 and called the church "The Cathedral of the Plains"; it still deserves the title.

There are thousands of "Victorias" in the United States— so many that we do not notice them. Nor do we notice the corollary; that there are so *few* Victorias in the developed world *outside* the United States—communities which, almost within living memory, have created themselves from nothing. Here lies a key source of the temptation of exceptionalism; of the sense that Americans are both uniquely blessed and uniquely capable, such that any fall from grace is greeted with cries of woe as if the world had ended. From John Winthrop to Ronald Reagan, Americans have always had a sense that they were something special. "The greatest single effort of national deliberation that the world has ever seen" was how John Adams, for example, described the Constitutional Convention of 1787; modesty when describing public achievements has never been a conspicuous American characteristic.

But then, Americans have had little to be modest about. Think, for a moment, of the marriage between brain and brawn which typified Detroit in the 1940s. This did not arrive unbidden from the vasty deep, devoid of precursors. Neither America's passionate commitment to education nor its entrepreneurial drive—nor the combination of the two— was a function purely of the exigencies of World War II. Americans had been founding universities by the score long before 1945. Harvard was founded in 1636, William and Mary in 1693, Yale in 1701. This passion for higher education wasn't limited to a cosmopolitan, developed, Atlantic seaboard. The University of Michigan was chartered in 1817; it had been in Ann Arbor since 1821. By 1940, the campus already had 12,000 students. The land grants that would underpin the finances of state universities originate in ordinances of 1785 and 1787. Once Americans moved west, colleges were founded almost as soon as plow first turned the virgin sod. In eastern Kansas, for example, the Methodist church founded Baker University at Baldwin City in 1858; in 1865, seventeen miles away, the Baptists founded a university in Ottawa; the next year the University of Kansas was opened in Lawrence, fifteen miles north of Baldwin City. Three universities, opened in eight years, within a little more than a day's trip by horse and buggy: yet in 1860 the total population of Kansas was just 107,000. Nowhere else in the world would such a high value be placed on education.

Not just on education for the sake of it—but education for a social and economic purpose. By 1900, the great northern universities, located in industrial centers like New York, Boston, and Philadelphia, were pollinating local commerce with their research. Indeed, for forty years this had been an axiomatic part of their mission. The Massachusetts Institute of Technology, first planned in 1846, was chartered in 1861. The charter dedicates the school to "the advancement, development and application of science," and quite soon after its founding MIT's labs were assisting both Thomas Edison and Alexander Graham Bell. Such developments were not limited to the Northeast. What was later to be the California Institute of Technology was founded in a Los Angeles suburb in 1891; Berkeley, on the edge of industrial Oakland, was chartered in 1868, Stanford in 1891. Even in the South, where the links between education and industry were of less significance than in the North or California, it was understood that universities were a source of local prosperity. Georgia Tech opened its doors in Atlanta in 1888, and one of its early graduates, I. H. Hardeman, was a genuine southern hero—he saw that air-conditioning would be a godsend to the textile industry.

Just as higher education has a long pedigree, so does the energy of the American economy. By 1850, the National Road, financed by the federal government, stretched from east of the Appalachians to Vandalia, Illinois, linking the seaboard to the agricultural heartland. The Erie Canal connected New York to the Great Lakes. There is a famous passage in Tocqueville worth quoting at length: "A stranger is constantly amazed by the immense public works executed by a nation which contains, so to speak, no rich men. The Americans arrived but as yesterday on the territory which they inhabit, and they have already changed the whole order of nature for their advantage. They have joined the Hudson to the Mississippi, and made the Atlantic Ocean communicate with the Gulf of Mexico. . . . The longest railroads which have been constructed, up to the present time, are in America." In short, as early as the 1830s, capitalism in the United States was simply more big-muscled, just more damn thrilling than anywhere else.

By 1851, the year of the Great Exhibition in London, America's industry, science, and technology had shaken the Old World out of any economic complacency. The mechanical reapers with which Cyrus McCormick broke the prairies caused a sensation in London. (The British government set up a committee of inquiry to figure out the sources of their cousins' economic strength.) Mid-nineteenth-century American industry didn't just rely on mass production (an American invention) and the application of unskilled labor. It also had a significant presence in high technology. In the 1850s, firms in Liverpool started ordering ships for the Australian trade not from British shipyards but from those of New England. Donald McKay's yard in Boston turned out clippers—the space shuttles of their time—which could sail more than 400 miles a day. McKay's ship *The Champion of the Seas*, in whose honor Liverpool's children still sang songs a century later, made 465 miles in the southern ocean on December 12, 1854. Europe had nothing to match it.

Sixty years later, on the eve of World War I, America was

the world's largest economy—accounting for a little less than a quarter of world output. According to the economic historian Gavin Wright, the United States led the world in the production of natural gas, petroleum (no less than 65 percent of world output), copper, coal, and silver. It was far and away the world's largest producer of iron ore—the ore-rich hills of the Mesabi Range, deep in the frozen northeast of Minnesota, were the source, beyond any other, of America's industrial might. America lagged behind only South Africa in the production of gold. America did not have a *monopoly* of power—an important point. Germany had an economy as advanced as that of America, with great strengths in high-technology sectors like precision engineering and chemicals. It was Germany and Britain—not the United States—which had the ships and weapons that could project their military power to the far ends of the globe. (Indeed, the American army was small and poorly equipped. With the exception of the Spanish-American War—little more than an extended skirmish—and the colonial wars in the Philippines, the army had spent most of its time since the Civil War involved in police actions against Indians.)

This older America, the America on the cusp of World War I, is worth recalling. For today's America much resembles the country as it then existed. The dislocations and fragmentation, the sheer *messiness* of modern American life, have precursors in an earlier time. If America is to search for models in its past to ease its way into the future it might look to life as it was led at the beginning of the century.

Then, as now, America was a country of immigrants, and then as now, the immigrants came from "new" countries of origin. In 1910, the number of immigrants from Germany was only a third what it had been in 1890, and the number from Ireland little more than a half. But in the twenty years from 1890 to 1910, the annual number of immigrants from Italy more than quadrupled, and from Russia it grew fivefold. In those two decades, for example, the Massachusetts mill town of Lowell, which had seen earlier immigration from French Canada and Ireland, received waves of immigrants first from Poland and other parts of Eastern Europe, and then from much more exotic locations—Syria, Armenia, and elsewhere in the Ottoman Empire. In 1900, 43 percent of Lowell's population was foreign-born.

Through the rosy-hued spectacles of hindsight, the immigrants of the first years of this century look familiar: a bit like Grandma, and not at all like the Mexicans and Southeast Asians who now flock to American towns—Lowell among them. But that was not how it seemed at the time. Nativist sentiment ran rampant. Foreign agitators were blamed for labor unrest. Leon Czolgosz, a Polish anarchist, had shot President McKinley; in the recent past, political violence like the Haymarket incident in Chicago had been laid at the feet of foreigners. During the great 1919 steel strike in the Monongahela Valley of western Pennsylvania, posters urging the workers to return to their jobs had to be printed in eight languages—English, Polish, Croatian, Italian, Lithuanian, Slovak, Hungarian, and Russian. On the poster a stern Uncle Sam (of course) claims that few workers ever left their jobs—"only a few foreign-born—most aliens who allowed themselves to be swayed by the un-American teachings of radical strike agitators. . . . Nothing short of 100% Americanism," bellows Uncle Sam, "can hope to win out in this country." Nor was it just the bosses who took such a dim view of those from abroad. Samuel Gompers of the American Federation of Labor (himself an immigrant from Britain) had opposed literacy tests for immigrants in the 1880s, but later endorsed them, as did most union officers.

Probably two out of every five immigrants at the turn of the century were unskilled and just one out of five skilled (many of the rest were originally farmers). In 1910, more than 65 percent of all laborers in mining and manufacturing were either foreign-born or the children of immigrants. These unskilled workers were welcome in America because there was a shortage of labor. Just the same is true today. From the 1920s to the 1970s, few immigrants arrived in Lowell, and the proportion of foreign-born fell to 9 percent in 1970. But now Lowell is reliving its past. New immigration has changed the face of the town once again: since 1980, more than 25,000 Southeast Asians—most of them Cambodian—have poured into the town, and now make up about a quarter of Lowell's population. By the mid-1990s, Lowell was a sorrily depressed place, and Cambodians have been blamed for taking jobs that belonged to "real" Americans. But the immigrants came to town because its employers couldn't find local labor. During the "Massachusetts Miracle" in the mid-1980s, Lowell's unemployment rate was less than 4 percent (effectively, a labor shortage); only the Cambodians would take the low-paying assembly line jobs that locals didn't want.

Inevitably, given the size of the flows from abroad, the face and sound of America was changed by the great immigration of 1890–1910, just as it is now being changed again. For those who are worried about today's immigration, there's a convenient myth that the earlier incomers became painlessly assimilated into American life, as if they learned to love baseball and apple pie within weeks of landing in New York. Yet the most cursory research on the immigrant experience shows that there was always a tension between assimilation and the maintenance of national identities. Pittsburgh's immigrants played soccer—that European game—into the 1930s. In the words of a recent study of the Monongahela Valley steel towns: "Within walking distance of Jones and Laughlin Steel Works, a Polish woman could find the right ingredients for making kielbasa, golubki, or duck's blood soup; a Hungarian family could attend either the Hungarian Catholic or Hungarian Reformed Church, both with services in their native language; a Slovak worker in Homestead could practice gymnastic routines in the Sokol, or go to a wedding reception at the Russian Hall, with music by a local gypsy band." Now the Shop and Save supermarket in Lowell serves curry paste and fish sauce for its Cambodian clients, who have their own Buddhist temple just outside town.

The earlier immigrants didn't learn their English because—another of today's myths—some saintly teacher in bustled skirts, unencumbered by politically correct diktats on bilingual education, drummed it into them: since only about one in eight of all immigrants was aged under sixteen, the vast majority never saw the inside of a school at all. Instead, they learned to speak English in the factories, within supportive groups of their own people, sometimes from their own villages on the far side of the world. (In fact, earlier immigrants had things much easier than those of today: the factories have gone, and in an economy dominated by the service sector, immigrants' struggles with English are on display for all to hear—in 1994, Lowell did not have a single police officer able to speak Lao or Vietnamese.) Then as now, the currents that sustained ethnic identities were so strong that even those who did not approve of crude nativist sentiment worried that the country was becoming—though nobody used the word—"multicultural." "The one absolutely certain way of bringing this country to ruin," said Teddy Roosevelt, "would be to permit it to become a tangle of squabbling nationalities."

The parallels with an earlier America extend far beyond immigration, with all its tensions. At the beginning of the century, as at its end, the cities were thought to be havens of poverty and degradation. The photographs in Jacob Riis's *How the Other Half Lives*, the novels of Upton Sinclair, suggested alike that horrors lurked in the great metropolises. Those horrors (shades of today's debate on the underclass) were not assumed to be merely economic in nature. Explicitly, the state of the cities was considered to have a moral content, their unhappiness a natural outgrowth of dissipation, ungodliness, and corruption. Old-fashioned Americans deplored the trashiness of Coney Island. Evangelicals made common cause with the matrons of the heartland in fighting the Demon Drink, the curse of the working classes—whose popularity, for that matter, was often blamed, like so much else, on immigrants. "Prohibition," writes the historian Michael Kazin, "was *the* Protestant issue of the day. It had transcendent significance—both because it would cure a social evil and because it satisfied, better than any other isue, the urge to purify American culture." When the Prohibition Amendment was ratified in 1919, the evangelist Billy Sunday made the link between clean living and the state of the cities explicit. "The reign of tears is over," he cried. "The slums will soon be a memory."

At the start of this century, as at its end, class divisions were all too evident—indeed, for all our current troubles, they were far more vicious than they are now. From Paterson to Lawrence, from Gary to San Francisco, strikes erupted with an intensity now almost impossible to imagine. In June 1892, Pinkerton thugs hired by Henry Clay Frick landed at the Carnegie steelworks in Homestead to break a strike. In one day, twenty-four people were killed, all within view of a national press corps housed in a building that still stands between a library, built with Carnegie blood money, and the gray, empty slab of land where the steelworks once belched. In 1911 twenty-one people were killed when the *Los Angeles Times* printing plant was bombed. In 1914, in a day of shame and horror, company goons and National Guardsmen invaded a mining camp at Ludlow, Colorado. Thirteen people, including women and children (many of them immigrants, naturally), were killed in one morning. Between September 1913 and May 1914, no fewer than sixty-six people were killed at Ludlow. And the unrest continued after World War I. Wobblies were rounded up and lynched, while in the radical shipyards of the West Coast there was seething discontent. A general strike led by socialists paralyzed Seattle in 1919. "Classless" America? How soon we forget.

In the years before World War I, just as now, technology was transforming the nature of home, work, and play. Typewriters, assembly lines (by 1915, the Ford plant in Highland Park employed 16,000 men), and time-and-motion studies were the computers of their time. Electric lighting and water closets (and rolls of perforated toilet paper, invented just before the turn of the century) introduced cleanliness and light into what must have been dark and smelly houses. The movies took the country by storm; by 1910, says the historian Thomas Schlereth, there were "ten thousand movie theaters playing to a nationwide audience of over 10 million weekly."

Just as at the end of our century, before 1914 women were

demanding new political and social rights, and very often winning them. This wasn't just a question of listening to Margaret Sanger's lectures on birth control or wearing loose-fitting clothes in imitation of Isadora Duncan. Infinitely more important was an explosion of educational and employment opportunity: the defining characteristics of the "new woman" were not that she smoked in public or knew all about orgasms, but that she was well-educated and worked for a living. In 1902, 61 percent of high school graduates were women, and in the same year, according to the historian John Milton Cooper, women made up over half the undergraduate class at the University of Chicago. In 1870, only about one in fifty office workers was a woman; by 1910, four out of every ten were. And these women weren't all doing the jobs of menial drudges. In John Dos Passos's novel *The 42nd Parallel*, a marvelous passage describes the metropolitan self-confidence of Eleanor Stoddard, an interior designer, in 1917. "She had an office now all by herself and had two girls working with her to learn the business and had quite a lot of work to do. The office was in the first block above Madison Square on Madison Avenue and she had her own name on it. In the afternoon she'd ride downtown in a taxi and look up at the Metropolitan Life tower and the Flatiron Building and the lights against the steely Manhattan sky and think of crystals and artificial flowers and gilt patterns on indigo and claret-colored brocade. The maid would have tea ready for her, and often there would be friends waiting for her. She'd talk for a while before slipping off to dress for dinner." Just like an editor at Condé Nast, today.

There is one more striking similarity between America at the start of the twentieth century and at its end. In the 1980s and 1990s, it became fashionable to explain much of the modern world by reference to something called "the global economy." One of Washington's most influential think tanks is called the Institute for International Economics; the strange ways of portfolio managers in charge of pension and mutual funds are thought to be more determinative of foreign policy than the nostrums of old-fashioned diplomats; "emerging markets" have become the stuff of a thousand articles; America, we are told, must improve its "competitiveness." In this new "international marketplace" we are engaged, in the title of one best-seller, in a *Head to Head* competition with the Europeans and the Japanese. The "global economy" is so wondrous that one writer has described it in the following glowing terms: "The inhabitant of New York can order by telephone, sipping his morning coffee in bed, the various products of the whole earth, in such quantity as he might see fit, and reasonably expect their early delivery upon his doorstep; he can at the same moment and by the same means adventure his wealth in the natural resources and new enterprises of any quarter of the world, and share, without exertion, in their prospective fruits and advantages; or he can decide to couple the security of his fortunes with the good faith of the townspeople of any substantial municipality in any continent that fancy or information might recommend." And this celebrant of global capitalism continues to argue that the "internationalization" of "the ordinary course of social and economic life" is "nearly complete in practice."

Oops—wrong decade. For those words were not written in the 1990s, but in 1919. They appear in John Maynard Keynes's polemic *The Economic Consequences of the Peace*, describing the world as it existed in 1914. (Keynes buffs will notice that we have changed the master's use of "London" and "tea" to "New York" and "coffee." This is a trivial matter; if anything, New Yorkers were even more able to indulge in the pleasures of the pre–World War I global economy than were Londoners.)

In the pre-1914 precursor of today's global economy, where commercial men with letters of credit sauntered into banks anywhere in the world and great steamships carved the oceans, America played a full role. The value of American exports expanded almost threefold between 1890 and 1914, and the composition of those exports changed. Where once America had exported mainly raw materials from the plains and the mines of the West, now it increasingly exported sophisticated products—the share of exports accounted for by manufactured goods rose from 35 percent in 1900 to 47 percent in 1914. British writers, long (though mistakenly) thinking of themselves as denizens of the workshop of the world, wailed about the American goods, most of tip-top quality, which were entering their markets—everything from electric motors to clothing. Arthur Conan Doyle speckled his tales of Sherlock Holmes with muscular, confident American businessmen not just because he wanted sales in America (though he certainly did) but because such men were a commonplace in Britain.

Just as today, much of America's trade was with the developed economies of Europe. But just as today, American firms were increasingly looking to Latin America, where Elihu Root, Teddy Roosevelt's secretary of state, had negotiated a series of bilateral tariff cuts. Encouraged by the success of such tariff reduction, Congress in 1913 cut the general level of the tariff to a level which would not be seen again until the mid-1950s. Meanwhile, American multinational companies spread their operations all over the world. Ford, International Harvester, New York Life—all became as familiar overseas as

McDonald's hamburgers are now. President William Howard Taft reorganized the State Department to make it a more efficient representative of American interests abroad. (Seventy years later, Secretary of State Warren Christopher did exactly the same thing.)

Trade flowed both ways. Merchandise imports more than doubled between 1900 and 1914, and foreign direct investment in the U.S.—always important—continued its growth. In 1914, according to Mira Wilkins, an economic historian, no less than 20 percent of America's gross national product was accounted for by foreign investment—the overwhelming amount of it British. American railroad stocks had been quoted on the London Stock Exchange since the 1830s. In 1899, a British company bought Pillsbury, the biggest American miller. (In 1989, another British company bought it again.) True, British investment had not always been welcomed; America had seen its own crop of books warning of the perfidious nature of British bankers in the 1880s. But somehow the American economy managed to tolerate a level of foreign ownership that simply dwarfs that seen in the 1990s.

One man can serve as a symbol of how comfortable American business once was in the wider world. After graduating from Stanford, Herbert Hoover was sent to a mining camp in Western Australia. At the time of the Boxer Rebellion he was in Beijing. He met the Dalai Lama, prospected in the Gobi desert and Burma—in fact, just about everywhere. For two decades, he ran a mining consultancy headquartered in London, with offices in New York, San Francisco, Shanghai, and St. Petersburg. On the outbreak of World War I, he was offered a position in the British cabinet. At war's end, after his famine relief efforts had saved countless thousands of Europeans, Polish schoolchildren marched through the streets of Warsaw in his honor. "Mr. Hoover," said Keynes of the peace conference after the war, "was the only man who emerged from the ordeal of Paris with an enhanced reputation. . . . [He] imported into the councils . . . precisely that atmosphere of reality, knowledge, magnanimity, and disinterestedness, which, if they had been found in other quarters also, would have given us the Good Peace." The 1990s as the great decade of global capitalism? Oh, bunk. They haven't yet produced a single man who could hold a candle to Hoover.

And this illuminates a larger point. Hoover's combination of iron efficiency and philanthropy during and after the war epitomizes the extent to which America was a great power. Many Americans must have thought (as they always have, and always will) that the rest of the world could be left to its own devices. But people everywhere else knew better; by 1914, America was sufficiently powerful that it was, ineluctably, a part of the international order. True, America did not have the great armies or navies of Britain and Germany. But it had already proved that it could reshape the map of the world. From the time of the Spanish-American War and the annexation of the Philippines, through John Hay's "Open Door" policy to China, and on to Teddy Roosevelt's brokering of a peace between Russia and Japan in 1905, America had showed itself to be the dominant non-Asiatic power in the Pacific. Long before the doughboys reached Europe, it was plain that America had the power to make or break alliances. It was a country with which any other country pursuing sensible policies would want to be friends (as the British, but not the Germans, appreciated between 1914 and 1917). Just the same is true at the century's end.

In key respects, then, the America of 1914 feels familiar.

More familiar, surely, than the America of 1945—a strange and wondrous place. In 1945, America was not just a country with which everyone else wanted to be allied: it was, rather, a nation which, uncontestably, led the world. America's post-1945 self-confidence was not a matter solely for Americans; it affected everybody. America had not even entered the war when Henry Luce proclaimed the beginning of "The American Century"; at war's end, Winston Churchill said simply that "America at this moment stands at the summit of the world."

America escaped the destruction of World War II—virtually alone of all the countries whose soldiers fought in that horror. Indeed, the war was something of a savior of the American economy. It brought new demand for products after the long Depression, and (as Willow Run showed) it turned farmboys and city girls into skilled industrial workers. Those workers saved like Croesus, waiting for the moment when they could spend their new wealth.

At war's end, Europeans understood that they were dealing with something quite new—a giant. In the shattered economies of the Old World, girls scrounged nylons off American GIs and tried to ensnare them in marriage; boys chewed gum and scrawled "Kilroy was here" in imitation of the new demigods. In *Manhattan '45*, her love letter to New York, the Welsh travel writer Jan Morris describes an America whose prosperity and verve was awesome. The American nation, says Morris, "was realizing its stupendous strength, and as a result New York was emerging from a provincial, even a parochial sort of urbanity into true metropolitanism. The old brag 'biggest and finest in the nation' more and more evolved into 'biggest and finest in the world.' . . . Battered and impoverished London, humiliated Paris, shattered Ber-

49

lin, discredited Rome—the old capitals towards which, before the war, Americans had so often looked with sensations of diffident inferiority now seemed flaccid beside this prodigy of the West."

In the perfect symbolic gesture, the treaty establishing a United Nations was signed in America. At the end of older wars, diplomats had conferred at Versailles or Berlin, at Geneva or Greenwich. At the end of World War II, the road to peace started in San Francisco, and went via Lake Success, Long Island (the first headquarters of the United Nations), to the banks of the East River; quite a change.

At the same time, American culture was sweeping the globe. From Corn Flakes to Coca-Cola; from Barbara Stanwyck to Frank Sinatra; from musicals like *On the Town* and *An American in Paris* (a revealing subject for a post-1945 film) to novelists like Steinbeck and Hemingway, and so on to the Abstract Expressionist artists, America defined what was "modern." All was muscle, confidence, and color.

One other thing, vitally important, was new. America was now both the epitome and the guarantor of international democracy. Europeans such as Alexis de Tocqueville had long been interested in American democracy, but almost as they would examine a rat in a laboratory. Now, American democracy stood between humanity and an awful fate. In World War II America's democracy had provided the men and hardware which defeated fascism. Lumbering its guns to a new target, "Americanism" would soon stand as the only alternative to a communist totalitarianism just as hateful. American democracy provided the ideas, the moral basis, on which a new world might be ordered.

This was a huge change from the established order. In 1919, Woodrow Wilson and his bright young men had hoped that America would lead the democracies. But there was little appetite for such a project back home, and so America stood aloof from the League of Nations. In 1945, by contrast, Americans were prepared to try to remake the world in their own image. And they could try, in part, because there was so little competition. European democracies emerged from World War II far weaker, relative to America, than they had been in 1919. War turned the world upside down. Britain and France, Japan and Germany, were wrecked and in ruins. But war had also changed America. Though it had long been an economic giant, it had never before utterly dominated high-technology industries; but in 1945, it did. In 1914, America was a great trading nation whose business-men—like Herbert Hoover—knew that they had to live by their wits in a competitive world. Hoover would have thought it bizarre that America could ever have a hermetic, self-contained economy. Yet in 1945, that was the way the American economy was; since every other economy had been wrecked, foreign trade hardly troubled the American imagination.

The domestic economy, too, had been transformed. In 1945, the men and women at Willow Run spoke English; they had come a hundred miles or so from Appalachia. Had the factory been built thirty years earlier for World War I, it would have been a babel of Croatian, German, Italian, and Polish—just like the steel mills of the Monongahela Valley had been in 1919. By 1945, it hardly made sense to speak of America as a society of immigrants, since in the previous twenty years immigration had slowed to a thin trickle.

Nor, in 1945, was social class something which set Americans against each other and divided the country. There was a natural classlessness in the cars on the Willow Run Expressway, carrying everyone, whatever the color of their collar. The war itself had jumbled silk-stockinged WASPs alongside Italian and Irish working stiffs. Of course, it would be idle to pretend that there was a social homogeneity about America in 1945; there plainly was not. But unlike in Europe, politics was not overlaid on class divisions, such that political parties framed their appeal solely in terms of class solidarity. That would have been pointless: Americans may have had wildly different social circumstances, but they shared, as they always had, a common aspiration: they wanted to make life better for themselves and their families.

This marked quite a change from older patterns of American life. As World War I broke out, America was as keenly divided between rich and poor as most European countries. Americans could look at the palaces in Newport, Rhode Island, compare them with rat-run tenements in New York, and learn a quick lesson in class consciousness. In 1914, Americans knew that the troopers of a state government could massacre innocent women and children—as at Ludlow. In 1945, by contrast, Americans were already moving from the farms and the tenements to the suburbs, where everyone would live lives rather similar to each other. And they knew (think of the migrant workers' camp in *The Grapes of Wrath*) that the federal government would look after them. The feds made sure, for example, that Willow Run had every modern amenity. When FDR died in the spring of 1945, thousands of Americans lined the tracks of the railroad as his body was brought home from Warm Springs, Georgia. The federal government was a friend; not a threat.

No immigrants; less bitter class divisions; a benign federal government; utter domination of the world economy. That was how America was in 1945. America had *never* been like that before, yet in our addled national memory, we think of such exceptional times not only as the way that America has always been, but as it should be in the future. This is a cruel self-delusion—one that we can only overcome if we learn what it was that made the years after 1945 so memorable; and so peculiar.

CHAPTER THREE

The Golden Age: Society

Why do Americans look back on the years after 1945 with such longing? Because they were a time of great—unprecedented—national cohesion. The United States had just fought and won a "good war," a war in which more than 400,000 Americans had lost their lives, and to which the resources of the whole nation had been dedicated. At the war's end, the country continued to come together, in all sorts of ways, large and small. It is the memory of this national unity that is so powerful today.

Of all the aspects of this unifying process, none was more important than the steady integration of the South into economic and social structures common to the rest of the nation. In 1945 the South was another country; over the next thirty years it became Americanized. To understand the importance of this, we need to recognize how peculiar the South had once been.

We can start on a hill just south of Birmingham, Alabama. A statue of Vulcan, god of fire, patron of metalworkers, stands watch over the city. Down below, you can see the site of the giant Slosser iron foundry. If you could crane your neck over the corrugated hills, rich in iron ore, that surround Birmingham, you would see the town of Bessemer to the southwest. Most towns are named for a geographical feature, or after their founders. Bessemer was named in 1873 for the man (Sir Henry Bessemer) who, in England, had discovered that blowing cold air through molten pig iron would magically transmute the iron into steel. Birmingham's prosperity depended on Bessemer's invention.

Vulcan was built in 1904 for the World's Exposition in St. Louis. At that time, said W. J. Cash in *The Mind of the South*, Birmingham, "Planted black and ugly upon her mountains of iron, was reddening the night with multiplying sullen fires. . . . Atlanta, remembering her ashes, was proudly piling mythology upon mythology and boasting herself a phoenix city." The unwary visitor may assume that in 1904 Vulcan stood for something rather grand: the revival of southern industry and civic pride after the Civil War. Looked at narrowly, the state of southern manufacturing was worth celebrating. The South's railways, wrecked by Sherman, were rebuilt within five years of Appomattox; investment in manufacturing surged in the 1870s and 1880s. Yet for all the talk of a New South, Cash's sly description of Atlanta was accurate; this was all a myth. The South's economy was a colonial one; northern capital controlled its industry and commerce. By national standards, southern industrial workers were poor, and for the first half of the century, would remain so.

In 1900, the annual national income for agricultural workers was $260, and for non-agricultural workers $622. In New York, agricultural workers earned an average of $330; non-agricultural workers $638. In Alabama, by contrast, farmworkers earned just $120 in 1900, or less than half the national average; industrial workers in Birmingham earned about $450, or 70 percent of the national average. The South almost completely missed the immigration of the late nineteenth century, and all the economic activity that immigration brings. In 1900 the South accounted for only 3 percent of the urban foreign-born population, and 7 percent of the rural foreign-born population. And the South also largely missed the breakthroughs in science and business techniques which, after the Civil War, made the North into the greatest economic power on the globe.

Universities provide an acid test. By 1900, the great northern universities, based in cities like New York, Boston, and Philadelphia, were intimately connected with local businesses. Most southern universities had a very different vocation. They were squirreled away in rural backwaters, in bucolic towns with unreddened skies like Oxford, Mississippi, or Chapel Hill, North Carolina. These were places where romance and literary traditions flowered but where the animal instincts of modern capitalism did not. Students sensed this. The novelist Thomas Wolfe entered the University of North Carolina in 1915. In *Look Homeward, Angel* Wolfe wrote, "The university was a charming, an unforgettable place . . . buried in a pastoral wilderness . . . one felt its remoteness, its isolated charm. Its century-long struggle in the forest had given it a sweetness and a beauty. It had the fine authority of provincialism—the provincialism of an older South."

This Old South was a cotton monoculture—just as world demand for cotton, and hence its price, was collapsing. The first patent for a mechanical cotton harvester was granted in the 1850s. But the planters had a ready supply of cheap black labor and little access to credit, so they had neither the money nor the incentive to invest in new machinery. Instead, the planters turned to sharecropping. Sharecroppers often lived in penury, while southern landowners, often unable to get decent prices for cotton, were chronically debt-ridden.

These mutually reinforcing trends meant that the long decline of the South, which had started before the Civil War, continued after it. In 1840, average income in the South had been 76 percent of the national average; by 1860, it was 72 percent. By 1900 that figure had fallen to just 51 percent. In the East South Central census region (Kentucky, Tennessee, Alabama, and Mississippi) it stood at just 49 percent of the national average. No amount of light from Vulcan's torch could transform the bleakness and peculiarity of southern poverty. This was another country indeed; America could not become a truly cohesive place if it remained so.

In the fifty years after 1900, southern income per head gradually improved. By 1925 the South had more than 50 percent of the nation's spindles and looms. But there wasn't much else. In 1934 a standard economic history of the South discussed industry with a few pages on textiles and rather less on minerals like iron, oil, and sulfur. But change was coming, and it was led by the federal government. In hindsight, it is clear that 1929 marked the beginning of a period marked by three great national crises—the Depression, war (hot and cold), and the battle for civil rights. In each case the federal government became the main agent for addressing the national crisis. And this new role for the federal government was nowhere so important as in the South.

Shortly after his election, Franklin Roosevelt declared that the South was the nation's "Number One economic problem." The Tennessee Valley Authority brought electricity to the hollows of Appalachia; the Agricultural Adjustment Administration tried to raise commodity prices by taking surplus land out of production. Land grant colleges and the federal Agriculture Department's extension service improved the husbandry of southern farms. And, eventually, the cotton harvest was mechanized. In Arkansas, for example, virtually none of the cotton harvest was picked mechanically in the 1940s; by 1972 all of it was.

All this led to a great migration to the cities, North and South. Prewar, there was little defense work in the South. But after Pearl Harbor, towns along the Gulf Coast like Mobile, Alabama (which doubled its population during the war), hired workers by the thousands. Aircraft, synthetic rubber, and all the other hardware of war began to be manufactured; the South increased its industrial capacity by around 40 percent during wartime. Those who left the farms found wages beyond the dreams of avarice (in Willow Run, according to local lore, some hillbillies didn't believe that bills could come in denominations of more than $10).

Industrialization and urbanization gathered pace after 1945. Between 1940 and 1970 the number of southern manufacturing jobs more than doubled. And the structure of industry changed. In 1940 about two-thirds of all southern manufactures had been nondurable goods like textiles. By the 1970s only about half were. General Motors and Ford built assembly plants in Atlanta; Allis-Chalmers and International Harvester built plants in the South to meet the demand for mechanical cotton pickers. By the 1980s North Carolina had more of its labor force employed in manufacturing than any other state.

Technological change much assisted the South. Industries no longer needed to be located close to natural resources, ports, and harbors. With the coming of the transistor (perhaps the single greatest invention of post-1945 America) and the microchip, industry became "miniaturized." Whole sectors of the economy developed not on the manipulation of mounds of ore and coal, but of electrons. In this new world, the South lost its comparative disadvantage.

In the post-1945 years, southern governors discovered "economic development." They tramped the country and the world looking for investment. They offered subsidies and tax breaks, but their great card was the cost of southern labor, always cheaper than that in the North. And they could promise those who bothered to ask (and every industrialist did) that there was a "good labor climate" in their region, which meant that unions were barely tolerated. Textile towns like Spartanburg, South Carolina, sought investors from Europe—such as the German textile company Hoechst—and later from Japan. Luther Hodges, governor of North Carolina in the 1950s, dreamed of a "research park" in the woodlands of the Piedmont, equidistant from the campuses of Duke, the University of North Carolina, and North Carolina State. By the 1990s his dream, now called Research Triangle Park, would quietly hum with laboratories from some of the world's leading companies.

In the 1950s, the federal government continued to assist the southern economy, locating federal offices, defense plants, and military bases in the region. On the back of federal investment at Cape Canaveral, north-central Florida became one of the world's centers of the space and aerospace industries. Prewar, the area had been part of the inward-looking Deep South. Now its industry is about as unprovincial as anywhere in the world, and it can thank the federal government for the change.

The effects of all this were dramatic. By 1950, after fifty years of long, slow improvement in their position, the four poor East South Central states had an income per head equal to 62 percent of the national average. Then came the great leap forward. By 1970 that figure had risen to 74 percent, and by 1990 the figure for Tennessee was as much as 87 percent. Looked at purely as a matter of economics, southern peculiarity had ended; the South was no longer different in kind from the rest of the nation.

In 1945 the South, of course, had been different from the rest of the country not simply because it was poor and rural. The differences went much deeper than that; so deep that they stretched America's fabric to the breaking point. It is one thing for a society that spans a continent, and that is almost exclusively composed of immigrants or their descendants, to tolerate diversity of views and beliefs among its members. It is quite another to allow one region to crush the dignity of some of its members solely on the basis of their race.

In 1937, the Swedish sociologist Gunnar Myrdal was commissioned by the Carnegie Foundation to supervise a study of blacks, published as *An American Dilemma* in 1944. Myrdal insisted that the place of blacks in the South diminished all Americans. The question of race, he argued, was a "problem in the heart of the American." Myrdal's "dilemma" was the need to reconcile "the American creed" of equality and democracy with local interests. But Myrdal's contribution went beyond moral philosophy; he constructed a rich data set from which he drew blunt conclusions. "The economic situation of the negroes in America is pathological," said Myrdal; "the masses of American negroes are destitute." He drew attention to the "tradition of illegality" in the South, and, in a much-quoted passage, said that "The white southerner practically never sees a negro except as his servant and

in some other standardized and formalized caste situation"—
and the use of the word "caste" was no accident.

The Jim Crow laws had become so pervasive that Myrdal's
extraordinary claim was true. Indeed, while Myrdal and his
team were still at work, the discrimination laws were extended to new situations. Atlanta segregated its taxis in 1940;
Virginia segregated its airports in 1944. Yet by the mid-
1990s, though researchers could no doubt find racism and
segregation in the South, the systematic legal discrimination
which Myrdal identified had gone. In that respect, too, the
South has become like the rest of the country. How did this
happen?

From the distance of the 1990s there are two salient aspects of the struggle for civil rights in the South. The first
was the heroism and moral authority of blacks themselves:
not just the obvious bravery of those like Martin Luther
King, Jr., John Lewis, and Medgar Evers, but the unsung
heroism of old cotton-chopping women who overcame fear
and registered to vote within weeks of being free to do so.
The second was the extension of national institutions to the
South. To be sure, there was often backsliding, or worse.
President Eisenhower, convinced that laws could not change
the deeply ingrained folkways of men, often treated the civil
rights movement with the impatience he would have
brought to a troublesome fly on the golf course. President
Kennedy equivocated, compromised, wheeled, and dealed.
And yet the totality of the record is clear. In the 1960s it was
the federal Congress which gave meaning to constitutional
amendments that had been passed after the Civil War. It was
the federal Supreme Court which, in a fifteen-year sequence
of cases, chipped away at legal segregation until the foundation of the southern temple was undermined by *Brown v. Board*

of Education. It was the federal judges of the Fifth Circuit who implemented *Brown* and the other desegregation cases, though ostracized by their neighbors and spurned by their churches. Judge Frank Johnson of that court, an old college friend of Governor George Wallace of Alabama, at one time or another placed under his jurisdiction Alabama's prison and highway patrol systems, property tax assessment program, mental health agency, and public education system.

The federal government also showed its military might. It sent hundreds of federal marshals to the South; state National Guards were placed under national control. Armed forces of the national government were deployed. In 1957 Eisenhower sent the paratroopers of the 101st Airborne Division to Little Rock. In 1962, during the battle to register James Meredith at Ole Miss, the federal government mobilized no fewer than 23,000 members of the armed forces, soldiers, marines, and airmen, to put down the state's resistance.

Arguably, the federal government's most significant deployment of military power had happened earlier, in 1948, when President Truman signed an executive order to integrate the armed services. By the time the forces were on the firing line at Oxford, Mississippi, they were already the best evidence for the virtues of integration in the nation—and, ironically, the army has always recruited heavily among white southerners.

Other national institutions similarly extended their influence to the South. Walter Reuther of the autoworkers bankrolled many civil rights campaigns. Though the editorial line of many local TV stations in the South remained sympathetic to segregation, they could not control the national debate. The nationwide TV networks—and TV, though still a novelty, was in most American homes by 1960—showed dramatic pictures of Bull Connor's dogs in Birmingham and broadcast, live, the great march on Washington in 1963.

When it was all over—when Vulcan could look down on a Birmingham that neither smelled of tear gas nor echoed the sound of breaking glass—the country had changed forever. Atlanta and Birmingham, Memphis and Jackson, had the same glass-walled skyscrapers as cities in the West and North. Their workers did the same kind of jobs as workers in the North; the farmers in the fields used the same kind of equipment as on the Great Plains. In 1992, Mike Espy, a black from the Mississippi Delta, "the most southern place on earth," where blacks had once chopped cotton in peonage, became secretary of agriculture in Washington—at a time when his brother was mayor of Clarksdale, a Delta town that had once been rabidly racist. By the end of 1994, the president and vice president, the speaker of the House of Representatives, and the majority leader of the House all had their homes in the old Confederacy.

Not everyone welcomed the end of southern peculiarity. As early as 1931, a group of writers based at Vanderbilt University in Nashville had written a manifesto against the imposition of economic and social systems "foreign" to the South. These "southern agrarians," as they came to be called, were often criticized for looking at southern life solely through white men's eyes. Yet they nonetheless touched a chord among those who were not racist. In 1980, Marshall Frady, a southern journalist, lamented that "For the past few decades the South has been mightily laboring to mutate itself into a tinfoil-twinky simulation of southern California, and in the process has unwittingly worked on itself a spiritual impoverishment. . . . The mischief is that, in its transfiguration into What-a-Burger drive-ins and apartment wastelands, the

South is being etherized, subtly rendered pastless, memory-less and vague of identity." That jeremiad is much too pessimistic. Southern exceptionalism yet endures. Arrive in a southern airport on a summer night and the air still smells softer, more mysterious. But the cruel oddity of southern ways—of naked racism and a colonized economy—has been ended.

The transformation of the South after 1945 was part of a much larger demographic phenomenon. America saw two great movements of population. The first involved the growth of the "Sunbelt"—a relative decline of the Northeast and the Midwest and a boom in the South and the West. The second was a massive shift of people from farms, small towns, and central cities to the suburbs. Together, these movements helped create a more unified nation.

In 1940—to adopt the definition of Carl Abbott of Portland State University—the United States had a "core" with two outliers. The core was a rectangle at whose corners were Boston, Philadelphia, St. Louis, and St. Paul. Within this area were half the nation's population, and nearly three-quarters of its industrial output. The first outlier—the West—was scarcely populated, with an economy based on the extraction of natural resources, and with few cities (which tended to be treated with amused contempt by the sophisticates of the Northeast). The second outlier—the South—was an economic basket case with its own peculiar social customs. By the end of the Golden Age, however, this division into core and outlying regions no longer made sense. In 1940, the population share of the core was 54 percent, with the South at 32 percent, and the West at a little more than 14 percent. By 1980, the core had 48 percent of the population, the South had increased to 33 percent, and the West accounted for nearly 19 percent. Climate and topography ensured that the distribution of the population was not smoothly perfect, but the pattern of settlement was now pretty uniform.

Both the growth of the Sunbelt and suburbanization are critical to understanding modern America. Neither the Sunbelt nor the suburbs are homogeneous. There are real differences in the patterns of settlement, prosperity, and prospects within both. There are big patches of "Sunbelt" states that demonstrate none of the demographic and social characteristics that are meant to typify the region; conversely, "Sunbelt" traits are well-marked in some communities that are cold and wet. In fact, as Abbott has argued, the period since 1950 has seen two distinct regions of relative population growth. One starts south of Delaware, stretching from the foothills of the Appalachians to the Atlantic Ocean, encompassing the Chesapeake Bay states, most of the Carolinas (but not the hilly backcountry), parts of Georgia, and all of Florida. It excludes much of the mid-South along the Tennessee Valley and the old cotton kingdom of the Deep South. The second region of growth stretches from Texas into parts of Oklahoma and thence to the west through the desert to the Pacific Coast. And it includes almost all of that coast, the Willamette Valley and Puget Sound as much as southern California. True, to place Portland, Oregon, in something called the "Sunbelt" does violence to the language; but it is the term that is at fault, not the inclusion of that rainy city in its boundaries.

In two important ways the movement of population to the Southeast differed from that to the West. The first was a matter of timing. The empty spaces and rich natural resources of the West—especially California—have exercised a pull on America's imagination for more than two centuries. It is true that post–Civil War immigration to the West was small compared with that to the northeastern cities like New York and Boston. But the better comparison is with the South. The great immigration from Europe of 1880–1910 passed by the South. Though early figures for the movement of native-born Americans are not always reliable, the picture there is plain, too. Between 1870 and 1910 the white population of the South increased by two and half times, while the white population of the West increased sevenfold. Clearly, there was substantial internal immigration by native-born whites from the South (and from everywhere else) to the West. But there is very little evidence that before World War I there was significant internal migration from any other region to the South.

This picture—of the West leading and the South lagging as the destination of both American and foreign migrants—was true for two-thirds of this century; you don't have to read *The Grapes of Wrath* to know that. As we have seen, World War II brought a boom to the South; but it brought a much bigger boom to the West. Defense contracts flooded southern California; San Diego became one of the continent's great cities; while Portland became the site of an important shipyard.

This boom, just like the mining boom at the end of the last century, sucked in foreign immigrants. Mexicans, thousands of whom had been expelled from America in the 1930s, flocked back to Los Angeles. But the renewed surge of foreign immigration to the West was insignificant compared with the flow of native-born Americans there. Between 1950 and 1965 the annual average net migration from other regions to California was 320,000. By the 1980s, by contrast, internal migration flows to the West were only about a quarter of the size they had been in the 1950s.

What had happened? Simple: the South had caught up.

Using calculations made by John Kasarda of the University of North Carolina, a transformation in the relative attractiveness of the West and the South since the 1960s is apparent, at least as regards native-born migrants (immigration from overseas is another story). Between 1955 and 1960, for example, the South had a net outmigration with the West of 380,000. By the period between 1970 and 1975 the picture had reversed; 75,000 more westerners moved to the South than in the opposite direction.

These flows from the West to the South were dwarfed by migration to the South from the Northeast and Midwest. By the 1950s, northerners moving their home preferred the South to the West; by the 1970s, so did midwesterners. Farmers and their families moved from Iowa to Atlanta; retired steelworkers settled in the Ozarks and Florida. Between 1955 and 1985, the South received a net 3.4 million people from the Northeast and 3.1 million from the Midwest. Peak migration from the Northeast to the South was in the 1970s; from the Midwest (badly hit by the recession of 1980–82) it was in the early 1980s.

Internal migration to the South, then, was later than that to the West. The second difference between South and West is more subtle. Measuring westward internal migration is a simple matter, because so few people have left the West; the flows have all been one way. (Though there has been some internal migration out of California in recent years, most of those who have fled the smog have settled elsewhere in the West, especially in the mountain states.) But in the South two enormous flows of population have had to be set off against each other. Blacks and poor whites have left the South for the rest of the country; whites (and, lately, a few blacks) have flocked to the South.

This two-way flow is of long standing. Gavin Wright, an economic historian, estimates that 500,000 blacks left the South between 1915 and 1920, as northern factories recruited cheap black labor. World War II saw a new burst of southern migration (both black and white) to northern cities like Detroit and southern ones such as Mobile. The mechanization of the cotton harvest did the rest. More than 350,000 workers left southern farms in the 1940s, and more than 1 million in the 1950s. Hence despite the massive immigration to the South of whites from the Northeast and Midwest in the 1950s, it was not until the very end of that decade that the South was a net importer of population.

These differences between the movements to the West and the South had important consequences. The West stopped being an outlier much earlier than the South. Mass internal migration to the West started before 1900 and had ended by the late 1960s. By that time, the West was as "settled," by the same kinds of people, engaged in much the same kind of economic activities, as anywhere else in the country.

The consequences of flows into and out of the South are more complex. In theory, the influx of people from other parts of the country may have helped "modernize" racial attitudes in the South. Perhaps a bigger change has been an "export" of the South to the rest of the country. In World War II, in places like Detroit, this was thought to be a real problem, as southern whites (with their peculiar racial attitudes) poured into a city which was already a tinderbox. More recently, white southern politicians and their positions have assumed a new prominence. Since politics in the South remains more conservative than anywhere else, national politics, too, has become more conservative. Southern voters as a group remain more individualistic than other Americans, more likely to be "tough on crime" (no southern state has abolished the death penalty, though many northern ones have). Southerners remain suspicious of all things which emanate from Washington (which shows great ingratitude). As the southern vote has become more important, so all these "southern" attitudes have become "mainstream."

Beyond this spread of white southern attitudes, the main significance of the "export" of the South has been a rapid dispersion of the black population. In 1940, America was not a multicultural place; in fact, most of the country wasn't even biracial. In 1940, when the long boom was just about to start, 77 percent of the black population lived in the South. In 1980, by which time the boom was over, only 53 percent did. In those forty years, the black population grew quite modestly, from about 10 percent of the nation's total to about 12 percent. But look at the changing nature of the population in three non-southern states over those years and a far more dramatic change is evident. Michigan was 4 percent black in 1940, 13 percent black in 1980; Connecticut was 2 percent black in 1940, more than 7 percent black in 1980; and Washington State, which had only 7,000 blacks (or 0.4 percent of total population) in 1940, was home to 150,000 blacks, or 2.5 percent of the state's total, in 1980.

Here, in a nutshell, is one of the most profound changes of the Golden Age. At the end of World War II, most of America was racially homogeneous; even in cities like New York, which had a substantial black population, blacks tended to stay in their own part of town. In the 1950s, midtown Manhatttan was an overwhelmingly white place. Most of the country was so white that black faces were a rarity. After the restless currents of demography had swirled for forty years, such a statement could only be made of some sparsely populated regions like northern New England or the northern plains. "Race" could once be dismissed (cruelly and falsely) as a "southern" question; now, unequivocally, it was one for the whole nation.

In addition to the changing regional composition of the population, America was also completing a change from a society with its roots (and self-image) in small towns and farms to one that was relentlessly urban. This change has demanded much from Americans. It is commonplace that the supposed attractions of small, self-contained communities have been at the heart of one conception of what it means to be "American." And the image of small-town America has spread outside its shores. Ask Europeans to visualize an "ideal" American setting and they might conjure up a place like Woodstock, Vermont: white frame houses; a spire peeking above trees. Self-reliant but neighborly; churchgoing but ambitious for themselves and their families, as if determined to render their rightful portion to both God and Mammon— so appealing has the myth of the small town been that its strength is no surprise.

And it isn't all myth; American small towns were rather wonderful places. But they are dead. Indeed, they lived for a very short period; the high summer of small town America was extraordinarily brief. Take the High Plains as an example. After the threat of Indian raids was ended, boosters thought that great cities would cover the short grass prairie; that rain would follow the plow. They misread geography (and sociology, and climatology; they misread everything). The rural population of Kansas peaked sometime between 1910 and 1920 and then started to decline precipitously. In 1920 1,151,000 people lived in rural Kansas. In 1950 (when the census found, for the first time, that most

Kansans lived in towns or cities) just 912,000 did. By 1990 that figure had shrunk again, to 765,000. Although the population of Kansas increased between 1950 and 1990 by 30 percent, most counties saw absolute reductions. Between 1950 and 1990, North Dakota increased in population by just 3 percent; South Dakota by less than 7 percent. (During the same period, the population of the country as a whole increased by 64 percent.) In 1990, fewer people lived in North Dakota than had done in 1920.

The depopulation of rural America has not been limited to the High Plains, where the winters are long and the living is hard. It is just as marked in the South, as the mechanization of the cotton fields led to an exodus of the rural population. But the great emptying of rural America was not limited to farming communities. Ever since the first colonists chopped down New England trees to turn the timber into charcoal, there have been pockets of manufacturing and mining in rural areas. In southern Illinois, where Mother Jones, the great agitator of the coalfields, is buried among her boys, winding gear peeps above the grain fields; in the Black Hills of South Dakota, the spoil heaps of old mines soar like gray pillows over a blanket of conifers. The hills and hollows of Appalachia and the upcountry of the Carolinas are studded with mines, lumber mills, and textile plants. All these rural non-farming communities have lost population just as farming ones have done. Between 1950 and 1990 the population of West Virginia declined from just over 2 million to just under 1.8 million.

To some extent, the great emptying has been continuous for more than a century. As early as the census of 1920, more Americans (some 54 million) lived in urban areas than did those (51 million) who lived in rural ones. Still, the real change came during World War II and the Golden Age that followed it. In 1940 about 44 percent of the population lived in rural areas and 56 percent in urban ones. By 1970 the proportions had changed to 27 percent and 73 percent. About 7 million people left the farms in the 1940s and about 10 million in the 1950s. Between 1950 and 1970, total population increased by about 25 percent. But in the same period the population in towns with less than 2,500 people actually fell. The Golden Age was not, as Bill Clinton and Ross Perot pretended during the 1992 election, a time in which small-town America blossomed; on the contrary, it was the time of its death.

Where did they go in the years after 1945, these broad-shouldered farmers and their families; these deacons and cobblers, dairymen and schoolmarms? Well, along with everyone else, they went to the Sunbelt. But paradoxically, just as the movement to the Sunbelt was spreading Americans more evenly across the continent, so Americans were becoming more concentrated in urban areas—more precisely, in suburbs.

Suburbs can't be understood in ignorance of the cities they surround. Older American cities like Baltimore, New York, and Boston were ports; colonial outposts that imported finished goods and exported raw materials like timber, fish, and tobacco from their rural hinterland. Until this century, the industry of ports was conveniently clustered around the wharves. New York had its Garment District in downtown Manhattan, and in 1900, the vast majority of employed New Yorkers walked just a few blocks to work. Despite early attempts to "suburbanize" factories, much of the economies of America's city centers remained dedicated to manufacturing for a long time. Until the 1990s, you drove to Pittsburgh through the Fort Pitt Tunnel, popped out into the open air—and there, just a stone's throw from the city center, was a great steelworks, belching smoke and steam, barges and trains creaking and chugging their way toward giant blast furnaces. Detroit's first car factories—with iron foundries on site—were just a mile from downtown. The Chicago stock-yards and meat-packing plants were noxiously close to the Loop. As late as 1953, according to John Kasarda, 36 percent of the employment in central-city New York was engaged in manufacturing, as was 38 percent of comparable employment in Baltimore and 45 percent in Philadelphia.

Once again, the Golden Age was a time of great change. In the 1950s city centers lost millions of people and jobs to the suburbs. This doesn't mean that "the suburb" was plonked on an unsuspecting nation by Abraham, Alfred, and William Levitt, the father-and-sons team who built the Levittowns in the decade after 1945. As Kenneth Jackson of Columbia University has documented, suburban development in America has a long history. With the coming of the automobile, trucks made it easy to supply factories without depending on a river or a railhead. Forklifts, zipping supplies of raw materials to assembly lines, needed bigger sites; and all this led to the construction of plants in suburban greenfields. Indeed, in the 1930s, for the first time, more of the growth of metropolitan population took place in the suburbs than in city centers. By the 1950s, by which time "campus" or "parkland" industrial areas were fashionable, virtually all of that growth was in the suburbs. As places where a great mass of people wanted to live, America's city centers had a slightly longer time in the sun than small, rural towns—but not by much.

Yet though suburbs have had a long history, they came into their own in the Golden Age. In the 1930s the suburban population increased by 3.5 million, and in the 1940s by nearly 10.5 million. But in the 1950s it increased by more than 27 million, as it did in the 1960s. In the 1970s the increase in the suburban population, though substantial, was only about half what it had been in the 1950s and 1960s. In the 1980s the suburbs increased their population yet again, so that by 1990 more than half of all Americans lived in suburbs.

Who moved to the suburbs in the years after 1945? The short answer, happily also accurate, is "everyone did." Blacks did as well as whites (though black suburbanization was more important in the 1970s and 1980s than in the 1950s and 1960s). Working-class Americans left the tenements of the Lower East Side for Long Island; plutocrats left the town houses of the Upper East Side for Westchester County. Servicemen returning from World War II or Korea used subsidized mortgages to buy a four-room "Cape Codder" house in a Levittown. Farmers left western Kansas to buy a "ranch" house in the San Fernando Valley.

The television companies spotted the trend. NBC Radio's hit sitcom *The Life of Riley* (later transferred to television) was originally about a working stiff from Brooklyn. He was moved, postwar, to work in an aircraft factory in Los Angeles. Jackie Gleason's show *The Honeymooners*, the first great postwar TV sitcom, was set in a Brooklyn apartment. Its central character was a bus driver: definitely a city show. By contrast *Leave It to Beaver, Father Knows Best*, and *The Adventures of Ozzie and Harriet*, the hit shows that followed Gleason, were all identifiably suburban. The suburbs, in other words, were now the place where "real" Americans lived.

Once safely in the suburbs, America went on a binge of family life—and this became a defining characteristic of the

Golden Age, infusing its memory with a set of cultural values based on the sanctity of home, hearth, and kids. The median age of a woman's first marriage, which had been 21.5 in 1940, dropped to 20.5 in 1947. Some of that, no doubt, reflected a "demand" for marriage which had gone unsatisfied during the war, as young men left home to fight in the Pacific or Europe. But the median age kept on dropping. By 1956, its lowest point, the age was 20.1. A typical bride that year would have been only eleven at VJ Day—so she was not marrying early because she had spent the war pining for her sweetheart.

After they had gotten married, these postwar brides stayed married. A century-long increase in the divorce rate reversed itself in the 1950s. Europeans had long been scandalized by the ease with which Americans could get divorced, but in the 1950s Americans rediscovered virtue—or at least, one definition of it. In 1958, the divorce rate was actually lower than it had been in 1941.

And, notoriously, the married suburban women of the Golden Age had hordes of children. In 1916, the birthrate for women between fifteen and forty-four had been 123 per 1,000 women, much as it had been a century before. As better medical care lowered infant mortality, families needed fewer births to reach their ideal size. After World War I the birthrate dropped sharply. In 1936, its low point, the rate was just 76 per 1,000 women.

The birthrate leapt to 113 per 1,000 in 1947, as sex-starved men returned to lovesick women at the end of a war. The birthrate then dipped a little and then, against all expectations, started climbing once more. In 1957, it stood at 123 per 1,000 women of childbearing age, exactly where it had been in 1916. There were 4.3 million Americans born that year, a figure neither reached before nor matched since. (In fact, the Census Bureau predicts that the 1957 record will not be bettered until 2015, astonishing testimony to the fecundity of post-1945 America.) The average size of families, which had been shrinking for thirty years, suddenly grew once more. By 1980, according to demographer Richard Easterlin, the population was 15 percent more than the very highest forecast made by the Census Bureau in 1947. And so the famous cliché was born. But like all the best clichés, this one was dead true: there really was a baby boom.

Explaining why there was a baby boom is much more difficult than saying that it happened. The standard explanation goes like this: the postwar years were a time of unparalleled economic prosperity, which allowed women to stay at home and engendered the confidence to raise lots of children. Easterlin has argued that the boom can be explained by supply and demand. The relatively low birthrates of the 1920s and 1930s left young men at a premium in the 1950s. They could hence demand higher real wages, which allowed their wives to stay at home and have children. But even if there had been lots of young men instead of a few of them, the economy in the 1950s would probably still have boomed. In those circumstances, would there still have been a baby boom (in fact, an even bigger one)? Who can say? In some ways, the baby boom remains a mystery.

Two things are not a mystery. First, the 1950s saw a tremendous growth in family prosperity. In 1948 54 percent of families had a car; in 1956 73 percent did. Television became a "mass-ownership" commodity very quickly. In 1948 just 3 percent of families had a TV; by 1956 81 percent did— a single development which would have a profound impact on American cohesion. Betty Friedan, author of *The Feminine Mystique*, bemoaned the wave of gadgetry that dumped itself on suburbia in the 1950s, but some of her unhappiness must have been inspired by the terror of change. The very idea of what a "house" was, what "housework" meant, and what entertainment one could enjoy from the couch, were all transformed within less than two decades.

Secondly, the rate of female participation in the labor force grew far more slowly than the booming economy would have led one to expect. In 1945 36 percent of all women worked in the wartime economy. At war's end, that figure dropped to 31 percent, as women were laid off from munitions factories and offices. Then female labor force participation climbed slowly to 38 percent by 1960, and to 43 percent by 1970. But the early part of this rise was due almost entirely to older women reentering the labor force. Women aged from forty-five to sixty-four increased their participation rate by more than 16 points from 1946 to 1960; women aged twenty to twenty-four by less than 1 point. In 1960, single women were substantially less likely to work than they had been in 1946. Of married women with children under six, 19 percent worked in 1960—not much more than the 11 percent of such women who worked in 1946.

In fact, any apparent increase in women's work in the years just after 1945 is suspect. Between 1946 and 1960 the total female labor force grew by about 6.4 million people—rather more than the increase in the male labor force. But more than 17 million Americans left farms during that period, and though their labors never showed up in the statistics, American farmers' wives certainly "worked"—think of all the dressmaking and canning they did. Some women must have left the farm and gone into paying jobs. But most will not have done so; by any accurate use of the language, those women gave up work. So the truth is not just that young women, single or married, rarely worked during the fifteen years after the war; the total increase in female employment of all kinds was singularly modest. In other words, one important part of the myth of the Golden Age is quite accurate: Mom stayed home.

Put some of these demographic trends together and we can see why the years after World War II loom so large in America's collective imagination. For in that period America changed profoundly. The continent became much more evenly settled. The racial mix became better balanced as blacks spread out across the country; the South changed as it received an influx of population. The old divisions between city and country broke down as both lost population to suburbia. This, in sum, was the macro consequence of the two great population drifts.

But there were micro consequences, too—consequences which show up not in national statistics but in the way that families and communities lived their lives. Americans started to behave in different ways from their parents. In the suburbs, families had space and privacy. If they'd left a farm, as millions had, they could raise vegetables for fun; not because they had to. If they'd left a crowded tenement in the city, they could make love in privacy; not in embarrassment that in-laws would hear them. Families were stable; divorce was rare; women could devote their time to children.

This wasn't Utopia; that is clear. In her book *The Way We Never Were* Stephanie Coontz of Evergreen State University has detailed a sad catalogue of family dysfunctionality obscured by the statistics. Plenty of families were poor; plenty had alcoholic fathers (and mothers, too). Indeed, during the 1950s there was a rash of books, articles, and films on the awfulness of family life in the suburbs. William H. Whyte wrote

The Organization Man about Park Forest, Illinois, and though he admired some of the suburbanites' activities, he plainly did not like them. David Riesman, in *The Lonely Crowd*, worried about the "other-directedness" of the modern man, constantly looking for reassurance from a stifling peer group.

Suburbs were to blame. Suburbs bred sex-crazed wives whose detumescent husbands could no longer satisfy them; suburbs bred "juvenile delinquents," pouting and grunting like James Dean. Suburbs were right-wing. Had not William Levitt said, "No man who owns his own house and lot can be a communist. He has too much to do"? Had not Richard Nixon bragged in Moscow that the suburban kitchen—"designed to make things easier for our women"—was the epitome of capitalism's triumph? Suburbs, wrote the sociologist Herbert Gans, were supposed to breed a "new set of Americans, as mass-produced as the homes they lived in, ruled by the strictest conformity, incapable of real friendship, bored and lonely, alienated, atomized and depersonalized."

Predictably, the most dire warnings were reserved for those areas that combined the two population movements of the age—the suburbs of the Sunbelt. There is a moment in *Double Indemnity*, Billy Wilder's classic film of 1944, which encapsulates the intelligentsia's view of Sunbelt suburbia. An insurance salesman and his lover meet to discuss a murder. They meet not in a bar, not in an underworld dive, but in a Los Angeles suburban supermarket. This was evil among the Corn Flakes.

The most vitriolic attack on the suburbs came from two writers: Lewis Mumford and Betty Friedan. Mumford, an urban theoretician, published *The City in History* in 1961. It is not clear from his book if he liked any urban form that had been built later than, say, 1700. But he certainly loathed the suburbs. Suburbs were a "multitude of uniform, unidentifiable houses, lined up inflexibly, at uniform distances, on uniform roads, in a treeless communal waste . . . inhabited by people eating the same tasteless pre-fabricated foods, conforming in every inward and outward respect to a common mold. . . ." Suburbanites lived "an encapsulated life, spent either in a motor car or in the cabin of darkness before a television set." Los Angeles, needless to say, was the "reductio ad absurdum"; it was "grotesque," an "undifferentiated mass of houses." (One dares to wonder—had Mumford ever been there?)

Friedan, a journalist, published the The Feminine Mystique in 1963. For her, suburbs were "ugly and endless sprawls," a "national problem." They trapped women at home with children, doing work "an eight-year-old could do." If the suburban housewife didn't work she wouldn't have orgasms; she would soon be a lush. "Labor-saving" devices were nothing of the sort; they were ways of tying women to kids and the kitchen. Suburban women struggled with a "problem that has no name." "As she made the beds, shopped for groceries, matched slipcover material, ate peanut butter sandwiches with her children, chauffeured Cub Scouts and Brownies, lay beside her husband at night—she was afraid to ask even of herself the silent question—'Is this all?' "

Were things really that bad? Friedan (who had herself left the suburbs for the city) was on to something—life was not all roses for the educated American woman in the 1950s. But the intellectuals' critique failed the acid test. The suburbs, especially the Los Angeles suburbs, were the places in which Americans wanted to live. Farmers could now leave western Kansas and find comfort beyond their dreams. Excitement, too: after 1955, they could take the kids to Disneyland and enjoy safe, vicarious adventures. The intellectuals never understood that for Midwest farmers or the New York working class, a ranch home with a dishwasher and TV was seventh heaven. The attacks on suburbs, wrote Herbert Gans, were simply "upper-middle-class ethnocentrism."

Gans himself lived from 1958 to 1960 in a Levittown at Willingboro, New Jersey, across the river from Philadelphia, and in 1967 published a book about his experience. He found a society which formed more than 100 voluntary organizations within a couple of years. He found an informed interest in the local schools. He found substantial churchgoing (in no other rich country would such a book have devoted so much space to religion). He found little boredom or loneliness, little adultery (unsurprisingly, since it would have been impossible to hide it). He found little teenage delinquency. He found a society which had very little "unwanted conformity." Above all, he found a place that was "happy"; a good place to live.

The suburban Americans of Levittown had a stability and a cohesion in their lives. And, crucially, the twin movements of population across the country and to the suburbs had made such virtues portable. Though suburbs on the other side of the continent differed from those Gans studied outside Philadelphia, they were not so different that if a family moved it would be unable to "fit in." At least among white Americans, the twin population movements had made social cohesion all but universal. And this, in turn, provided a predictability to American life. Wherever they were, Americans knew what they were getting—the same PTAs, the same TV programs, the same design of houses, the same indicators of community spirit. Call this conformity, if you like: but it bred a relaxed comfort which has only grown in value in hindsight.

One other factor contributed massively to the sense of national unity in the Golden Age. There was no difficulty in knowing who was an "American." Why? Because there were so few immigrants.

Politicians of every stripe like to say that America is a country of immigrants. Yet within recent memory, it wasn't. After the great wave of immigration from 1880 to 1910, immigration was severely restricted. Tough national quotas, biased heavily toward Europeans, stopped almost all immigration from Latin America or Asia. The Great Depression did the rest. Since America was hit harder than any other developed economy, few potential immigrants saw it as a land flowing with milk and honey. In the five years from 1926 to 1930, for example, more than 121,000 Britons emigrated to the U.S. In the following five years, fewer than 15,000 did so. In 1933 there were only 23,000 new immigrants in total; a number so small had not been seen since 1830.

Indeed, in the 1930s as a whole, there was a small net out-migration of Americans. Some emigration from America was voluntary, but lots of it was not. As the labor market tightened in California and Texas, so Mexicans, who had long treated the border like a sieve, found themselves unwelcome. All told, about 400,000 Mexicans were forcibly "repatriated" during the 1930s—a number which certainly includes many who, born in El Norte, were actually American citizens. Anti-immigrant feeling survived into the 1940s. The disgraceful internment of Japanese-Americans during World War II is well known. Less remembered are the zoot suit riots in Los Angeles in 1943, when mobs of white youngsters attacked Mexicans and Filipinos, stripping many of them of clothes while the police looked on. For the next few years, Los Angeles imposed a nighttime curfew on Mexican kids.

The restrictions on immigration very quickly changed the

way the country looked and sounded. The period between 1940 and 1960 saw about 3.5 million immigrants; fewer than in any twenty-year span for a century. At the end of the 1950s, 178 million people lived in an America which was the world's economic, cultural, and military powerhouse. Yet that decade of American preeminence saw less immigration than the 1850s, when just 31 million lived in a sparsely peopled rural land.

In 1910, about 14 percent of the American population was foreign-born; the proportion was far higher in the major metropolitan areas. By 1940, the proportion of foreign-born had shrunk to just 8 percent—less than it had been in 1850. Since immigration remained tightly controlled until 1965, the foreign-born population continued to decline in relation to the native-born. The low point was reached in 1970, when a little over 4 percent of all those who lived in America had been born outside it—the smallest percentage since the founding of the republic.

It's difficult to comprehend quite what a change this was. Those who were middle-aged adults in the 1950s had been born into a country that was genuinely multicultural, particularly if they had been born in cities. Before World War I, New York, Chicago, San Francisco, and Los Angeles were a babel of foreign tongues, a bazaar of customs from around the world. But their children, those born in the Golden Age (and hence of middle age as this book is being written), grew up in quite a different place, one where everyone spoke English and where newly arrived immigrants were a rarity. This was quite new, even if it now seems like the height of a lost normality.

And there's more. With the exception of Mexicans crossing and recrossing the border, those lucky immigrants who were allowed into America in the Golden Age were overwhelmingly of white, northern European stock. In the 1950s, there were just 133,000 immigrants from the whole of Asia (many of them GI brides, which is how the number of Filipinos was augmented). In the same decade, there were nearly three times as many immigrants from Canada alone and four times as many from Germany. So rather than challenge America's sense of national identity with strange languages and stranger customs, the few immigrants who did arrive merely reinforced the dominant white, European culture.

In the hundreds of books written on America in the Golden Age, the absence of sustained analysis of immigration is striking. There's a reason for that. In the 1950s, upper-middle-class Americans—the sort of people who write books—could easily have thought that everything was normal, that immigration continued apace. These lucky folk met plenty of immigrants, because so many of those admitted were professional men, scientists, and scholars—often, refugees from the wreck of Europe. Hitler, as one academic has said, did a hell of a lot for Harvard. But for the vast majority of working-class Americans, it would have been quite possible to go through the 1950s hardly conscious of new immigration at all. The American population was more homogeneous than it had ever been before, or would ever be again. If, in 1955, one had asked the lunch-bucket crowd at a Monongahela Valley steel mill, "Who are Americans?" they would have replied, "People like us." And they would have been right. But not for long. Soon, renewed immigration, from places that weren't Canada or Germany, would shake up the postwar order itself: and this would be one of the reasons why the cohesion of the Golden Age broke down.

There is one final reason for the unity of American society in the Golden Age. America in 1945 was a country made by war. That much is plain and well-understood. Less remarked upon is a truth no less important: war continued. Not until 1995, and the fiftieth anniversary celebrations of VE Day in Moscow, could it accurately be said that war had ended. The *continuation* of a sort of war after 1945 had at least as great an effect on the United States as the real war had done.

The Cold War created institutions which were quite new to the American temper. Greg Bailey, now a lawyer and writer in St. Louis, spent much of his childhood in the 1950s and early 1960s at Bunker Hill Air Force Base in north-central Indiana. Bunker Hill was no ordinary military facility, and the kids who lived there were no ordinary base-brats. They were knowing, sophisticated; aged seven or eight, they could identify Berlin on a map and understood its significance. Their dads had told them; and since their dads worked for the Strategic Air Command—SAC—their words carried weight.

For forty-five years, SAC (motto: "Peace Is Our Profession") was one of the icons of the Cold War. Formed in 1946, it was knocked into shape by the larger-than-life figure of General Curtis LeMay. At its peak in 1957, SAC had thirty-eight domestic bases, and facilities in Europe, Canada, Africa, Puerto Rico, and Guam. Each base was equipped with the giant bombers which, loaded with nuclear weapons, could leave for the Soviet Union within minutes of an alert. And the possibility of such an alert was taken seriously. On training exercises, Bailey's father worked on the assumption that Russian saboteurs had slipped through the cornfields and poisoned the base's water supply.

It is easy to make a dread fun of such attitudes, and Stanley Kubrick's 1964 film *Dr. Strangelove* duly did so. On one level the film is just satire, with its LeMay figure discussing likely deaths in the event of war: "I'm not saying we won't get our hair mussed. Ten, twenty million dead, tops, depending on the breaks." But the satire is given a bite because Kubrick adeptly slipped in references to postwar culture—a B-52 pilot slyly reads *Playboy*, a general keeps a machine gun in his golf bag—as if to emphasize a nervy counterpoint between consumerism and the threat of death.

The end of that threat was formally acknowledged in September 1991, when George Bush stood down SAC from alert. For forty-five years LeMay's men had been at the ready: watchful, neurotic, regimented (the edges of lawns on a SAC base were clipped to an angle of precisely 45 degrees). SAC was staffed by men who, however crazy they may sometimes have seemed—and LeMay must often have seemed very crazy—thought that the defense of "our way of life" (a favorite *Dr. Strangelove* line) depended on the speed with which they could run from their houses to the bombers.

How did something as extraordinary as SAC come about? In 1946, "strategic" bombers were novel not just because their technology was of recent vintage, but—more importantly—because America had never before seen the need for anything like them. For almost all of its history the U.S. had been bereft of an enemy. Sure, Britain had been a rival during the nineteenth century, and sometimes an unfriendly one; but it was not an enemy. Nor did either Mexico or Spain, against both of which America had fought short wars, warrant that title. In World War I, of course, Germany had been an enemy—for all of eighteen months (compare this with the seventy-five years from 1870 during which it is reasonable to describe France and Germany as enemies). But in 1941 the U.S. had met a genuine enemy, and as the fog of war cleared, it was to find that it had another one. "I suppose," said Harry Truman as he left Washington in January 1953, "that history will remember my term in office as the years when the 'Cold War' began to overshadow our lives. I have hardly had a day in office that has not been dominated by this all-embracing struggle." Truman could not know it, but American lives would be overshadowed by the Cold War during the terms of the seven presidents following him. Plainly, of all the factors which made postwar America unique in the nation's annals, the fact that it was at war throughout the period ranks as high as any. This, incidentally, was a true war; more than 100,000 Americans lost their lives on the battlefield between 1945 and 1989. That little adjective "cold" can be awfully misleading.

Precisely because war forced America to have a particular view of the world outside its borders, it was bound to create a particular kind of nation within them. The Cold War contributed to national unity in two ways. First, it provided an ideology—a sense of national identity formed in opposition to a common enemy. Second, it shaped a set of economic and social policies which were cohesive in nature. But these developments, which were central to the construction of America in the Golden Age, should not obscure an obvious truth: the long state of war was a tremendous shock to the system.

The best evidence for that is in the position played in national life by the armed forces. For all of the Golden Age, and since, America has had a mighty military machine, whose offensive capability dwarfed that of any other nation. For twenty-five years, young men were conscripted into the colors; great emptinesses of desert were handed over to military exercises; a massive "defense industry" grew up to satisfy the Pentagon's wants and needs.

This was a complete break with the American past. Hith-

erto, when America's wars had ended, the army was dis-
banded forthwith; soldiers went home. Ten years from the
end of the Civil War, forces more than a million strong had
been reduced to an army and navy of just 35,000 men. After
the Indian wars ended, the army became little more than a
frontier constabulary. It was hated in the South (a memory of
the Civil War and Reconstruction), and not much more popular in the North, where the capitalists of the Gilded Age
thought the army a great waste of money. At the end of
World War I, the old pattern was repeated. Between 1918
and 1920 an army and navy with 2.9 million men on active
duty were reduced to forces just 340,000 strong. So the
natural policy in 1945 was never much in doubt. At VJ
Day there were about 12.1 million men and women on active
duty; two years later there were just 1.5 million. This was almost certainly the fastest voluntary reduction of military
might that the world has ever seen; and it turned out to be
unsustainable.

It was unsustainable because the U.S. found itself in a
Manichaean struggle with the Soviet Union. The literature
on the start of the Cold War is now immense, and controversial, but the sequence of events is pretty plain. An anti-
communist ideology came first; the "domestication" of the
Cold War into America's economic and social structures followed a few years later.

Americans lost faith in their wartime Soviet ally very
quickly. In opinion polls taken in the summer of 1945, more
than 60 percent thought that the Soviet Union would cooperate with the United States in the postwar world. By late
1947 less than 20 percent did. In the 1946 elections red-
baiting was already evident, and Joe McCarthy was elected
to the Senate from Wisconsin. In January 1947 George Ken-

nan, then at the National War College, deplored in a letter the "hysterical sort of anti-communism which, it seems to me, is gaining currency in this country." He might have deplored it, but he couldn't stop it; in March that year, just ten days after he had unveiled the Truman Doctrine before a joint session of Congress, the president announced an Employee Loyalty Program for government workers. Later in 1947, the House Un-American Activities Committee started its investigation into communist penetration of the movie industry. By the 1948 election the red scare was in full flood. The administration was riddled with communists; it was in the process of "losing" China; and so on. Between 1950 and 1954, McCarthy and McCarthyism would terrorize diplomats, professionals, writers, film-makers, and many others far less celebrated. The paraphernalia of thought control flicked through the lists of those employed by government departments and great seats of learning with mechanical zeal, picking out this teacher and that bureaucrat, flipping them into a professional trash can. In New York City alone, according to historian John Patrick Diggins, 321 schoolteachers and 58 college professors lost their jobs either because they had a communist blot on the copybooks of their past, or because they would not cooperate with investigations. (Diggins also reminds us that this witch-hunt was popular, noting an opinion poll in which 91 percent of Americans said that communists should not be allowed to teach. In 1954 nearly 80 percent of Americans thought that communists should not be allowed on radio.) Anti-communism merged with anti-intellectualism in a stultifying ideological grip: note how easily Adlai Stevenson was stigmatized as an "egghead" in 1952 and 1956.

In some measure, anti-communism was a rational response

(prosecuted irrationally) to the situation in which American policy-makers found themselves. At the end of the war, Americans had hoped, assumed, that they would be able to share the burden of remaking the wrecked world with their European allies. But Britain and France were much weaker than Americans supposed. The postwar world turned out to be bipolar, not multipolar. Especially after Russia got the bomb, power was held by a duopoly headquartered in Moscow and Washington. Since America and the Soviet Union were very different places, moved by very different national creeds and perceptions of their national interest, this unwelcome bipolarity meant that the U.S. and the Soviet Union became each other's opponents; they were bound to respond to each other's moves.

And the Soviet Union's moves were frightening. As early as February 1946, Stalin had argued that the fundamental contest between capitalism and communism might lead to renewed hostilities. Shortly after the speech, George Kennan's famous "Long Telegram" from Moscow argued that the Soviets had a "neurotic" view of world affairs; they wished to destroy the traditional American way of life. America and its allies, argued Kennan, had to meet attempts to expand Soviet power with resistance wherever those attempts might take place.

Within a year, Kennan's doctrine would have a name: containment. On February 21, 1947, the British informed the Americans that they were unable to meet their obligations to the security of Greece and Turkey. On March 12, President Truman announced that America would act as the guardian of democracy wherever it flowered. And so, at speed, the political structures of the Cold War were built. Congress approved aid to Greece and Turkey in April; General George

Marshall, the secretary of state, unveiled the plan for economic assistance to Europe that came to bear his name in a speech on June 5. In February 1948 a communist coup in Prague toppled the last hope for a noncommunist government in Eastern Europe. The same year, the North Atlantic Treaty formally bound the United States to the defense of Europe. In the summer of that year the Berlin blockade and airlift began and late in the summer of 1948 came the intelligence that the Soviets had the atomic bomb.

There's enough in that bare-bones account of three years' worth of crises to explain the demonization of communism. Granted, Soviet conduct could not reasonably be explained as a genuine threat to the lives of those in the American heartland, worries about the water supply at Bunker Hill Air Force Base notwithstanding. But by threatening America's weak allies in Europe, the Soviet Union forced America to act as if it were itself threatened. One could not be certain at the time that Soviet designs necessarily stopped at the Oder-Neisse line. Better to meet the Soviet threat early and head-on, while the U.S. was unquestionably more powerful than its adversary. On this view, turning the communist regime in Moscow into an enemy of the U.S. was the inevitable consequence of a rational policy choice. Besides, we know, in hindsight, that Soviet domination of Eastern Europe was despised by those who lived under its heel. However hateful many of its manifestations, history has not invalidated anticommunism as an ideology with noble intent.

There was one other reason for the force of America's anticommunist ideology. By 1950, America was involved in a real, shooting war with communist adversaries in Korea. The Korean War changed everything. It gave new life to the anticommunist witch-hunts. It solidified America's sense of itself as the embattled leader of "the free world." And it brought the Cold War home, transforming the domestic economy and society. Korea was crucial to the Golden Age.

Until Korea, defense budgets had been kept in check. There was virtually no increase in outlays on national defense between 1947 and 1950. But in January 1950, after the explosion of the Soviet atomic bomb, Truman asked the National Security Council to draft a full statement of American strategic aims. That statement was known as NSC-68—when completed, about 26,000 words long.

NSC-68 changed America. It marked a total rupture with the traditional American suspicion of standing armies. The paper called for a rapid buildup of political, economic, and military might in the free world, so that America and its allies would be able to challenge Soviet expansion wherever (literally) it occurred. The Allies were expected to contribute their share, but everyone understood that the main burden—which, over four to five years, the drafters of NSC-68 thought would be around $50 billion—would be shouldered by America. Many economists thought the plans were harebrained, or woolly, or both. But on June 25, North Korean troops swept south. America immediately offered assistance to the government in Seoul, and by June 30, Truman had given General Douglas MacArthur authority to engage North Korean troops. The three-year Korean War was underway. As Secretary of State Dean Acheson knew and said, NSC-68 was now safe. The plan was formally ratified by the full National Security Council on September 30. Expenditure on defense and international affairs was about $17 billion in 1949. By 1953 it had reached $52.7 billion; not even the most hawkish writers of NSC-68 could have contemplated that.

The level of spending on the Korean War transformed the country. In 1939, before the outbreak of World War II, government spending on defense and international affairs amounted to a little more than 2 percent of the economy and about 12.4 percent of the total federal budget. In 1949 the respective figures were still relatively modest: about 8 percent and 34 percent. But then came the once-for-all change of Korea. In 1951 defense spending accounted for more than 14 percent of the national economy. By 1955, after hostilities had ceased in Korea, defense spending still ate up 11 percent of the total economy and 62 percent of the federal budget. It was Korea—not Vietnam, much less the Carter-Reagan defense boom of 1979–86—which locked a large part of American business into dependence on the Pentagon. Not until the early 1990s would defense spending be scaled back, and even then, when America was at peace, its share of the national economy was three times what it had been in the 1930s.

But Korea did much more than change the economy. During the Korean War the dark side of the rational choice to demonize communism became apparent. Korea made absolutely sure that the loyalty boards and blacklists would continue for years. It was at the time of Korea that America found itself allied with the most reactionary, anti-democratic forces in the developing world—so long as they could pass muster as anti-communist. At the same time as it was fighting openly in Korea, America became committed to secret wars in Guatemala, Iran, Vietnam—anywhere that the logic of containment and NSC-68 dictated (which meant anywhere at all). It was Korea that made Washington an imperial, garrison city, circled by the citadels of national security—the Pentagon across the river in Virginia; the CIA over in Langley; the National Security Agency in Fort Meade, Maryland. All these gave, and still give, a military flavor to the nature of government in Washington quite different from that in Paris or London (but not different at all from that in Moscow). It was Korea that established that any man who aspired to be president had to be a putative "commander-in-chief." (To catch the novelty of this, consider whether Calvin Coolidge, say, would have passed the test.) Korea guaranteed that Bunker Hill Air Force Base would not soon revert to quiet pasture.

Anti-communism did not end with the Korean War, nor did the domestication of the Cold War. Between 1953 and 1956, the number of people who told pollsters that they wanted to "find out all the Communists in the country, even if some innocent people are accused" actually increased by 8 percentage points, despite McCarthy's fall from grace in 1954. In 1956 the Soviet Union ruthlessly crushed an uprising in Hungary. In 1957 a distinguished committee chaired by Rowan Gaither of the Ford Foundation found that the Soviet Union was just as threatening as ever. The Gaither report postulated (quite inaccurately) that the Soviets were so strong that a "missile gap" would soon be evident. The predictable response—shades of NSC-68—was yet another defense buildup, this time coupled with the suggestion for a huge civil defense program. Total cost of the Gaither proposals: a budget-busting $19 billion. In the 1960 election John Kennedy made the missile gap the centerpiece of his foreign policy criticism of Eisenhower. And in 1962, the Cuban missile crisis made the threat from communist aggression more terrifying than ever. After being fed a long diet of crisis, real or faked, it's hardly suprising that anti-communism had such a hold on the American imagination.

When the Cold War came home, however, it did so not just through the ideology of anti-communism. A whole set of social programs piggy-backed on the Cold War. Eisenhower used national security as a reason for building the interstate highway system. After the Russians launched *Sputnik* in 1957, Congress passed the national Defense Education Act to boost scientific education both in schools and in universities. Expenditure on health research, too, could be easily justified by the need to have a populace ready and able to beat back the Russians.

Most important, America's claim to be the guarantor of liberty abroad gave a new twist to the struggle for civil rights at home. The rhetoric of the Cold War was used by black leaders. In Martin Luther King's sermon on the very first night of the Montgomery bus boycott of 1955, he said, "If we were incarcerated behind the iron curtain of a communistic nation, we couldn't do this. But the great glory of American democracy is the right to protest for right." In a recent biography of John Kennedy, Richard Reeves has argued that "Kennedy was most concerned about domestic racial troubles as a foreign policy problem. He didn't want to see the problems give the country a bad name abroad." In 1961, at the height of the Freedom Riders' campaign, the *New York Times* made the link explicit. "In Birmingham and Montgomery the United States has lost another battle in the global cold war. The hoodlums, the screaming women, the citizens who stood and watched have done much to aid the communist cause throughout the world." In such unexpected ways did the Cold War double back from lands far away and make its presence felt at home.

Not the least important domestic aspect of the Cold War arose from the nature of the new standing army. Charles

Moskos of Northwestern University says that during World War II 80 percent of "age-eligible" American men served in the armed forces. As we know from Ernie Pyle's reports, from films and many memoirs, the American army in World War II jumbled white Americans together, of all classes and ethnic backgrounds. *Time* magazine said that those who raided Rouen "sounded like an All-American eleven" and proceeded to reel off six "ethnic" names, plus the "older, but not better, American names like Ray and Thacker, Walsh and Eaton and Tyler." Granted, armies aren't and can't be democracies; but they are melting pots.

The Cold War kept that pot boiling. The draft was suspended for eighteen months in 1947 and 1948. It was then reintroduced and maintained for another twenty-five years. In 1955–56, there were 2.5 million men and women in uniform, the greatest number ever in peacetime. In all, says Professor Moskos, five out of ten of all age-eligible men served in uniform from 1950 to the mid-1960s. The figure then fell, during the Vietnam War, to four out of ten; by the mid-1990s it had fallen to about one in ten. So during the Golden Age conscription became yet another way in which America was bound together. Since the military had been integrated before Korea, it is doubtful if there has ever been another American institution which so intermingled so many men, irrespective of their race, their social class, their ethnic background, or the region from which they hailed, as did the armed forces of the 1950s and 1960s. Moskos argues that the peacetime army "brought together millions of Americans who otherwise would have lived their lives in relative social and geographic isolation": as good a definition of the cohesion of the postwar years as one could wish to find.

Set all these factors together, and it is no surprise that

Americans should look back with longing on the world they have lost. American society was more homogeneous than it had even had been, united in the ways that it lived, the entertainment it enjoyed. West was more like east than ever before; south more like north. Underpinning it all were a common set of values and ideologies—values based on the central position of the nuclear family, ideologies based on a hatred of communism and a veneration of symbols of patriotism, like the armed forces. Immigration, that huge social force which had for generations brought the outside world to America's shores, was kept at a bare minimum. The federal government, continuing the role that it had been given by FDR during the Depression and World War II, bound the country together. It rebuilt the southern economy; it helped to kill Jim Crow; it funded a military which provided a common home to Americans of all accents and colors, and a military-industrial infrastructure which brought untold benefits to some backward regions. And while all this was going on, the economy was growing as never before, bringing prosperity to all. It is to that central economic phenomenon of the Golden Age, one now missed more than any other, that we turn next.

CHAPTER FOUR

The Golden Age: Economy

When Americans think back to the Golden Age, they don't just remember a nation that collectively moved to the suburbs and whose families had lots of kids. They also have a sense that those years were times of prosperity: that the economy was stronger then than it is now. Indeed, it was. America went through wrenching changes in the Golden Age, as people left behind their established patterns of life and forged new ones. Economic growth was the glue which made what might otherwise have been a time of social turmoil into one remembered for its placidity.

Habitually, we speak of "the American economy" as if it were as familiar as an old dog, an everyday presence whose mood can be checked by a handful of vital signs. Price levels, unemployment, the money supply, the Dow Jones index—we have a nodding acquaintance with all of these in much the same way that we know about the baseball standings or the TV schedules. Even those who are not economists know that this isn't the whole story; that "the economy" is an aggregate of activity in different industrial and commercial sectors, that different regions specialize in different businesses. But instinctively we feel, rightly, that all these slices of economic life come together to form a single whole.

Yet this sense of the American economy is comparatively recent. The United States spans a continent, with all the distance and variety which that implies. Understanding the growth of the economy after 1945 requires us to know how, for the first time, the myriad economic activities on this huge continent came to be combined in a single market.

America has wrestled with the idea of a single national market since the earliest days of the republic. For James Madison and Alexander Hamilton, a central criticism of the Articles of Confederation was their inability to provide for a true economic union between the states. Without such a union, they argued, the power of the United States would be less than its potential. In today's parlance, Madison and Hamilton wanted to establish a common market in which capital and labor, goods and people, could move freely. And so, in a series of clauses inconveniently scattered about the text, the drafters of the Constitution made the goal of a common market explicit. The famous commerce clause permitted Congress to "regulate Commerce with foreign nations, and among the several States, and with the Indian Tribes." The states, moreover, were prohibited from entering into foreign treaties. Seeing that none of them wanted to forge security alliances, the main purpose of this was to prohibit trade treaties with foreign powers. The states' ability to levy duties on imports and exports was limited. Most importantly, the Constitution declared that "No Preference shall be given by any Regulation of Commerce or Revenue to the Ports of one State over those of another: nor shall Vessels bound to, or from, one State, be obliged to enter, clear or pay duties in another."

The commerce clause has been doubly controversial. In the first place, the courts interpreting it have had to strike a balance between national powers and federalism; between the desire to create a nationwide, continentwide free trade area and the Constitution's reservation of all "non-enumerated" powers to the states. In the second place, the courts have had to choose between competing ways in which a free trade area might be guaranteed. On one view the national authorities— judicial and executive—are like the spectators at a bare-knuckled boxing match. They merely "hold the ring," or create an environment in which businesses compete with each other and in which states, so long as they do not deny the possibility of interstate commerce, legislate as they think fit. On a second view, the national authorities "shape the market"; they set bounds within which economic competition and free trade take place. In effect, the commerce clause asked courts to choose between a broad economic principle of laissez-faire, or one which contemplated a more interventionist role for the national government.

This abstruse stuff is vital to the history of modern America for one reason: the Golden Age started in the shadow of a Supreme Court decision which decisively answered both commerce clause questions in an expansive way. By the mid-1930s the correct reading of the commerce clause had transcended academic controversy. Between the stock market crash of October 1929 and the election of Franklin Roosevelt in 1932 American output had shrunk by more than 40 percent. The New Deal legislation which followed this catastrophe—agricultural support, wage and price controls, fair competition codes, public works—could only be constitutional if the commerce clause was read in a certain way. In 1935, the administration's National Recovery Act was struck down by the Supreme Court, prompting Roosevelt to ask, "Does this decision mean that the United States Government has no control over any national economic problem?" and to declare, "We have been relegated to the horse-and-buggy definition of interstate commerce." He would soon have his revenge. In *National Labor Relations Board v. Jones & Laughlin Steel Corp.*, decided in 1937, the court settled both questions on the commerce clause jurisdiction in favor of New Deal theory. The justices stressed the importance of a national common market. Congress, the court held, was not limited to regulating "commerce among the several states." It could also regulate anything else if such regulation was "essential or appropriate" to protecting commerce—even if the regulated activity took place solely within one state. True, the court made a nod in the direction of federalism; the commerce clause could not "effectually obliterate the distinction between what is national and what is local and create a completely centralized government." But this caveat could not conceal the fact that the reach of the federal government had been much extended. Moreover, the court acknowledged that to promote the free flow of internal trade the federal government was allowed to do more than "hold the ring." The government, said the court, could not only restrain barriers to trade but could also "foster, protect and promote" commerce.

Jones & Laughlin provided the legal basis for the mildly interventionist role that the central government was to play in the economy of the Golden Age. But an economic theory for that role was needed, too. Such a theory grew out of wartime. If the economy had continued its slow, peacetime recovery from recession in the 1940s, New Deal controls of the economy would have been gradually dismantled. Instead, after Pearl Harbor, they were intensified. In January 1942, the War Production Board was granted enormous powers over industry and raw materials. The Defense Plant Corporation invested in new plants making everything from aircraft to synthetic rubber. In April 1942, the Office of Price Administration was founded to control prices and rationing. After FDR's death, government intervention in the economy continued. Policy-makers were terrified that the war would end with economic gloom and chaos—just as had happened at the end of World War I, with hyperinflation in Germany and riots in Britain and America. On cue, the economy shrank by 1.6 percent between 1945 and 1946. By 1947, a net 2.6 million women had lost their jobs, with an immediate effect on family incomes. The government tried almost everything. Under the Surplus Property Act, for example, wartime facilities were sold, sometimes for just twenty cents on the dollar (which is how Henry Kaiser got Willow Run).

This does not mean that the country emerged from the war committed to social democracy and extensive government controls on the economy. Quite the contrary. As Alan Brinkley of Columbia University has argued, the war had not been a happy experience for the "economic planners." The War Production Board, says Brinkley, was an "endless bureaucratic ordeal," dominated by corporate executives—the "dollar-a-year men"—lent by Big Business. Economists had both been made skeptical of the market by the experience of the Depression, and made skeptical of intervention by wartime. They were groping for a new model for the role of government in the economy. They were given one by Alvin Hansen, a professor at Harvard who has a reasonable claim to the title of father of the postwar economy. In 1947 Hansen was sixty, and the leading American disciple of John Maynard Keynes, whose *General Theory of Employment, Interest and Money* had been published in 1936.

For Keynes, the central question of economics was the maintenance of adequate demand in the economy. He believed that government could ease the social consequences of the business cycle—poverty and unemployment—by pumping money into and out of the economy through fiscal policy. So when demand by the private sector for goods and services fell and hence unemployment rose, the government could cut taxes or increase spending to create additional demand.

Hansen agreed; in his postwar work the phrase "adequate aggregate demand" is repeated so often that it begins to sound like a Sanskrit mantra. He praised Britain's 1944 White Paper on employment policy (which Keynes had drafted) and admired the social cohesion of Sweden. But he was not a socialist. He understood the raw vitality of American business, the animal instincts which had made it an unparalleled source of wealth and innovation. And he noticed that, despite the prophecies of doom, the economy had started to expand in 1947. Hansen, in short, was a perfectly conventional capitalist (as, indeed, was Keynes) who was convinced that the American economy had to be based on a "price" or "market" system. For Hansen, government action should be limited, first, to "compensatory" fiscal policy intended to smooth the rough edges of the business cycle; and second, to investment in new airports, slum clearance, and schools— that which we now call the "infrastructure."

Hansen's views were plain in the original draft of the Full Employment Act of 1946, which was meant to be the economic centerpiece of Harry Truman's first administration. As originally drafted, the Act committed the government to "full employment" and implied that budget deficits were a permissible policy in times of recession. The bill's more radical proposals were watered down by Congress, and in its final form the bill established a Council of Economic Advisers as a voice of "orthodox" fiscally conservative, free market policies (which is what the Council has been ever since). But Congress still committed the government to some management of the economy. The crucial second section of the Employment Act (the word "full" was dropped in the legislative process) is worth quoting in its entirety:

"The Congress hereby declares that it is the continuing policy and reponsibility of the Federal government to use all practicable means consistent with its needs and obligations and other essential considerations of national policy, with the assistance and cooperation of industry, agriculture, labor and State and local governments, to coordinate and utilize all its plans, functions, and resources for the purpose of creating and maintaining, in a manner calculated to foster and promote free competitive enterprise and the general welfare, conditions under which there will be afforded useful employment opportunities, including self-employment, for those able, willing, and seeking to work, and to promote maximum employment, production and purchasing power."

It's easy to read that long sentence as boilerplate—easy, and wrong. In fact, the Employment Act embodied a consensus on economic policy which continued for the next thirty-five years.

The consensus—often called conservative Keynesianism—accepted the importance of a single national market and welcomed the interpretation of the commerce clause which had assisted its creation. It granted the government a role in the management of the economy as a whole. But in contrast to the experience of the European democracies, America's consensus implicitly frowned on government intervention at the level of an individual firm. Unlike their European counterparts, America's economic policy-makers never contemplated taking the "commanding heights" of the economy into public ownership. The rescue of Chrysler and the nationalization of the rail passenger business through the medium of Amtrak were controversial precisely because they were examples of a kind of intervention which has been so rare. Proof of the limited nature of government economic intervention is quite easy to find. Between 1929 and 1949, government's share of national output just about doubled. Yet between the late 1940s and the early 1990s, government's share increased modestly from about 28 percent of the GNP to around 33 percent. In all that time, federal tax revenues stayed within a narrow range of 17 percent to 19 percent of the economy.

In 1958, John Kenneth Galbraith, also a Harvard economist, attacked the "conventional wisdom" (a phrase he coined) of conservative Keynesianism precisely because it was indeed conservative. Galbraith argued that the dominant economic ideas of the postwar years had led to insufficient investment in "public goods" like health and education. Instead, said Galbraith, government had limited itself to maintaining demand for the goods and services of the private sector. Hence (simplifying a complex argument) Galbraith's claim that America combined private affluence with public squalor.

Yet even if Galbraith's critique were true, it is also true that American governments have never attempted the impossible—to withdraw entirely from management of the economy. Though it was not until John Kennedy's presidency that an administration publicly committed itself to Keynesian demand management, every postwar president did it. Some pumped money into the economy in the guise of defense buildups—as during the Korean and Vietnam wars, and again from 1978 to 1986. Some cut taxes—in 1948, 1954, the early 1960s, and the early 1980s. But just as every postwar American president accepted that the prime motor of economic growth should be the private sector, so did every one try to shape the environment in which the private sector operated.

For proof of the strength of the postwar consensus, read the annual economic reports of the presidents. Over thirty-two years, from 1948 to 1980, they are strikingly similar. Of course, different things were stressed at different times by different presidents. But consider the two following phrases: "The Federal government will use its vast powers to help maintain employment and purchasing power"; and "The government does not have a stop and start responsibility [for economic management] but a continuous one." In both cases, the author was not a Democrat but Dwight Eisenhower; there are similar sentiments in the reports signed by Richard Nixon.

It was not until the 1982 report—the first signed by Ronald Reagan—that the tone changed. "In the year just ended," wrote Reagan (or rather, his advisers), "the first decisive steps were taken towards a fundamental reorientation of the role of the Federal government in our economy." This, said Reagan, was "long overdue" because "The policies of the past have failed." Some failure. In the previous thirty-five years, the United States had seen prosperity grow like no country had ever seen before. It had done so on the base of a solid, unshakable consensus both on the nature of the American economy and the role of government in managing it. Lucky old America; by comparison with the lurches in economic policy seen in other countries since 1945, this was stability indeed.

By the end of the 1940s, then, America had a firm theoretical base for the development of its economy. Legal barriers to the creation of a true national market had been removed, and a specific, limited role for the government had been defined. Now the dream of a single market had to be made concrete, which took muscle, money, technology—and, indeed, concrete.

Long before the Civil War, John Calhoun of South Carolina had argued that a system of federally financed roads and canals would "bind the Republic together." Albert Gallatin, Jefferson's great treasury secretary, offered a Report on Roads and Canals to Congress which said that improved transportation would "cement the union." In the nineteenth century, the federal government granted land to railroad companies; from Tocqueville's time, America led the world in railroad construction. Later, the South was linked by the railroads to the North (though less well to the natural resources of the West); the mines and farms of the West were linked to Chicago, and, thence, to the East. And America soon led the world in the construction of roads. In 1907 ground was broken for the Bronx River Parkway in New York—the world's first "limited access" highway. In the 1920s, Rand McNally's maps showed drivers the best way around the continent. By the 1930s, Los Angeles's streetcars had been replaced by wide roads. Robert Moses, master builder and power broker, linked New York City to beach and glade with a series of "parkways." During the New Deal, new roads were built to lift areas out of recession; Asheville, North Carolina, went collectively wild when it was announced that the route for the Blue Ridge Parkway would kiss the edge of town.

Still, at the end of the 1930s there was nothing like a national highway system—despite intense lobbying by the rubber, cement, and asphalt industries. But in 1940, just as the Golden Age was about to begin, the first 160 miles of the Pennsylvania Turnpike were opened from Carlisle to Irwin. This was the first true freeway, designed for commercial vehicles (banned from Moses' parkways) as well as private cars. The war saw new roads like the one that ran to Willow Run. Between 1947 and 1951, an average of 18,700 miles of federal highways were built annually, compared with an average of just 13,700 between 1936 and 1940.

The great breakthrough, however, came with Eisenhower's election in 1952. In 1919 he had spent fifty-six days crossing the continent in a motorized convoy. As president, he had the opportunity to improve on this record, and took it. The interstate system was endorsed by Congress in 1956. On its face, the legislation was concerned with national defense (those deadly Canadians . . .); some in Washington saw the program as a Keynesian device to pump demand into the economy. But whatever justification was offered for the 42,500-mile system, completed in the 1990s (and 90 percent funded by the federal government), its impact was clear. As Calhoun and Gallatin had dreamed so long ago, the roads were to bind the republic together.

The interstate system remains unique in the world; to this day, no superhighway crosses Canada. Granted, when they entered urban areas, the interstates did more harm than good. The new roads carved through cities as if some latter-day Moses had parted a new Red Sea. The Dan Ryan Expressway in Chicago isolates one of the world's largest (and most awful) public housing projects from the rest of the city. New freeways ruined the waterfront of San Francisco and Seattle; they nearly wrecked the sublime classicism of Washington, D.C. There was nothing particularly American about this vandalism. But the hatred which some came to feel for urban freeways was just enough to cloud the success of the whole program. And that success was real. New roads and bridges lifted areas like Maryland's Eastern Shore out of rural poverty; they linked Colorado's ski resorts to Denver (through a tunnel aptly named after Eisenhower). Throughout the country, they bound places that had once been backwaters into a national consciousness.

The freeways virtually created long-distance trucking. In 1946, at the beginning of the Golden Age, 9 percent of the volume of intercity freight traffic was carried on trucks and 68 percent of it by rail. By 1975, rail's share of the total had shrunk to 37 percent. The volume carried by trucks, meanwhile, had increased more than fivefold, and now stood at 22 percent of the total. New factories were built by the side of the interstate; courtesy of Uncle Sam, trucks drew up right to the main gate. Tractor-trailers, big rigs, CB radio, and truckstops became part of American folklore, joining heavy petting in the back seat as slices of Americana which depended on the internal combustion engine.

The new roads did more than bind the country together, like a vast spider's web without a center; they did more than disperse and yet link economic activity more capably than rail could ever have done. They enabled Americans to live more like each other. And, for that matter, sleep like (and with) each other. Hotel chains sprang up as if dragon's teeth had been sown around the new roads. Fast-food chains—

Colonel Sanders's Kentucky Fried Chicken and McDonald's—dotted the littoral of the highways. The fast-food joints were so successful that, by the 1990s, the search for authentic regional cuisine had become a spectator sport, as upper-income travelers searched for that hard-to-find joint which sold chicken-fried steak.

There were other links, other webs binding the country together, creating the national market. In 1945, there were 200 telephones for every 1,000 Americans; in 1960 more than 400. Between the end of the war and the early 1970s, the number of long-distance conversations each day increased sixfold—but the price for a three-minute call from San Francisco to New York tumbled to a quarter of what it had been. Phones in the kitchens, phones in the cars, teenagers spending unrationed hours on the phone with their friends— no other country in the developed world had anything like this.

And no other country had internal air travel. Those wonderful ads in the *National Geographic* magazine in the 1950s, with sleek Grace Kelly look-alikes flitting off to San Francisco—nobody else had them, or anything like them. America had always led the world in aviation; the first regular airmail service linked Washington, D.C., to New York City in 1919, and within five years had been extended across the nation. But after 1945 the business matured to span the continent. In the thirty years from 1945 to 1975, airlines' route mileage increased four times, their revenue passenger miles twenty times, and their freight tonnage no less than a hundred times. Elsewhere, airlines were usually owned by the government. Only in America were private-sector airlines, like United, Eastern, and TWA, household names. True, it was not until 1972 that more than half of all Americans had ever flown. But it is also true that in the 1950s and 1960s air travel was commonplace and affordable for both business and pleasure. This was unique on the globe.

Still, for all the ways in which the Golden Age saw the country become linked together in a single market, that market was still asked to span a continent—a tall order. In the forty-eight contiguous states there were still four time zones, great topographical ruptures (nobody had abolished the Rockies), and, not least, significant differences of climate. The last of these, however, was about to change.

Say that it's 1950, and you are a banker in Charleston, South Carolina. Your house has a porch, with wide halls; you keep the windows open but the blinds drawn. In the summer, you drink as much iced tea or lemonade as you can stomach, and escape whenever possible to the coolness of movie theaters. State and local government offices are cooled by an ineffective fan (the federal building down the street does better—typical of the Yankees). Your son says he wants to live in Phoenix, about which you know nothing save that it is in a desert. So he must be mad. An acquaintance has just asked for a loan to develop nearby Hilton Head Island, which you know is both buggy and humid. So he must be mad, too.

But he wasn't. In 1945 Henry Kaiser—the same man who bought Willow Run and built the Portland shipyards—started building prefabricated homes for GIs, complete with air-conditioning. In 1951, the Carrier Corporation started selling cheap window units. The window units were noisy, but did the the job. Then, in 1960, central air-conditioning became available, and by 1965 40 percent of new homes in the South had it. According to historian Raymond Arsenault, in 1960 18 percent of all southern homes—new and old—

had air-conditioners; by 1970 more than 50 percent of them did, and by 1980 more than 73 percent. Even among blacks in Mississippi—the poorest of the southern poor—40 percent of households had air-conditioning by 1980.

The air-conditioner did as much as any single artifact to make America a unified economic market. Along with the automobile and the television, it is one of the products that remade and, to an extent, homogenized America. It absolutely transformed the South—changed the architecture, the food and drink. In fact, the air-conditioner changed the very fabric of social interaction, since it was now more comfortable to stay locked indoors than to chat on a porch. It doubled the length of the tourist season in Florida, and it made possible the construction of Walt Disney World in Orlando, opened in 1973. (Southern California, home of the original Disneyland, does not need air-conditioning to make the summer bearable; central Florida does.) It made the South attractive to immigrants from the North who had hitherto shunned its summers. All in all, says Arsenault, "General Electric has proved a more devastating invader than General Sherman."

Texans took to Carrier's machines as to the manner born. In *The Right Stuff*, Tom Wolfe described the arrival of the Apollo astronauts in Houston on July 4, 1962. The city, wrote Wolfe, was "an unbelievably torrid effluvial swamp, with a mass of mushy asphalt, known as Downtown, set in the middle." The astronauts were taken to the Houston Coliseum, where "A bone-chilling chill hits them. . . . The place is air-conditioned Houston style, which is to say, within an inch of your life. . . . Everybody's bone marrow congealed. It made you feel like your teeth were loose."

Wolfe had a point. The Gulf cities and desert Southwest have been changed utterly by the air-conditioner. The two states which have grown fastest since 1950 are Arizona and Nevada. Nevada has gone from 160,000 leathery ranchers to 1.2 million people who race from their pool to the central air-conditioning when the going gets really tough. In 1950 Arizona had a population less than that of tiny Rhode Island; now it has one bigger than Connecticut. Phoenix and Las Vegas, Palm Springs and Houston—none of them could have grown the way that they have without the air-conditioner.

Perhaps the best example of the way in which the webs of a national market transformed America is Hilton Head. In the late 1940s, the island had a population of about 1,000, of whom fewer than 50 were white, and fifty-four varieties of mosquito. You could only reach the island by ferry (itself a recent innovation). Old Sea Island cotton plantations had disappeared and the island's economy depended on hunting and lumber. Less than fifty years later the island had 25,000 permanent inhabitants and attracted 1.5 million visitors (who spent $500 million) each year. The visitors came from all fifty states and from foreign countries oceans away.

Charles Fraser, who planned the island's development, says that air-conditioning was a crucial breakthrough which made success possible; he discovered the technology by selling Carrier's window units during his junior year at the University of Georgia. But think of all the other ways the national market contributed to Hilton Head's growth. In 1956 it was linked to the mainland by a bridge. Later, as I-95 made its unlovely way down the Eastern Seaboard, you could drive there from Washington in a day, from New York in a little longer. Planes would bring people from Boston and Los Angeles. Cheap telecommunications would let travel agents call, and call, and call again, until they got the deal they wanted. Trucks would bring merchandise from factories to hundreds of ritzy shops, stocking and restocking shelves in a trice. Workers whose parents had rarely left their hometowns would come down and play those boom sports of the Golden Age, golf and tennis (by the 1990s Hilton Head had twenty-seven golf courses and 300 tennis courts). Granted, there have been tourist booms in other parts of the world. But Hilton Head is not in an undeveloped country; it doesn't offer cheap sun-and-sex vacations. It's got spacious oceanfront condos and expensive shops. Yet it is not plutocratic; it could not attract 1.5 million visitors a year if it was. Most of its visitors are just ordinary folk; small businessmen from Atlanta and Columbia, retired lawyers or military men. Its golf courses are as popular with your local Oldsmobile dealer as they are with a visitor from Japan.

That is the true achievement of the post-1945 American economy. From the commerce clause to the air-conditioner, Americans used tools and theories to shape the richest integrated economic market the world had ever seen. The benefits of that market were distributed to more ordinary people than any economy had ever before managed. The great American middle class was able to enjoy a lifestyle that in other countries was the exclusive prerogative of the exceedingly rich.

There was, moreover, one other important characteristic of the postwar economy—one that contributed much to the sense of national cohesion in those years. In a way that marked it apart from the trading nation that had been America before World War I, the economy of the years that followed World War II was remarkably self-contained.

At first glance, this is counterintuitive. For after the war, American policy-makers explicitly adopted an "international" economic policy. In 1944, the United States had sponsored conferences at Dumbarton Oaks, in Washington, D.C., and Bretton Woods, New Hampshire, and the conferences led directly to the formation of the World Bank and the International Monetary Fund—both to be headquartered in Washington. Under American leadership, the western nations adopted a set of economic policies broadly consistent with the "conservative Keynesianism" of post-1945 America. Post-1945 global capitalism was Made in America.

That, of course, made it an object of suspicion. Foreigners began to think the whole purpose of the postwar order was not to create benign conditions for economic growth, but rather to create new markets for American goods. Europeans had once scrawled "Kilroy was here"; soon they would write "Yankee go home." In the mid-1960s, the French writer Jean-Jacques Servan-Schreiber wrote a best-seller—*The American Challenge*—whose thesis was that American capitalism was undermining Europe's economic and cultural independence. In America itself, it became fashionable to explain the whole of the postwar settlement as a plot by American capitalists to secure foreign markets and to strangle any politico-economic system which threatened their interests.

Yet despite the zeal with which Americans promoted global capitalism, a striking truth remains. In the 1950s the "international economy" was not nearly as important to America as is often assumed. No doubt the unsung work of the U.S. government's statisticians does not uncover all the mysteries in the mind of man, but it does shed light on one or two. And it pretty much disposes of the argument that the postwar settlement was just a veil for the ambitions of American capitalism.

The crucial data are those for trade flows. Take 1950 as a

starting point, since by then America's trading partners in the advanced economies were able to afford American goods. In the ten following years the value of American exports did indeed double, and the trade surplus in merchandise goods increased from $1.4 billion to $5.9 billion in 1960. But as a share of the American economy, exports went nowhere. They accounted for 3.6 percent of output in 1950 and the same figure in 1959. Exports rose to 4.1 percent of the economy in 1960 and oscillated around that share for the next decade. Compared with the export growth of other leading industrial countries at the same time, this was quite insignificant.

Far from demonstrating the rapaciousness of American capitalism in the postwar years, the trade figures prove, rather, how self-contained the American economic miracle was. In 1955, for example, combined imports and exports made up less than 7 percent of the economy. Given that any national economy, however large, cannot satisfy all the wants of its consumers, that is quite a measure of self-sufficiency. The postwar output of what we can call "Friedan goods"—the dishwashers, televisions, and everything else that was remaking the American home—went overwhelmingly to American consumers. Exports of consumer goods grew much slower than those of other goods. By 1970, exports of Friedan goods were a smaller share of total exports than they had been in 1950.

There was a corollary to this history of American exports: there were very few imports, too. At no time in the 1950s did imports account for more than 3.1 percent of the economy; they did not account for more than 4 percent until 1970. Apart from a few enthusiasts for British sports cars, American consumers ignored foreign goods. Take any episode of *Leave*

It to Beaver. Just about the only foreign product in the Cleaver home would have been the coffee in a gleaming, aluminum percolator—and even that might have come from Hawaii. No Korean televisions; no German cars; no British coats; no French wine. Moreover, had a screenwriter suggested an episode in which Ward Cleaver's company was bought by a Japanese firm he would surely have been thought mad. True, as Servan-Schreiber noted, American multinational firms were investing abroad quite heavily (though this was not a new phenomenon—it had been seen in both the 1890s and 1920s). But foreign direct investment in America was so small as to be hardly noticeable. As late as the mid-1970s, around the end of the long postwar boom, foreign-owned businesses employed only a little over 1 percent of American workers.

Of course, when the economic figures from the 1950s are picked apart, you can see the beginnings of developments that would later become controversial—like the rise of Japan. As early as the mid-1950s, there was political opposition to the imports of Japanese textiles. By 1960 (much earlier than most suppose) the value of Japanese imports was greater than those from the United Kingdom. Moreover, as other economies grew stronger, so they nibbled away at America's monopoly of Friedan goods. In the immediate postwar years, America's imports were dominated by foodstuffs and industrial raw materials. But the share of imports taken by consumer goods grew steadily, from 6 percent in 1950, to 13 percent in 1960, to 19 percent in 1970. To most Americans, this rise in import penetration must have seemed imperceptible. One day, it would have profound political consequences.

The postwar economy, then, was "new" in two ways. For

the first time, America had a truly integrated national market; and that market was self-contained. Both of these factors contributed enormously to the sense of national unity which typified the Golden Age. But there was more to the postwar economy than that. The economy "grew" like never before.

"Economic growth" is one of those little terms that hide a lot. At its simplest, it is the source of prosperity for individuals and their families. People like prosperity; and since the years after 1945 were, for most Americans, prosperous beyond their wildest dreams, it is hardly surprising that they should look back on them with longing—and when they do, they unwittingly thank growth for their good fortune. In fact, economic growth was the bond that bound together a society which was actually going through quite wrenching change—from farm and city to the suburbs, from small families to large ones.

The sources of economic growth are a mystery. Yet there is no doubt that in the years after 1945 the economy did grow in a new way, and that such growth changed the face of America; in fact, made it a happier place. Two industries make the point: computers and steel.

There's a curious absence in *The Organization Man* and *The Lonely Crowd*, those two books which tried so hard to define America's character in the years after 1945. W. H. Whyte and David Riesman hardly mention the three initials IBM. Yet those who worked for the giant computer company were the very apotheosis of "other-directed," organization men. They were expected to conform to a strict dress code: blue suits, white shirts, stiff collars. Faces were scrubbed and hairless; alcohol was banned on company premises or at company functions. IBM (and IBM men) prized above all else "marketing"—that quintessence of the American business ethic, a word which has a settled meaning in no language other than American English.

Yet the apparent, easily mocked conformity of IBM hid a richer truth—one utterly missed by Whyte, Riesman, and other critics of the post-1945 dispensation. Those hardworking marketing men were at the heart of a period which made America the envy of the world. In the twenty years between 1945 and 1965 IBM's annual gross revenues in the U.S. increased twentyfold to $2.5 billion. And having reached a position where they controlled two-thirds of the world's computer market, IBM then bet the company. In the late 1960s IBM gambled $5 billion—that's real money now and was astonishing then—on the System 360 family of mainframe computers. It was a winning bet; the System 360 and its successors underpinned IBM's fortunes right into the 1980s.

IBM offers almost a caricature of America's modern social history. Its first headquarters were in Endicott, New York, a gritty industrial town on the Chenango River, where it was said that a prudent IBM manager would draw the shades before having a cocktail with his wife (Thomas Watson, Sr., the patriarch of the firm, replaced a row of honky-tonk bars in Endicott with a research center). After World War II the firm moved to Manhattan, during those few years when New York was the undisputed if uncrowned capital of the world. Then, in the 1960s, the company moved again—naturally, to the suburbs, where most of its marketing men and technicians already lived: IBM settled in Armonk, in Westchester County, New York. And those suburban conformists made a little miracle. Instead of moping around in the anomie which Lewis Mumford and Betty Friedan said was their lot, they built the tools that gave America international economic dominance. In 1965 there were 386 computers for every million managers in America, compared with 125 in prosperous Switzerland and just 65 in France—a vital American technological advantage which yet endures.

The beardless, white-shirted men of IBM did well from the Golden Age: they traveled, they bought TVs and hi-fis. But the fruits of the economic success of post-1945 America were not limited to the tree-shaded suburbs of Westchester County, or to those who worked in high-technology industries. They were widely spread; in their own way, they were just as noticeable, for example, in the steel towns of the Monongahela Valley, south of Pittsburgh—towns which nobody would ever confuse with Westchester County.

The steel industry in America has been stained with blood. One writer calls the mills at the turn of the century "charnel houses"; in 1906 no fewer than 405 men were killed in accidents in U.S. Steel plants. The history of the Mon Valley towns, each with a steel mill lining the river, a few blocks from downtown, had been bloodier than most. In July 1892, a pitched battle between Pinkerton men and workers at the Carnegie plant in Homestead left twenty-four dead. In the 1950s, this history of strife and danger had not been forgotten. It lived on, for example, in the loyalty workers gave to their unions. But it was a history of little relevance to the conditions that most workers now enjoyed. The demand for American steel after 1945 was such that employment was all but guaranteed. Moreover, the profits of the steel companies were so great that even unskilled hands could earn money beyond the dreams of their fathers—let alone their grandfathers, the men who had trekked to western Pennsylvania from Wales and Ireland, from Croatia and Slovakia.

Many of the Mon Valley towns peaked in population in

the early 1930s. But though their population was slipping between 1945 and 1970, the towns had never before been as prosperous as they were in those years—nor would they ever be so rich again. This was not nirvana; labor relations were only marginally better than they had been, and the valley suffered all the hardship of a long and bitter steel strike in 1957. Still, the steel towns had thriving shopping centers, good jobs, decent opportunities for leisure. The steelworkers had television, of course. But they also had limitless deer to hunt in the woods; they could fish or go boating on the lakes that dot the western Pennsylvania mountains. As much as in the suburban villas of Armonk, it was in the row houses of McKeesport and Homestead, squashed between the Monongahela, the steel plants, and the timbered woods above them, that the American dream of middle-class comforts for all was made real.

Why did IBM—and not some German, French, or Japanese company—come to dominate the world's computer industry? Why did the Mon Valley have a brief period of prosperity? Part of the answer lies far beyond the Golden Age. The republic had long had a stunning abundance of untapped natural resources. Given such a bounty, you would have had to be singularly dumb and lazy to do anything but become rich. Americans were neither. It was the Americans themselves, for example, who developed transport technology, first by water, then by railroad, so that raw materials could be taken to the factories where they were alchemized into goods with a higher value. But ingenuity alone didn't build the American economy; other nations were just as clever. According to one modern study, in one or another of the forty years before 1913, Canada, Australia, all the Scandinavian countries, France, and Germany all had rates of productivity growth higher than that of the United States; and after 1918 Japan joined them. In 1914, it was far from axiomatic that a world-changing industry based on the manipulation of electrons could have developed only in the suburbs of the United States. Many would have assumed that Germany, for example, would be the home of the computer. In 1914, America did not have a monopoly of higher education. The Great Depression was much deeper in the United States than anywhere else. The American economy contracted in size by roughly two-fifths in the early 1930s; no other developed economy shrank so much. It would have been a particularly confident forecaster who would have said, in 1939, that America would shortly be the economic hegemon that it became. So: why IBM?

Partly, because of war. We can't pretend that the gun-thundered years of 1914 and 1939 didn't happen. War made all forecasts moot. Twice within three decades, world war stood an expected, "normal" development of the global economy on its head and produced in its wake something quite extraordinary.

The size of the American nation, the abundance of its endowment of natural resources, would always have made America a huge economy, but world war twice held back America's competitors, wrecking the economies of Britain, France, Germany, Japan, and Russia. And whereas the economic wreckage after World War I was typified by financial disaster—like hyperinflation in Germany, or the liquidation of Britain's portfolio of foreign assets—the wreckage after 1945 was all too physical: twisted girders and rubble everywhere from Tokyo to the Ruhr. The damage that war did to other economies provided a space in which the unscarred muscles of Americans could flex themselves. Canada, similarly protected from the ravages of war by the Atlantic and Pacific, is the only other country whose economy delivered such riches to its people so soon after the end of World War II.

Yet war explains only part of the mystery of America's growth in the Golden Age. After 1945 the American economy did not just outperform that of other nations; it was also strong when measured against America's own past. According to figures by Kumiharu Shigehara of the Organization of Economic Cooperation and Development, between 1900 and 1913, American gross domestic product per head grew by an annual average of 2.0 percent; between 1913 and 1950, it grew by an annual average of 1.6 percent. But between 1950 and 1973, it grew by an average of 2.2 percent each year.

The war and its aftermath certainly helped that happen. American exports grew in the Golden Age; but they could not grow much, since wrecked economies cannot fund huge flows of imports. At the same time, however, total imports into America in the early postwar years were very low, much lower than they would have been if the other industrial economies had escaped the ravages of war. This no doubt gave some American businesses opportunities in the home market that they would not otherwise have had. The Mon Valley steelmakers, for example, did not have to compete with imports from Europe and Asia. But neither imports nor exports were sufficiently large for international trade to explain more than a part of the growth of the economy as a whole.

Economies can "grow" in all sorts of ways. They can annex new territory and markets; they can put new workers (like women or children) into jobs. Some of America's postwar growth can be explained in this unexciting way; the movement of more than 15 million Americans after the war from farms to factories and offices was a source of growth. The great emptying of rural America shifted resources (broadly speaking) from an inefficient sector of the economy to a more efficient one. But there comes a time when you run out of new workers or new land. In the end, productivity alone is what counts. As Paul Krugman of Stanford University says, "Productivity isn't everything, but in the long run it is almost everything. A country's ability to raise its standard of living depends almost entirely on its ability to raise its output per worker."

American productivity did increase dramatically in the Golden Age. But hasn't the American economy always been tremendously productive? Hadn't the American worker's sheer vitality, his energy and skill, knocked Tocqueville's socks off? Wasn't "Yankee ingenuity"—that great old synonym for productivity—something at which European visitors to American shores stood in awe?

Well: yes and no. The American worker has indeed always been productive and skillful; the early American colonists, for example, had to invent tools unknown in Europe to break and harvest the virgin land. But over the long term, there is little evidence that Americans have been more inventive, more hardworking, than anyone else—or at least, by enough, for long enough, to make a massive difference. The post-1945 triumphs of the American economy, in other words, did not depend on some God-given, exceptional capacity of Americans. Other factors mattered.

Measuring productivity growth is an inexact science, but just about everyone agrees on the broad picture, if not the exact details. In the fifty years before 1930, American productivity grew at an annual rate of about 2 percent a year.

During the Depression it slumped to an annual growth rate of less than 1 percent a year. Then, in the years between 1945 and the early 1970s, productivity growth soared to an annual rate that sometimes reached 4 percent and averaged about 3 percent over the whole period. These broadbrush trends obscure important differences—for example, the second half of the Golden Age saw less productivity growth than the first half. But the trends do show that the Golden Age was mighty unusual.

Unfortunately, economists find it no easier to explain the causes of productivity growth than to measure it. In a large sense, no doubt, the postwar spurt of growth was a mere "catch-up" by the American economy from the Depression. During the 1930s, and especially during the war, a host of technological breakthroughs had been made. Many prewar inventions were displayed before a salivating public at the New York World's Fair in 1939; some wartime inventions were at the heart of the success of companies like IBM. But during wartime itself, there had been little incentive, and less demand, to turn new technologies into goods for sale to ordinary Americans. After 1945, that changed; which is why Betty Friedan had a TV and washing machine.

Moreover, the war raised the rate of savings. In the 1930s, at the heart of the Depression, there had been little on which to spend money. In wartime, there was, in effect, a system of compulsory savings through rationing and war bonds; in 1944, the amount of total personal saving was fourteen times as much as in 1939. Not until the Vietnam War period did the federal government "dissave" through persistent budget deficits; in the sixteen years from 1950 to 1966 the federal budget was in surplus as often as it ran a deficit, and only once (in the short-lived recession of 1958) did the deficit approach 2 percent of the GNP. So in the years after the war there was a tidal wave of savings—unappropriated by the government—available for investment in new plants and new technologies. As this investment took place, so the productive potential of the economy rose; and as that happened, so did the wealth of its people.

Put all this together, and we can start to explain the postwar growth. The application of new technologies led to a "catch-up" from the years of low growth. A huge pool of capital was available for investment. There was an open world-trading system to which America's potential competitors came, if not crippled, then at least bandaged. Conservative Keynesianism brought stability to macroeconomic policy. All these factors reinforced each other. And at the level of the individual company, like IBM, or an industry, like steel, they provided grand new opportunities. Those commercial opportunities, in their turn, were translated into wages and profits which created a massive middle class, able to enjoy amenities beyond the dreams of their parents.

Many modern economists think there was one more element. They look not just to "capital" of the familiar, green kind—the cash, stocks, and bonds which provide nourishment for growing companies—but to the "human capital" which each individual invests in himself. Economists are now fascinated by the effect that education—the acquisition of knowledge and skills—has on economic growth. And they have noticed that, for one more reason, the Golden Age was remarkable. America's educational system was transformed.

Here, too, the postwar economy had deep roots. Between 1870 and 1940 the population tripled, while the number of students in secondary schools increased by a multiple of almost ninety. By 1940 about three-quarters of all those aged from five to nineteen were enrolled in school. Even allowing for the usual differences between the South and everywhere else, and between blacks (anywhere) and whites, this effectively meant that everyone was offered a secondary education. Hence one of the icons of the Golden Age—the local high school with its hordes of teenagers, each one with perfect teeth, clear skin, and the keys to the car.

In 1940, 12 percent of the male population and 16 percent of women had completed four years of high school; thirty years later, the relevant figures were 30 percent and more than 37 percent. This improvement was impressive, but hardly dramatic. Much the same judgment could be applied to the burst of interest in high school scientific education after the Russians launched *Sputnik* in 1957—it was important, but not earthshaking. But in higher education, the Golden Age was a time of such change that the word "dramatic" hardly does justice to the case.

To catch what happened to higher education in the postwar years it is useful not to look at the aggregate figures but at just one institution—or rather, a set of them: the University of California. It isn't a perfect example—the system is bigger and better than anything anywhere else. But understanding how California created a system of mass higher education that, at its finest, was the envy of the world gives some indication why the American economy grew so much after 1945.

California's constitution of 1849 made provision for a state university, and in 1853 Henry Durant, an alumnus of Yale, opened the Contra Costa Academy, in Oakland, with three students. Within two years he had written the charter for a private College of California. In 1861 the trustees acquired a larger site that they named Berkeley. The land was hilly and foggy; lousy for farming. The next year President Lincoln signed the Morrill Act, which granted states 30,000 acres of land for each member of Congress, so long as they used the income to establish colleges "to promote the liberal and practical education of the industrial classes." In 1868, California rechartered the College of California, on the Berkeley site, as the University of California. By the turn of the century Berkeley had 2,550 students and was considered to be among the best colleges in the country, with a medical and law school. In 1891 the private university of Stanford was founded just south of San Francisco, presenting the state university with a competitor; in order to preempt something similar in Los Angeles, the regents established a second campus there in 1919. From 1930 to 1958, under the presidency of Robert Gordon Sproul, the system expanded to eight campuses— and the federal government arrived.

Once again, war mattered. War brought the feds to Berkeley, just as it did to Ann Arbor. And the Cold War kept them there. The enormous expenditure on defense technology of the 1950s and 1960s bred a near-dependence on Uncle Sam. After 1947, the Lawrence Radiation Laboratory at Berkeley, whose scientists had participated in the Manhattan Project, was supported almost entirely by the U.S. Atomic Energy Commission. By 1965, Lawrence scientists had discovered about a third of around eighty known atomic particles and had revolutionized man's concept of matter. Pre-1941, the federal government had supported little university research outside agriculture. By 1964, 58 percent of the University of California's research expenditures came from federal grants, contracts, and appropriations. From the hills above the campus, visitors could look down on a jumble of cyclotrons and laboratories, all of it courtesy of Washington.

Research money wasn't the half of it. In 1944, when the war was far from won, Congress passed the Servicemen's Readjustment Act, universally known as the GI Bill of Rights. Among other benefits, the GI Bill gave veterans help with books and tuition fees, and paid them a small stipend while they studied. The bill had its opponents, like Robert Hutchings of the University of Chicago, and few ever thought that the chance of four years at college would be as attractive to battle-hardened soldiers as proved to be the case.

Yet the GI Bill was a staggering success. In 1946, more than a million veterans enrolled at universities, doubling total student numbers. At Berkeley, enrollment nearly tripled in the two years between 1944, when 7,748 students were on the books, and 1946, when 21,909 were. In Quonset huts and crowded classrooms, professors taught students who were often as old as them and much more wise in the ways of the world. Nationally, at the peak of the GI graduations in 1950, 496,000 degrees were awarded, more than twice as many as in 1942. Not until 1962 was the 1950 figure surpassed. By the time the program was over, more than 2.2 million veterans had used the GI Bill to go to college. And then off those veterans went, off in their blue suits to IBM; off to scurry, clipboard in hand, after Robert McNamara at Ford and the Pentagon. They headed for newly air-conditioned Houston, and (still in blue suits, still in crisp white shirts) joined in the partnership between the public and private sectors which became the Apollo space program. The GI Bill graduates were not just the organization men; they were also the best and the brightest.

In California, as elsewhere, the GI Bill turned higher education into an "expected entitlement": young people now felt that they had a right to a period in a college. But by the mid-

1950s, this sense of entitlement threatened to overwhelm the state. The first wave of baby-boom children were making their way through the high schools, and California was absorbing more than 300,000 immigrants from the rest of the United States each year. In 1955, a report for the state predicted that within a decade the state's colleges and universities would have to more than double their number of students. To avoid chaotic, unplanned growth, the state drew up a master plan in 1960 for the integrated development of junior colleges, state colleges, and the university system; the plan was passed into law by the state legislature. Under the plan, each sector of higher education was allotted a distinct role. The university was to recruit among the top 12.5 percent of high school graduates and had prime responsibility for post-master's study and research. The state colleges (later brought together as California State University) were to recruit among the top 30 percent of high school graduates, and had a key role in teacher education. The junior colleges, later to be known as community colleges, were to be open to virtually all high school graduates: the goal was to have such a college within commuting distance of almost all residents. Modular degree courses and the system of "credits" (an American invention, incidentally) made it easy for students to move from one university to another or to take some time off from their studies. And the state provided the funds, with hardly a murmur: Clark Kerr, who was president of the university at the time of the master plan, says that he can recall only one conversation at a senior level about resources.

By the mid-1990s, the University of California enrolled over 166,000 students a year on nine campuses. Not just Berkeley, but also UC Los Angeles, Davis, San Diego, and Irvine have international reputations as leading research universities. There are now nineteen campuses of California State University and 106 community colleges. If you are looking for a monument to the energy of America in the Golden Age, and to the way in which the federal system can work wonders, higher education in California would be hard to beat.

Why is this story so central? Because it transformed the American economy. Economists are still perfecting techniques that enable them to assess the rate of return to investment in human capital—in education and skills—but the results are striking. Gregory Mankiw of Harvard reports, as a consensus view, that each year of schooling raises a worker's wage by about 8 percent. That implies that for the average American worker with thirteen years of schooling, two-thirds of his earnings represent a return to investment in education. Put like that, it begins to be clear that the GI Bill, and the expectation of an entitlement to higher education, suddenly moved the American economy to a new level of productivity. In 1940, a teenager working in an aircraft factory in Long Beach might have developed the skills to fix a welding machine if it broke down on the job. Ten years later, the same kind of boy might have earned a degree in aeronautical engineering. You do not have to despise the first, humdrum skill to appreciate that the acquisition of the second, higher skill is more likely to provide a higher standard of living for those who get it—to say nothing of those that boy may one day employ. Multiply that example by a few million, and you begin to understand how the GI Bill changed the American economy.

The reference to boys in the last paragraph is not the slip of an unthinking sexist. It is deliberate. For there were not one but two, overlapping, extensions of higher education in the postwar years. In 1920, there were about twice as many bachelor's degrees awarded to men as to women. But the GI Bill naturally benefited men. So by 1950 the gap had grown; there were now three times as many bachelor's degrees awarded to men as to women, and Betty Friedan was quite right to note that the position of women on campuses in the 1950s was less happy than it had been in the 1930s. It wasn't just that those women who made it to the university were expected to look for a man rather than a degree. In relative terms, there were simply fewer women around. Between 1940 and 1960, the numbers of first degrees awarded to men went up by 133 percent, to women by just 79 percent.

But then look what happened. Between 1950 and 1970, men's first degrees went up from 329,000 a year to 451,000 a year, a rise of 37 percent. But the number of first degrees to women exploded from 103,000 to 341,000, or by 231 percent. By 1980 (when men were awarded 474,000 first degrees, women 456,000) there was virtual parity between the sexes; and by 1982 women were ahead. In that year (and every subsequent year) women earned more first degrees than men. In short, the step-change in the productive potential of the economy that started with the GI Bill took nearly forty years to show its full colors. First, veterans were raised to a new level of skills; then the veterans were joined by nonveteran men; then came the younger sisters and daughters of those men.

So there are a number of lessons from the expansion of higher education. The first is that it was a critical factor—almost certainly the most important—in explaining the unprecedented economic growth that took place in America in the thirty years after 1945. That growth in turn was the bedrock, the essential underpinning, without which America could not have been its self-confident self.

Second, the new opportunities in education both led and followed the creation of a new kind of economy; one which placed far more emphasis on brains than on brawn. Between 1940 and 1970, the total civilian labor force increased from about 52 million to about 79 million. During that time blue-collar workers increased from 26.6 million to 39.4 million. But white-collar workers more than doubled their numbers, from 16 million to nearly 38 million; by the mid-1970s the labor force would be predominantly white-collar. Moreover, within blue-collar trades, by far the greatest growth was in the service sector, not in manufacturing or mining. The number of cleaners, for example, increased six times, the number of blue-collar workers in hospitals seven times. Those blue-collar workers employed in mines and quarries, by contrast, dropped from 845,000 in 1940 to just 164,000 in 1970. In short, though both those who worked for IBM and those who worked in the Mon Valley did well in the Golden Age, only the IBM workers were on the right side of history.

By the end of the Golden Age, the economy was one of white collars and clean hands. Since education is the ticket of entry to the huge American "middle class," the new economy helped smooth away class resentment. After the GI Bill, there was little reason and less excuse for our talented boy on the shop floor in Long Beach to think that he was doomed to a life of baloney sandwiches and beer while the children of his boss took their girlfriends to the Cal-Stanford game. Educational opportunity was expanding for everyone. Its distribution may not have been perfect, but it was more systematic than any other society had so far managed. And this strengthened social cohesion. Post-1945, universities became (as the wartime armed forces had been) places where men of very different social backgrounds could mingle relatively freely. The system of "mass" higher education became a way in which "middle-class" cultural norms were spread around the population. In the beer cellars and dorms, everyone could talk, equally knowledgeably, about Jackie Gleason or Lenny Bruce; everyone could dance to Elvis.

The economic and social significance of the explosion of higher education had a flip side. Both IBM and the Mon Valley had benefited from the prosperity of the Golden Age, and both had been the source of new middle-class spending patterns—TVs, vacations, new cars, bigger houses. Yet the nature of economic growth meant that, quite soon, the experiences of the marketing men from Armonk and the steel-workers of the Mon Valley would diverge. In the 1950s, everyone was becoming more prosperous; workers in Armonk could look forward to continued prosperity based on their monopoly of a new technology, workers in the Mon Valley could rely on unions to protect their gains. But as the economy became more white-collar, so institutions of working-class solidarity were weakened. The best (though partial) proxy for measuring this is the proportion of the nonfarm labor force that was unionized. This reached a high point of 32.5 percent in 1953, after which unions started a steady and persistent decline, first in their share of the labor force and then, in the mid-1970s, in absolute numbers. By the early 1990s only about 16 percent of the nonfarm labor force was unionized, and even once-strong unions like the Steelworkers had been unable to stop the Mon Valley lurching into a terrible depression. Of course, the decline in union strength was not solely a function of the changing nature of the economy; it was also linked to anti-union legislation and to the unions' terrible public image. But it was partly driven by Americans' new educational opportunities. Much later, a few Americans would have cause to wonder whether this decline of labor unions was an undivided blessing.

Although it would not come into focus until the 1980s, the way in which a new, educated middle class made a new economy created an unexpected problem. Those without higher-level skills were left unable to partake fully of the benefits of the new economy, and bereft of working-class social institutions from which they could draw succor. In Armonk this didn't matter; in the Mon Valley, it did. The working class started to get left behind. In time, the American economy would stop generating the low-skilled, high-waged jobs on which the Golden Age had been built. Those who were left in declining industries and declining areas would start blaming anyone in sight. Blacks, for example: as affirmative action took root in the 1970s, so white workers began to think that their travails could be explained by misguided social engineering. Later, in the 1980s, foreign countries would be blamed for the decline in economic opportunities, as low-skilled work moved offshore, to Latin America or Asia. And by the 1990s, immigrants, prepared, according to myth, to work for far less than American workers would accept, also came in for a share of the blame for the declining fortunes of the working class. Playing off blacks, foreign competition, and immigrants, a degree of class and racial resentment would eventually develop in the white working class, of a kind and intensity unknown in the Golden Age.

Moreover, it gradually dawned on Americans that the expansion of higher education after World War II was easy compared with what would come later. By the 1980s, America was being asked to raise the level of skills not of a great middle class which had never before gone to college, as it had done in the 1950s; but to transform the skills of those for whom a college education was not necessarily appropriate. Of course the boy on the shop floor in Long Beach in 1940 had talents that were being wasted; everyone knew that, and everyone knew that all it would take to unlock those talents was the application of rather a lot of money and a place at Cal State. Later, America would be faced with a tougher nut to crack. It would be asked to raise the skill levels not of un-fulfilled youngsters, identifiably part of a society that shared much in common; but of kids sullenly alienated from their surroundings. And these new kids would not be in Long Beach or places like it; they would be in Compton, Watts, and other of the nation's ghettos.

So growth had its problems. Yes, from Armonk to the Mon Valley, to Long Beach, it created a middle class that, by the 1960s, was the envy of the world—richer, healthier, more self-confident. But even during the Golden Age, it was al-ready clear that some groups within the middle class were doing much better than others. The economy became, more and more, one that placed a premium on education. And so were sown the seeds of a class division which would not be fully obvious until the late 1980s. That specter, however, should not let us forget what an amazing time the period af-ter 1945 was. If you want to know what made the Golden Age golden, the answer is: the economy, stupid.

CHAPTER FIVE

An American Tragedy:
The 1960s

America had been very lucky in the years after World War II; and the luck ran out. Something happened—indeed lots of things happened—to America between the 1960s and the 1990s which wrecked the cohesion and self-confidence that had been so powerful in the Golden Age. The Golden Age had many endings, not one. Every one of the factors which for twenty years had brought Americans together weakened, and then changed. Like a machine gone mad, the cogwheels and driveshafts that had once turned out some perfect bolt of cloth ground to a halt, reversed themselves, and started tearing it up.

At the end of this process, America was a much more divided, messy society than it had been during the cohesive, stable years after 1945. It was often said that America was in decline, and indeed in some senses it was. Much of this decline was quite inevitable, a consequence of the rebirth of other nations and the end of the peculiar social conditions which had marked the Golden Age. To that extent "decline" is only problematic if we take as a starting point the years after 1945, which are a false comparator. But some aspects of America's decline are real and deeply disturbing, particularly the way in which it is becoming sharply divided by social class.

There's no neat sequence to the way in which the nation fractured. Different factors, different themes overlapped. Broadly, it is possible to identify three distinct periods. In what we often call "the 1960s," a period which really ran from 1963 to 1974, the federal government was stripped of much authority. In "the 1970s," really from 1968 to 1981, the nature of the American family was stood on its head. In the 1980s, new and troubling divisions emerged, both between regions and between social classes. In each of these three periods, and for each of the fractures which they epitomize, economic changes were a crucial determinant. By the 1990s, a fourth aspect of the extent to which America had changed had become apparent. America's place in the wider world had been transformed, as the external threat diminished, unprecedented numbers of immigrants arrived, and the economy became internationalized. All of these developments contributed to a sense of fragmentation of the nation, so much so that by the 1990s, at a time when vicious shooting wars raged in Eastern Europe, intellectuals could talk loosely of the "Balkanization" of America, and do so without obvious irony.

"Balkanization" overdoes the case; yet there is little doubt that America has changed dramatically since the Golden Age. Consider life in 1960, when Americans could look back on a period of great political stability. Only three men had held the office of president in the previous twenty-eight years. Never before in the republic's history had the shortest of three successive presidencies lasted more than seven years.

Of course, there were many issues which distinguished Eisenhower from FDR and Truman, but on the large questions the three men were cut from the same cloth. All believed in free enterprise economics, yet all recognized an economic role for government; all were committed to a strong national defense; all saw the United States as the leader of a bloc of like-minded democracies.

The next fourteen years were devastating, and though the tale of devastation is as familiar as an old book, it is still chilling. One president was murdered. His successor was forced from office, his spirit broken by an unpopular foreign war. The next president was the only one to have resigned while in office. Along the way, Robert Kennedy, one of the country's most popular politicians, and the man who perhaps more than any other tried to bridge the nascent gap between white-collar elites and blue-collar workers, was murdered while running for the presidency in 1968; George Wallace was crippled while campaigning in 1972. Both Martin Luther King, Jr., and Malcolm X were shot dead. This is just the bare bones of what happened; it does not dwell on riots, tear gas, or a pattern of crime and lies orchestrated from the White House, not to mention demonstrators who glorified the leader of an enemy nation, students shot dead on campuses, homemade bombs, a corrupt vice president, and a disgraced justice of the Supreme Court. A well-received book on the events of 1968 was called *An American Melodrama*, but it is hard to think of a more inapt title. What happened that year was not a melodrama, studded with cries of woe and wicked uncles. It was a full-blown tragedy, and one which made not just America but the whole world a less happy, more dangerous place.

In the horrors of the twentieth century, many nations have

suffered invasion, war, pestilence, terror. But since 1945, no modern democracy has seen anything like the political disasters that visited America in the 1960s and 1970s. If you watch the silent, red-eyed visitors to the museum in the old Dallas Book Depository, you can understand why the novelist Don DeLillo once spoke of the "confusion, chaos and sense of randomness" of the years since November 1963. But somehow America survived the fearful litany. In any other country the consequence, in all likelihood, would have been civil war, or a military coup, or both. Americans should take that lesson to heart: if they could get through the terrible years between 1963 and 1974, they can certainly survive whatever vicissitudes fate throws at them between now and the end of the century.

The political tragedies were in the future when Todd Gitlin, now a professor at Berkeley, graduated from Harvard in 1963. An activist at Harvard, Gitlin, like others, had been moved by the civil rights struggle in the South and had seen his faith in JFK tested by the Bay of Pigs. He had read and admired the statement that a group called Students for a Democratic Society (SDS) had drafted in the summer of 1962 at a United Auto Workers camp at Port Huron, Michigan. After Harvard he headed for Ann Arbor. The University of Michigan campus was not bristling with radicalism; Gitlin thought it had a pastoral nature a world removed from the bustle of Detroit. But some leaders of the SDS were there, including Tom Hayden, who had been editor of the student newspaper and had helped draft the Port Huron Statement.

The statement is about 40,000 words long, as big as a small book. For some, it is a seminal document, a divining rod which revealed that the post-1945 "American way of life" was but a pool of stagnant water. For others it is merely sophomoric, naive, and idealistic. Still, it was written mainly by people in their early twenties, who are entitled to be naive and expected to be idealistic. The oldest person intimately involved in the project was Michael Harrington, a campaigner against poverty and author of *The Other America*, and he was only in his early thirties. Some parts of the document were misconceived, and some of its language silly and ponderous.

Yet cumulatively, the paragraphs of the Port Huron Statement had a rare power. It was rooted in a belief in the potential for change—the revolutionary potential of American democracy, especially if such democracy could be transformed by the adjective "participatory." The statement owed a debt to the English socialist tradition of William Morris and G. D. H. Cole, at once pragmatic and utopian, grounded in the idea that communities can transform the lives of their members. And it had a great first sentence, one that sticks in the mind. "We are people of this generation," wrote the SDS men and women, "bred in at least modest comfort, housed now in universities, looking uncomfortably to the world we inherit."

In the end, the Port Huron Statement is spooky. Its writers were engaged in parricide, in slaughtering the assumptions by which their parents, the children of the Depression, had chosen to live. Economic growth, the New Left argued, was not an end in itself; suburbanization did not bring fraternity and mutual respect; prosperity had not been spread as widely as conventional wisdom assumed; the international hegemony of the United States was not something of obvious benefit to the world.

These beliefs did not spring fully formed from the heads of a few students in Ann Arbor. They had their roots in the

Golden Age themselves, in a sort of underground opposition in (and to) the dispensation of the 1950s. That opposition included artists and Beats, Old Left unionists and communists, poets and academics, and was perhaps best personified by the Columbia University sociologist C. Wright Mills. A Texan who loved riding motorbikes and was proud of his sexual vigor, Mills was all-American. He was not effete; he wrote a carpentered prose with echoes of Hemingway; he lived hard and died young, of a heart attack, after a night preparing for a televised debate on Cuba. Hayden, drafting the Port Huron Statement at the time, was shattered.

For Mills, the American "state" (using the Marxist term) was not a source of cohesion and prosperity. To the contrary, in *The Power Elite*, published in 1956, Mills had argued that America was run by a network of Big Business, the rich, the military, and their lackeys in Washington. Under cover of economic growth, this "elite" had consolidated its control of the nation. In the book's last pages Mills lost all semblance of academic discipline. "America," he said, "appears before the world a naked and arbitrary power, as, in the name of realism, its men of decision enforce their often crackpot definitions upon world reality. The second-rate mind is in command of the ponderously spoken platitude," and so on and so on, ending with an attack on the "commanders of power" and the "American system of organized irresponsibility."

Mills is important not because the *The Power Elite* is a great book (it reads like random facts strung together, until expense-accounts seem as corrupting of the soul as the bomb). His importance lies in his challenge to the legitimacy of the state, that state which, since the time of FDR, had been a source of great strength and cohesion to America, winning wars, transforming the South, ameliorating the worst effects of poverty. All this, Mills, and his young acolytes, dismissed. And so armed with a theory, SDS activists went out to do community work in Appalachia and the northern cities. They now had a guiding light: the American state and the federal government, its organizing committee (in Lenin's phrase), was not a benign force in society. In truth, it systematically ignored America's needs. "We live among a national celebration of economic prosperity" said the Port Huron Statement, "while poverty and deprivation remain an unbreakable way of life for millions."

Yet Mills and the SDS led their followers into a trap. Notwithstanding commitments to autonomous community action, they looked mainly to government—who else was there?—to ameliorate racism in the cities and poverty in Appalachia. Yet if the government was illegitimate, if Washington was in the hands of a reactionary elite, what good was served by seeking its help? Better to tear things down and start anew. And so, remarkably soon, the New Left developed a revolutionary edge which both alienated it from mainstream "liberal" opinion, as was clear from the time of the Democratic party convention in 1964, and which was an enduring foundation of deep cultural divisions within the country. "Revolutionary," incidentally, is not a word used lightly, or with deference merely to the music of the time which celebrated the concept ("Look what's happening out in the streets," sang Jefferson Airplane. "Got a revolution"). Gitlin himself, the author of a fine history of the New Left, reckons that in the winter of 1969–70 there were no fewer than 250 serious bombings associated with the white left.

The principal aspect of domestic policy on which the left sought governmental action became so controversial that it made its own devastating contribution to the collapse of government authority. This was the demand for a second, "economic," phase of civil rights legislation to accompany "political" reforms, like the Voting Rights Act of 1964. Survey evidence shows a steady, marked retreat from support for racial segregation after World War II. According to the authors Benjamin Page and Robert Shapiro, the number of those favoring black and white children going to the same school rose from 31 percent in 1941 to 50 percent in 1956 and 66 percent in 1973, and had reached 88 percent in 1980. But predictable divisions continued. In 1964, for example, nearly 80 percent of northern high school graduates favored school desegregation compared with just 40 percent of southern high school graduates.

Support for civil rights was one thing when the term meant an end to legally protected segregation in the South. When civil rights came to mean fair housing laws, equal employment policies, and busing to undo racial segregation in schools, all accompanied by higher property taxes, the situation was altered. The year 1965 was pivotal. That summer, the palm-treed Los Angeles ghetto of Watts erupted, kindling four years of riots in cities throughout the country. The civil rights movement became more threatening. No longer led by men of peace and the cloth, its leadership was grasped by black nationalists. "We shall overcome" was an inclusive motto; "Black power" was not; "Burn, baby, burn" was horrifying.

A change in the way in which black political demands were framed contributed to a falling off in white support for civil rights. Though white voters supported equal rights in the abstract, they were wary of supporting policies designed to redress racial imbalances on the ground. In 1964, when pollsters asked whether "the government should see to it that white and black children are allowed to go to the same schools" 42 percent of white respondents agreed. In 1968, three years after Watts, only 36 percent did, and the figure declined still further in successive years. Page and Shapiro argue that "large majorities of Americans have opposed busing virtually every time they have been asked about it." Support for equal employment legislation did not increase at all between 1964 and 1974.

All this was mirrored by a change in political loyalty. By the mid-1960s, as Lyndon Johnson well knew, the Democratic party had become closely identified with social legislation to help blacks. Between 1964 and 1968 the combination within FDR's party of both the white working class and a liberal elite was shattered.

In the 1964 election, the year of the Johnson landslide, the Democratic party received 61 percent of the popular vote; more than it had ever received before or has won since. Four years later, at the end of Johnson's Great Society presidency, Hubert Humphrey, the Democrats' presidential candidate, won just 43 percent of the popular vote. That is an astonishing turnaround of political fortunes in just four years. Those four years had seen the Vietnam War escalate and grow unpopular; at the end of 1964 there were 23,000 American soldiers in Vietnam, a number that grew to 536,000 by the end of 1968. Yet Kevin Phillips's book *The Emerging Republican Majority*, the definitive study of politics in the middle-to-late 1960s, hardly mentions Vietnam. For Phillips, Richard Nixon's majority in 1968 was not formed out of the crucible of war. Instead, that majority "spoke clearly for a shift away from sociological jurisprudence, moral permissiveness, experimental residential, welfare and educational programming and massive federal spending by which the Liberal (mostly

Democratic) Establishment sought to propagate liberal institutions and ideology."

In the phrase used by the authors Tom and Mary Edsall, a chain reaction was under way. The 1960s saw the growth of a new social activism, often expressed in lawsuits, which stressed the rights of those who had once been denied them. Blacks, welfare recipients, homosexuals, women, the mentally ill, prisoners—all were the subject of new campaigns and new laws. At the same time, the programs of the War on Poverty increased spending on welfare. Between 1965 and 1975, recipients of basic welfare programs like Aid to Families with Dependent Children increased threefold, as did the money spent on such programs. Many such programs helped the white working class, particularly the old and sick. But some of the new money went to those who might be thought "undeserving," like teenage mothers, and at least some voters resented having to support such wards of the state (especially if they were black). Inflation was moving families into higher tax brackets (in fact, during this period many working-class families paid income tax for the first time). And so white working-class voters left the Democrats, the party of governmental activism, in droves.

Like a lot of postwar America's history, you can find those voters in the environs of Detroit. Macomb County, north of the city, is typical Golden Age suburbia, settled by working-class families, often Catholic, often employed in the car factories, and after the riots of 1967, often in flight from Detroit. In 1960 John Kennedy won 63 percent of the vote in Macomb; Michael Barone, coauthor of *The Almanac of American Politics*, claims that it was then "the most Democratic major suburban county in the United States." Macomb remained solidly Democratic in 1964. But in 1968, a year after the Detroit riots, the politics of race relations had moved into a new phase. The Democrats carried Macomb once more—Hubert Humphrey was popular with working-class white voters in the Great Lakes states—but they won just 55 percent of the vote, while 14 percent (compared with 10 percent statewide) went to George Wallace, the candidate of white resentment. In 1972, when federal courts considered busing children to Detroit, the Republicans won the county easily, and by 1984, Macomb County was solidly Republican. The "Reagan Democrats," as they were now called, delivered 66 percent of the county's vote to the president.

Here was the first ominous fracture in America's postwar cohesion. The political consensus which had linked the white working class and liberal elites behind an activist federal government—FDR's legacy—had all but vanished. Life for the Democrats from now on would be an uphill struggle. Yet in a more important sense, the fissures in the road from Ann Arbor transcended politics. They represented decisive social divisions. As the memory of the "good war" receded, so did the mood of national unity of purpose which it had engendered. And this decline of national unity was made all the more deep when "the war" came to mean not the heroism of 1941–45, but something much worse. The politics of Vietnam and (later) Watergate, which between them dominated political discourse for nine years between 1965 and 1974, shattered whatever confidence was left in the federal government.

Remember John Kennedy's inaugural speech. While the rest of the "civilized" world was still crawling from a wreckage of its own making, here was a young man committing a nation to be generous with its blood. Kennedy was elected, he believed, to expand the area of freedom in the world. As biographers have made abundantly clear, he found all domestic policy, even civil rights, an irritating diversion from foreign affairs. If there was a single city whose fate was at the center of his presidency it was not Birmingham, but Berlin. And, in the spirit of the times, Kennedy's emphasis on foreign affairs met little resistance.

But Vietnam changed everything. For those who had crafted America's foreign policy at the end of World War II, Vietnam was a nightmare made flesh, exposing tensions which they had hoped to keep hidden. "Vietnam," writes the historian H. W. Brands, "lay at the end of the line of America's Cold War reasoning, the conclusion of a chronological and syllogistic chain that stretched from the origins of the Cold War to the 1960s." Eventually, Vietnam would cause all the Wise Men—the group of diplomats who forged post-1945 foreign policy—great heartache. George Kennan had warned against involvement in Vietnam before 1950; Paul Nitze, who had drafted NSC-68, came to oppose the war; so did Dean Acheson, the epitome of containment; so did Walter Lippmann. Yet even early opponents of the war could never have dreamed that the demonstrations against it would be so bitter and violent, or that some Americans would one day hope that a Stalinist state would defeat their own country in war.

Every question about Vietnam had two equally plausible answers. Who led North Vietnam? Men who were nationalists but also communists. Who led South Vietnam? Corrupt little tyrants who could only be replaced by something worse. What was America's interest in Vietnam? Nothing; it was a wide ocean away, with few natural resources. Yet if Vietnam fell to communism, so might Indonesia, and Thai-

land, and Malaysia—and at some point in that baleful sequence, America's interests would be very much at stake.
Containment was designed to do good; and yet, as Lippmann had prophesied, and Kennan had come to believe, it
would require America to compromise with great evil.

The effects of all this were profound. After the troops had
come home, dead or alive, Vietnam left a sullen division of
opinion within America. Much of the foreign policy "establishment" remained committed to the containment of Soviet
power and was prepared to act unilaterally in defense of that
policy. On the other hand were those who now found containment to be corrupting; who disavowed foreign intervention, adopted "human rights" as a compass of policy, favored
multilateralism, and opposed the arms race.

Some good came out of this split. The absence of popular
support for Vietnam spurred the military to define in advance
the circumstances in which it was sensible to deploy American force overseas. But much damage was done, too. Once
support for containment was weakened, the Soviet Union
could expand its influence in the developing world at will, as
it did throughout Africa in the 1970s. Vietnam made the
world a more dangerous place.

And this takes no account of the war's effect on America's
soul, on ordinary Americans' sense of their society's goodness
and abilities, which had been so burnished during the Golden
Age. The government lied; over and over. The armed forces,
so admired in the Golden Age, were incapable of winning a
war against a Third World army of peasants. The military
seemed to be staffed by men who had left their decency at
home; who would destroy villages to save them; who would
massacre innocents; who would spend their R&R getting laid
and stoned in Thailand. Many middle-aged Americans had

memories of the "good war" fought as much in the Pacific as Europe; for them, especially, Vietnam was a source of boundless shame.

Vietnam helped fracture America in other ways. It set the young, who would have to fight, against the middle-aged, who would not. World War II had been the quintessential "classless" war, with all kinds of Americans jumbled up in platoons together. One important legacy of that war was the sense, throughout the Golden Age, that America had avoided the social divisions of the kind under which Europe labored. Vietnam reintroduced class as a way of explaining differences within the nation. Primarily because of student deferments, the war bore much more heavily on working-class Americans than on rich ones. The proportion of draft-eligible males who actually served in the military dropped sharply between the 1950s and the Vietnam era. Working-class children had to defer employment while college students completed their degrees. Though there is dispute over whether poor people were more likely to die in Vietnam than rich ones, those who did serve plainly resented those who did not. And this sense that Vietnam sharpened class divisions lingers still: as late as 1992, the young Bill Clinton's draft-dodging looked likely to deny him a shot at the presidency. In 1993, as president, he was roundly booed by Vietnam veterans when he spoke at their memorial.

Class divisions over Vietnam later become evident elsewhere. Opposition to the war by young people often went hand in hand with a "1960s" lifestyle, with a new dispensation on sex and the recreational use of drugs. At least that is how things must have seemed to those watching on television, as hippies planted flowers in the guns of National Guardsmen, and yippies tried to levitate the Pentagon. Typically, by the late 1960s those who opposed the war supported the whole liberal agenda of social issues, and some went beyond liberalism. In 1967, reporting for *The New Republic* on a meeting between anti-war Americans and Vietnamese "revolutionaries," Christopher Jencks noted that the Americans "saw the war as an inevitable by-product of some ill-defined sickness in the American system, which could be cured only by radical political remedies. . . . They were contemptuous of liberals who . . . think that when the war is over America will get on with rehabilitating a flawed but redeemable society."

Protestors burned both their draft cards and Old Glory; one action seemed to imply the other. Inevitably, the anti-war protestors were deeply unpopular with those working-class Americans who deserted the Democrats. Todd Gitlin writes that by the time of the Democratic convention in Chicago in 1968 "the antiwar movement was detested—the most hated political group in America." This is not suprising; in any society, those who oppose a war in which other people's sons are being slaughtered can expect some heat. But plenty of anti-war protestors—in Chicago and elsewhere—just fanned the flames.

By 1972, when many Democratic party activists came from the anti-war ranks, the party's platform read like the Port Huron Statement, full of rights and entitlements for the very groups and practices most suspect to the white working class. Working-class Americans therefore made snap judgments of guilt by assocation: those who opposed the war were long-haired flag-burners who also wanted to raise taxes to support black welfare mothers. That didn't help the welfare mothers, and it bred a division which lasted for years. The activists of the 1960s have carried their attitudes with them. The journalist and author E. J. Dionne has noted, for example, that the issues which galvanized the Democratic party in the 1970s and 1980s were precisely those which had their roots in the 1960s, like abortion and the environment. By the 1980s, some Democrats seemed concerned about everything except the economy and the redistribution of wealth. Yet that was what mattered in Macomb County, where postwar prosperity was on the slide. Todd Gitlin was more right than he knew. The real point was not, as he saw in 1962, that the University of Michigan was a world away from Detroit; it was that after Vietnam, Ann Arbor and Macomb County were in different universes.

And then came Watergate. In 1972, Norman Macrae later wrote in *The Economist*, "The presidential election was won with the largest majority in America's history by two men who were at that moment chargeable as accomplices of different felons." Watergate, that shabby, foul-mouthed tissue of lies and half-truths, was intimately connected to Vietnam. The historian Stanley Kuttner argues that "The two events played on one another." The first adventure of the White House "plumbers" was the burglary of the psychiatrist of Daniel Ellsberg, the man who had leaked the Pentagon Papers.

As the scandal unfolded from 1972 to 1974, America was made privy to a government that was dishonest, profane, and devious. The nation's top lawyers broke the law; the president's spokesman stood at the lectern in the West Wing and lied. "Follow the money," Deep Throat told Bob Woodward and Carl Bernstein, and there was plenty of it to follow; the government was revealed to be sodden with illicit cash. The administration had an "enemies list"; those who ran the most powerful nation on the globe were exposed as having the morals of a schoolyard bully. Americans have, perhaps, always been suspicious of the workings of their capital city. But from the time of FDR, they could, legitimately, think that Washington had been inhabited by men and women who at least tried to do good—and whose efforts had often succeeded. No more; by the time Watergate was over, it had combined with Vietnam to leave a residue of cynicism about Washington and all who worked there; a cynicism which was still palpable more than twenty years after Richard Nixon had left for California in August 1974. In nine awful years, the federal government had been stripped of respect, and without respect, found itself devoid of authority. And so one of the principal sources of America's post-1945 cohesion lay bleeding, unable to help a country which desperately needed help.

It's often said that Vietnam had one more effect—that it was the source of a long economic malaise. During the 1960s and 1970s, the economy did indeed decline from its postwar heights, and Lyndon Johnson's attempt to both fund ambitious social programs and prosecute the war—the classic guns and butter strategy—did indeed place intolerable burdens on public finances. But to blame Vietnam for the economy's fall from grace is much too simple.

There's a conventional wisdom about the "1960s." We think they were a set of social and economic progressions that ended in anarchy, revolution, and a counterculture. (In 1972, when student radicals were on the City Council, Ann Arbor slashed penalties for possessing drugs.) The "1960s," on this view, started with Elvis in a GI uniform and ended with Jimi Hendrix playing a psychedelic version of "The Star-Spangled Banner" to a blissed-out, sex-mad, anti-war crowd at Woodstock. It's easy to read backward from what we think the 1960s were and elevate early prophets like Mills into a pantheon.

Yet that is only half the story. The early 1960s were marked by conservative activism on campuses as well. Both ends of the political spectrum rebelled against the nostrums of the Golden Age. Both had their roots in the 1950s; for every C. Wright Mills, there was a William Buckley, raging against the absence of God at Yale and the moral vacuity of the New Deal.

The left concentrated on the social failures of the Golden Age. The unsung contribution of the right was to challenge the economic consensus of conservative Keynesianism, that theory which underpinned the prosperity of the Golden Age. There had always been doubters. From the 1940s, Friedrich von Hayek, an Austrian emigré and frequent visitor to America, had argued that "economic planning" was inconsistent with political liberalism; indeed, that it led to totalitarianism. A group of economists at the University of Chicago had never signed on to Keynesianism. Throughout the 1950s "Chicago" theorists like George Stigler, George Shultz (later to hold four cabinet positions), and Milton Friedman challenged the prevailing orthodoxy. By 1961 the academic winds were in their favor. The long consensus on economic policy was about to end.

That year two crucial papers refounded the intellectual basis of free market (or "classical") economics. Ronald Coase of the University of Chicago argued that the case for government intervention because of "externality"—a cost borne by others than the parties to an exchange—was much weaker than the Keynesians supposed. Intervention in the economy could not be justified as easily as Alvin Hansen and his followers had said. John Muth, at Carnegie-Mellon in Pittsburgh, argued that because market actors would anticipate and discount in advance intervention in the economy, government meddling would rarely achieve its objectives. In fact, it would probably make things worse. Above all, there was Milton Friedman. A bureaucrat in Washington during World War II, Friedman quickly became both an economist of technical brilliance and a committed conservative libertarian. Throughout the late 1950s, he gave a series of lectures on the virtues of free markets, collected in his book *Capitalism and Freedom* in 1962. His presidential address to the American Economic Association in 1967 was seminal, challenging a whole generation of economists to return to "classical" theories and, by implication, scale back the role of the Rooseveltian state. By 1964 Friedman was advising Barry Goldwater in his presidential campaign. The Republicans were trounced, but the attack on conservative Keynesianism, which Friedman would continue to popularize through a regular column in *Newsweek*, was now firmly in the political mainstream. The New Deal was not yet dead; but like the senators waiting for Caesar, its enemies were a-gathering.

The critique of the conservative economists had much force. Just as the New Left was right to claim that the Golden Age had not delivered equal opportunity for all, so conservatives were right to spot a change in the American economy. By the latter half of the 1960s, the productivity gains seen earlier in the Golden Age were waning, though economists usually mark the "break-point" in productivity growth to 1973, the year of the Yom Kippur War and the first oil shock. The economist Angus Maddison calculates that America's growth rate from 1950 to 1973 averaged 3.7 percent a year.

But from 1973 onward, the rate of productivity growth in the economy returns to something like the "trend" of 1.5 percent (or less) a year seen before 1945.

Why did growth slow down? The Vietnam War certainly played a part, even if less of one than myth suggests. In 1968 the country was spending about as much on national defense as it had at the height of the Korean War (though as a proportion of the economy, the spending on Vietnam was much lower). But until President Johnson took extraordinary measures to balance the budget in 1968 he had been unwilling to raise new taxes for the war—and he was, in any event, spending far more money than previous presidents on social programs. So the budget deficit grew, and has pretty consistently continued to grow ever since.

The Vietnam period also saw the start of a great inflation. By and large, the Golden Age had not seen large price increases, though there had been a small upward blip in the mid-to-late 1950s. In none of the years from 1960 to 1965 did the annual percentage change in the consumer price index exceed 2 percent. In only one year between 1986 and 1995 (1986, when the oil price collapsed) did it go under that figure. Inflation introduced a troubling new uncertainty to the American dream. It debauched the currency; it allowed Americans, particularly those on fixed incomes, such as senior citizens, to think that their hard-won prosperity could disappear before their eyes.

Since some of the economic indicators started to turn down during the period of the war, it's easy to blame Vietnam for all the ills, real and imagined, that have plagued the economy since. But though much can be laid at the door of the war, declining growth and productivity cannot. For a start, many of the indicators that changed in the United

States changed elsewhere, too—a fact almost entirely missed by American public opinion.

There is now broad agreement that the huge gains in productivity in postwar Germany, for example, had passed their peak as early as 1960. Bradford de Long and Lawrence Summers estimate that in the 1950s the annual average rate of productivity growth in Germany was 6.4 percent; in the 1960s it was just 4.1 percent, and in the 1970s 2.5 percent. Japan shows a similar pattern. Its highest decade of productivity growth was the 1960s (an annual average rate of 8.4 percent); in the 1970s the average dropped to 4.4 percent. The Vietnam War certainly did not account for these reductions.

No one factor explains the post-1973 slowdown in growth. To some extent, as many economists now argue, there is nothing to explain. The growth of the postwar years was an aberration; sooner or later, the underlying trend was bound to reassert itself.

Still, since the slowdown has so colored modern America, we need to look at some relevant factors. Most economists now discount the importance of the oil shocks of the 1970s. The energy sector of the economy is not big enough for a rise in the price of oil to explain slow growth. There is a decent real-world test for this proposition. If oil explains everything, we would have expected a great leap of growth when the oil price collapsed in the mid-1980s, but that didn't happen.

Demographic changes may have contributed to the slowdown. The period between 1948 and 1964, argues Michael Darby of UCLA, was typified by slow growth of the labor market. The children of the baby boom were still in school, and immigration was almost nonexistent. At the same time the quality of the labor force rocketed. In the period between 1965 and 1979, Darby argues, the conditions were reversed. The baby-boom children entered the workforce in huge numbers, immigration picked up, and, partly because of these new entries into the labor force, its quality diminished.

That no doubt is part of the picture; but as a determinative reason for the slowdown of growth, the labor-market theory is implausible. The quality of the labor force did not collapse after 1973; on the contrary, in many ways it kept rising. There were more women in universities. The median number of school years completed actually increased from 10.6 in 1960 to 12.1 in 1970 and 12.7 in 1980. You could argue, of course, that the quality of the education that American high school students received was less good in the 1970s than in the 1950s (though it is implausible to argue that its quality declined enough to account for the slowing of growth). And you could argue (more plausibly) that the type of employment required in the new American economy demanded higher skills than the education system was giving its students. But the safest conclusion is that though the "GI Bill" increase in labor quality contributed mightily to the rapid growth of the economy in the Golden Age, the later decline in labor quality (if there was one) was a much smaller factor in the slowdown of growth.

The slowdown may also have happened because, as Norman Macrae once argued, intriguingly, American business lost its animal instincts. The verve and self-confidence which had once made American businesses the wonder of the world was lost. In 1975, Macrae found an American private sector which had become wrapped in bureaucratic red tape (perhaps, after all, there was a downside to the triumph of Organization Man). And Macrae thought that

America had developed an "anti-business" ethos rather like that of Britain's. "The entrepreneurial fervor seems to be dying," said Macrae. "In 1965–75 what name of a new and domestically based entrepreneur springs to mind?" There were none.

There was more. We know that after 1960 real levels of investment in public infrastructure declined. But some of that is explained easily; the peak period of investment in schools, for example, coincided with the time the baby-boomers entered the classrooms. America's infrastructure was "finished" earlier than that of other countries. There's no point punishing people for the sin of being first, though Americans often punish themselves in just that way. American real investment in new highways (for example) was less in the 1970s and 1980s than in the 1950s and 1960s, and less impressive than that of, say, France, but that just tells us that America had built modern roads much earlier than other countries. The more pertinent criticism is that America never fully appreciated how much it would cost to maintain an old infrastructure in good repair. Scarce funds were appropriated for pointless pork-barrel projects rather than for the vital task of upgrading essential facilities, which is one reason why, in the 1990s, virtually no bridge or tunnel linking Manhattan or Long Island to the mainland was free of construction crews.

Inflation was certainly a factor in the slowdown of growth. Kumiharu Shigehara of the Organization of Economic Co-operation and Development calculates that whereas the annualized growth rate of inflation was 3.6 percent between 1960 and 1973, it leapt to 8 percent from 1973 to 1979, and was still 6.3 percent between 1979 and 1985. The effect of inflation on growth is, like much in economics, a bit of a mystery. But Shigehara's view is persuasive. "High and variable inflation affects productivity performance adversely by distorting the investment decisions that are made. . . . It is difficult to forget the twisted allocations of time and re- sources that came from the interactions of inflation with ac- counting and tax systems, and the anguish felt by the least sophisticated investors as they saw the value of their savings diminished." And that's just technical economic jargon: what it really means is that poorer, working-class Americans saw their nest eggs shrink, and the dreams of undiminished pros- perity shattered.

Partly because inflation nibbled away at the value of capi- tal, the 1970s also saw a reduction in both private savings and government "savings" (budget surpluses), while the 1980s saw persistently high federal budget deficits. You can't invest a deficit. Without savings, an economy does not generate the cash with which it can invest in new productive potential, and America's overall investment certainly declined after 1973. The share of that investment going to research amd development also declined, and the rate of growth of invest- ment in industrial equipment slowed quite markedly from a point somewhere in the mid-to-late 1970s. For too many American businesses in the 1970s, the temptation to build a new corporate headquarters or hire a new lobbyist took precedence over modernizing capital equipment. To put it at its lowest, none of this helped.

And so we come to the big unknowable: if economic growth had continued at the pace of the Golden Age, would the crisis of government have been averted? Not entirely; but it must be the case that as economic slowdown became en- trenched, programs to help Americans, especially blacks, faced an uphill political struggle. Had the economy grown between 1973 and 1980 at the rate seen in the Golden Age, there would have been literally billions more dollars available for such programs or, more to the point, for tax cuts.

Instead, a set of perceived threats to the prosperity and stability of the Golden Age became linked with one another. The "threat" to the prospects of working-class Americans represented by the economic slowdown became muddled with the "threat" of higher taxes to pay for social programs. This, in turn, became muddled with the "threat" of employment policies which seemed to discriminate in favor of blacks, and the "threat" of a culture antithetical to the white working class.

The Golden Age had been a time of unlimited promise. For the generation that had grown up in the Depression, who had left the farms and the tenements for the suburbs, that promise had very largely been met. They were able to live lives far more comfortable than those of their parents, and were able to dream that their children would enjoy yet higher standards of affluence. But these expectations of a constantly growing standard of living depended implicitly on continued growth. Without such growth, there was bound to be a crisis one day; not necessarily just an economic crisis, or even a political crisis, but a crisis of the spirit.

And the day of reckoning came. But not just because John Kennedy was shot, or because of Vietnam, or because white working-class families lost faith in government. And the day of reckoning didn't just come because growth stopped— though for a variety of reasons growth and the increase in family incomes did indeed come to an end.

Cumulatively, these changes transformed American prospects; they shattered the dream of continued abundance. Paul Krugman reminds us that in 1967, when the futurist Herman Kahn looked at the prospects for the economy in the year 2000, his most pessimistic prediction was annual productivity growth of 2.5 percent; Kahn thought that 4 percent growth was more likely. The reality was rather different. As Krugman was to say in 1990, "productivity crept up by little more than 1 percent a year, while hourly wages fell through the 1970s and 1980s, [and] poverty grew in absolute terms." Kahn and his associates, thought Krugman, would have regarded such an outcome as a "disaster." Indeed, in 1990, millions of Americans did. They felt they were being asked to adapt to circumstances for which they had not been prepared and which were not their fault. America's disaster at the end of the Golden Age was not what it might have been. After all that had gone wrong, the wonder is that America came through the 1960s and 1970s in as good shape as it did. But the endpoint was bad enough. The Golden Age was over.

CHAPTER SIX

Values and Families:
The 1970s

Through the late 1960s and early 1970s, while the authority of the federal government collapsed, social divisions grew and the economy took a downturn. At the same time some core values of postwar America came under attack. The nuclear family, whose heyday had been the 1950s, started to go out of fashion, its ethos attacked as narrowly constricting and antithetical to the pursuit of individual happiness.

The assault on the values of the Golden Age, paradoxically, grew out of the very abundance which had been the hallmark of the people of plenty. Just as the long economic boom was coming to an end, Americans went on a binge. By the late 1960s Americans felt more affluent than they had ever done before; and they indulged. At just the moment that the nation needed retrenchment, needed to rediscover the old American values of thrift, hard work, and sobriety, it got hedonism. It was like wearing Oscar de la Renta to do the yardwork.

Daniel Bell of Harvard has argued that this binge was inevitable. American capitalism had once taken its moral compass from the small-town Protestant ethic, which prized thrift, effort, and a resistance to the temptations of the flesh. But the link between capitalism and a moral ethic had long been sundered; first by the excesses of the Gilded Age, then by the metropolitanism and modernity of America in the 1920s. "The Protestant ethic," says Bell of the 1960s, "served to limit sumptuary (though not capital) accumulation. When the Protestant ethic was sundered from bourgeois society, only the hedonism remained, and the capitalist system lost its transcendental ethic. . . . The cultural, if not moral, justification of capitalism has become hedonism, the idea of pleasure as a way of life."

That was true only up to a point. The share of their incomes which Americans spent on alcohol and meals outside the home actually dropped between 1950 and 1970. If any category of spending grew markedly in the Golden Age it was on personal health—hardly the mark of a sumptuary society. Yet, intuitively, Bell is right. In the Golden Age "consumerism" became aggressive, showering Americans with stuff, equating the "good life" with a life of plenty. Sexual and other taboos were cast overboard. As consumerism took off, so did a politics which stressed the sanctity of individual preferences and lifestyles—and a jurisprudence to protect them. Public thrift was lost in a race for "entitlements," irrespective of moral worth. However good or bad the moorings of the Protestant ethic may have been, America certainly lost them. Foreign perceptions of what it meant to be an American changed radically. For example, in 1956 Grace Kelly, all cool, controlled elegance, arrived in Monaco to marry her prince; in 1971 Jim Morrison, who had once waved his penis at a crowd, died, bloated and addled, in a cheap Paris hotel. "Get your own thing"—the consumerist ethic of the late

1950s—had become "Do your own thing" in the 1960s and "You have a right to your own thing" in the 1970s. For some, like Morrison, this declension would prove fatal. For America as a whole, it was the welcome mat for a time of troubles.

All this, in the shadow of a sluggish economy, would have caused some social stress. But not all Americans had been seduced by consumerism, nor had deified individual rights, nor ever thought unbridled entitlements were such a great idea. For many, the traditional ethical base of America and American capitalism—a base with roots much deeper than the Golden Age—was worth defending. Those who held such views were neither a small minority nor silent. Their resistance to the social changes of the 1960s and 1970s would prime the guns of the culture wars.

Wherever you are in America, the scale of religious observance is extraordinary. From tarpaper shacks in Kentucky where preachers handle snakes, to great, somber cathedrals; from the long sermons in black churches, to a quiet meeting of the Society of Friends, the range and fervor of churchgoing is remarkable. Around 60 percent of Americans say they belong to a church, a number which hasn't changed much since 1950. Few Americans know how peculiar this is. International surveys consistently show that outside small countries like Ireland, the level of churchgoing in the United States is much greater than in any other advanced society. Europeans in America often know more neighbors who attend church every week than they have European friends who worship once a decade. Garry Wills has suggested that Michael Dukakis, the Democratic candidate for the presidency in 1988, was the first truly "secular" national politician in America, and not much good it did him. Outside America, a politician who is openly devout is considered an oddity.

Still, many Americans miss the obvious. Not all of their compatriots thought the ethos of the 1960s and 1970s—do your own thing, and damn the consequences—was such a great idea. On the first day of the Republican party convention at Houston in 1992, a lunchtime rally was held in honor of God and country. Within minutes, the room was packed like a tin of sardines; 3,000 people got in. They were all ages; there were hundreds of children, scores of babies. After a few songs, Pat Boone led the crowd in prayer, and then started to declaim from II Chronicles 7:14. "If my people, which are called by my name, shall humble themselves, and pray, and seek my face, and turn from their wicked ways," he said, as the voices of the crowd joined him, "then will I hear from heaven, and will forgive their sin, and will heal their land." And with that the multitude broke into Amens and Hallelujahs. Soon the podium was taken by Dan Quayle, then the vice president. Just a few weeks before, he had given a speech on "family values," criticizing the heroine of a popular TV series for calling the decision to have a child out of wedlock just another "lifestyle choice." For his pains, he had been much mocked by the "cultural elite" of Hollywood and New York. At Houston, Quayle told the crowd, "It wasn't me they were laughing at"—pause for dramatic effect—"it was you." And his audience erupted.

At the back of the room, meanwhile, the ladies and gentlemen of the press looked on, tripping over television cables, one minute amused, the next scornful. None murmured Amen; none bowed their head in prayer; none changed their view that Quayle was a bit of a buffoon. None recognized that he was speaking for a large portion, perhaps even a majority, of decent, hardworking Americans, who did *not* think the family was funny, did *not* think that illegitimacy was something to be laughed away. In the overworked phrase of the early 1990s, the press didn't get it.

For those who thought that Quayle was on the right side of the cultural wars, the central issue was the family. The importance of the nuclear family to America's understanding of itself was absolutely crucial to the Golden Age. The unit of husband, wife, and children provided, in miniature, the stability and cohesion which was an attribute of the whole postwar dispensation. Yet since the Golden Age ended, the family has gone through remarkable changes.

The basic data are easy to lay out. In the Golden Age, to exaggerate only a little, everyone got married and everyone got married young. Betty Friedan may have lamented the fact, but that was the way it was. Nineteen out of every twenty women who reached their twentieth birthday in the mid-1950s got married. In 1956 the median age at marriage of women was an all-time low—just over 20. By 1970 the median age had crept up to 20.5 years, and by the mid-1990s it had reached 24.5, the highest in the century. That's the first change. But by the 1980s Americans were not just marrying later; many were deciding not to marry at all. In 1970 one in nine of all women aged 25 to 29 was unmarried; by 1991 nearly a third were. That is quite a shift.

Next, the downturn in the divorce rate of the 1950s and early 1960s came to a dead stop and rapidly reversed itself, whizzing into uncharted territory. The 1970s were the period when things changed. In 1970 there were 3.5 divorces for every 1,000 people; a figure which rose rapidly to 5.3 in 1981—the year when there were more divorces than any other before or since. Since the early 1980s the rate of divorce has moderated, which makes predictions of the future difficult. Still, in 1992 Andrew Cherlin of Johns Hopkins University estimated that, based on current trends, about half of all recent marriages would end in divorce or separation. That's something of a consensus view, but it is a consensus which would have appalled most Americans in the 1950s.

Patterns of childbearing changed as well, and here, too, the 1970s were critical. After the baby boom peaked in the mid-1950s, birthrates dropped very sharply to reach a low point in the mid-to-late 1970s before picking up once more. Along with the later age of marriage, women had children much later than they had in the Golden Age. Between 1970 and 1992, the number of total live births increased only slightly, from 3.7 million to 4 million. But during the same years the number of births to women aged over 30 doubled to 1.3 million—more than a quarter of the total compared with just a sixth in 1970.

One consequence of the greater numbers of older mothers is that there are fewer teenage pregnancies. In 1986, the low point, there were just 472,000 births to teenage mothers compared with 656,000 in 1970. Many observers miss this fact because births to unmarried women as a whole have increased as a proportion of total births, from about 11 percent in 1970 to 30 percent in 1992, but fewer unmarried mothers are teenagers than they used to be. Another thing you don't hear often is that, in raw numbers, the real increase in out-of-wedlock births has come among white women. There were 175,000 such births in 1970, about 722,000 in 1992.

The increase in such births to black women has been much more modest. It's easy to miss this point, because married black women have far fewer children than they did in the Golden Age. If married black women had continued having children at the rate they had in the 1950s, much thoughtless commentary on the state of the black family would have been avoided. But they didn't, so in the black population, out-of-wedlock births have grown as a proportion of all births from about 30 percent in 1970 to about 68 percent in 1992.

How can we sum up these changes? Perhaps by mentally killing off Ozzie and Harriet. It is now quite useless to think of the American family as a unit with a man and a woman who get married, have at least two children quite early in their marriage, and stay married forever—the model which underpinned American social relations in the Golden Age. The state of marriage, and particularly a first marriage, takes up much less of an American's lifetime than it used to. Those who do get married are quite likely to have just one child, and to have it when the mother is in her thirties; and they are quite likely to marry more than once.

All that is quite easy to swallow, however, compared to the rise in single-parent families. There were 3.8 million such families in 1970 (13 percent of all families) compared with 10.5 million in 1992 (30 percent of all families). The rise is just about equally marked among white and black families. Proportionately, black families were about three times as likely as whites to be headed by single parents in 1970 but only about twice as likely in 1992. But because the base of single-parenthood among blacks started higher than among whites, the endpoint seems more alarming. In 1992 62 percent of black families with children were headed by single parents. Anyone who, in the 1950s, would have predicted such a state of affairs would have been thought crazy. We should not be surprised if such dramatic changes prove very hard to cope with.

How are we supposed to explain such radical changes in family life? A partial answer is that there is nothing to explain. In many ways it was the Golden Age that was peculiar, not the period that came after. Steven McLaughlin of the Battelle Institute in Seattle has argued that the daughters of the baby boom live lives that are much more similar to their grandmothers' than to their mothers'. Their mothers married early; the baby-boom daughters don't, nor did their grandmothers. Their mothers had at least two children; the baby-boom daughters don't. Their mothers had their children when they were in their early to mid-twenties; the baby-boom daughters don't, nor did many of their grandmothers. Their mothers spent their years of middle age when divorce was becoming more rare; the baby-boom daughters don't, and neither did their grandmothers.

You can push the comparison even further. While divorce and illegitimacy have led to many single-parent families and stepfamilies, within living memory there were plenty of such families because of the death of a spouse in a first marriage. The number of marriages ending in death or divorce hardly changed as a proportion of all such marriages between 1860 and 1970. As divorce became more common, so the in-marriage death of a spouse became less common. With a bit of nerve, you could push the point even further. For example, while it is true that many children today live in single-parent households, two generations ago they might have lived in orphanages. Insouciant observers might ask: what's changed?

Well, two wrongs don't make a right. We can't dismiss the stunted life chances of children in single-parent families—the weight of evidence on that is now compelling—by arguing that they are lucky not to be in an orphanage. The evidence suggests that children cope with the death of a parent much better than they cope with divorce. In any event, divorce became so common after 1970 that marriages now break down (by any method) far more often than they have ever done before. Raising children is difficult enough with two parents; the doubling of children in one-parent families between 1970 and 1990 can't be wished away by appeals to the past, especially since we now know that a single parent is the best predictor of family poverty.

If the scale of family breakdown at the end of the Golden Age was not just a return to old patterns, how should it be explained? Why did the traditional family, the bedrock of post-1945 America, suddenly go out of fashion? Because of an unhappy meeting of the culture and the economy. Changing cultural norms made marriage less popular and much reduced the stigma attaching to both divorce and illegitimacy. At the same time, a changing economy provided new opportunities for women. Some women, indeed, were forced to take those opportunities as the only way of maintaining family income. In short, women were pushed out of the kitchen and into the workforce—at just the time when a life tied to the drudgery of the kitchen was, in any event, considered a cultural backwater. All of this combined to change the pattern of family life so that millions of children were brought up either with only one parent (in which case they would very likely be poor) or with a stepparent (in which case they would quite likely be unhappy). As Christopher Jencks of Northwestern University has written, "It is the conjunction of economic vulnerability and cultural change that has proved so disastrous." And the little euphemism "cultural change" in that sentence brings us, at last, to sex.

Suppose it's the summer of 1969, and you're in Amsterdam, or Athens, or Rome—any city in Europe will do. Find the American Express office. Look closely and you'll see that there are lots of European students hanging around—German, British, Dutch. They're not there to pick up their mail from home, and they're certainly not there to book plane or rail tickets (these guys hitchhike). They are there, gentle reader, to meet the American girls inside, and get laid.

And they will. By the end of the 1960s, it was an incontrovertible truth of a European summer that American girls were easy. Their reputation swept the old continent. This was not old-fashioned 1950s flirtatiousness—a Vassar girl granting some Lothario a moonlit kiss by the Trevi Fountain. This was the real thing; one-night stands, shared sleeping bags, techniques which came as a joyous surprise to the poor Europeans, some of whom have never quite recovered. Doubt it not; there really was a sexual revolution, and it has changed America. It is quite useless to think about the transformation of America since the end of the Golden Age without thinking about sex.

From the mid-1960s to the mid-1970s the nation lived through an all-encompassing transformation of sexual mores. What had once been thought deviant quickly became an unremarkable fact of life. The age of first sexual experience went down, the average number of lifetime partners went up. Homosexuality became more accepted; a variety of hitherto unusual sexual practices became commonplace. Christopher Jencks dryly notes, "In the space of a decade we moved from thinking that society ought to discourage extramarital sex, and especially out-of-wedlock births, to thinking that such efforts were an unwarranted infringement of personal liberty. Instead of feeling morally superior to anyone who had a baby without marrying, the young began to feel morally superior to anyone who disapproved of unwed mothers."

The sexual revolution has changed America more than most are prepared to admit. It's changed newsstands so that parents have to hurry their children past the exposed flesh.

It's changed the way we speak—TV stars now use language for which your grandmother would have banished you from the table. It's changed whole areas of cities—anyone who thinks that the innocence of burlesque is but remotely connected to what now goes on around New York's Times Square hasn't been there lately. It's almost certainly changed what we do in the marital bedroom. It's changed our sense of available happiness. We all feel entitled to a "good sex life," which is a phrase that means something different now from what it once did (if, indeed, it ever meant anything at all to most people). Something of the speed of the change can be gleaned from movies (though any branch of popular culture would do). In the film *Double Indemnity*, made in 1944, the star-crossed lovers share the occasional frustrated kiss. When the film was remade as *Body Heat* in 1981, the heroine performs oral sex on the hero in view of a child. In *Shampoo*, released in 1975 but set on election night in 1968—and perhaps the single work which best revealed the moral ambiguities of the period—the hero has sex with his girlfriend, his girlfriend's best friend, the best friend's lover's wife, and the lover's wife's daughter. His behavior is not thought remarkable.

The revolution combined a change in attitudes with a change in sexual practice: the first is almost more important than the second. In a sense, the change in attitude was the coming of honesty: a willingness to bring into the open things that had long been hidden.

It would be difficult to understand American popular culture in the 1990s, for example, without knowing what oral sex is. (Think how often you hear someone say "That sucks!") Not long ago, oral sex was on the very outer edge of popular discourse; it's moved mainstream damn quickly. But that's not the same as proving that behavior changed as radically. True, oral sex is common; according to the Battelle Research Institute, around 80 percent of all American men have received blow jobs. But in some of the groups that Alfred Kinsey studied in the late 1940s, 60 percent of men said they had received oral sex—and given taboos, the real number may have been higher. Homosexuality makes the same point. It is true that homosexuals are less "in the closet" than they once were, and that their lifestyle has had an impact on everything from fashion design to advertising. It is (probably) also true that, at least between the late 1960s and early 1980s, more homosexual men had sex with more partners, more often, than before the sexual revolution. But, to state what should be obvious, it is very much not true that greater acceptance of homosexuality has somehow produced more homosexuals. A careful Battelle study in the 1990s found that only 1.1 percent of American men were exclusively gay; it is frankly impossible to believe that the number of exclusively gay men was *less* than that in the Golden Age.

Yet behavior has indeed changed, too. Research shows that only 7 percent of white women born in the 1920s had premarital sex. Of those born in the 1950s, 45 percent did; by 1979, 50 percent of those aged fifteen to nineteen were sexually experienced. We know the turning point; it was the few years at the end of the 1960s and beginning of the 1970s, just when college girls were swamping American Express offices in Europe. (This was also the time when pornography became socially acceptable, when earnest semioticians took *Deep Throat* seriously—nasty, exploitative film though it was.)

To an extent, the new sexual adventurism of women was to be welcomed. It marked the end of a double standard. Men had always had sex. Until the 1960s, the number of unmarried men who were sexually experienced was double the number of white women the same age. The difference between men and white women of the same age has since attenuated—though not quite vanished—entirely because women are having sex earlier.

There is still a lot we don't know. We do not know with certainty how much the age of first sexual experience for men dropped between the 1950s and the 1970s, though drop it certainly did. We are just starting to learn about multiple sexual partners. The Battelle study found that 9 percent of men had more than four partners in an eighteen-month period. Freya Sonenstein of the Urban Institute has found that a typical adolescent male might have just two partners in a year, of which several months would be sex-free. These findings seem quite conservative; but we have little to compare them with from, say, the 1950s.

So much is still guesswork. We don't know why the change in attitude or practice happened, though we do know that the seeds of the sexual revolution were sown during the Golden Age. Did sex become a thing of fun because penicillin, that gift of World War II, reduced the risk of venereal disease? Was it all due to the pill? Did reliable contraception lead to "recreational sex," which rather later became socially accepted? Maybe; there are studies which show that the change in attitudes to sex lagged change in behavior. It was not until the mid-1980s that a majority of Americans said they did not disapprove of premarital sex, although by then around 70 percent of nonmarried Americans were sexually experienced.

Were other factors at work? Perhaps Daniel Bell is right; perhaps once American capitalism lost its connection to the Protestant ethic it was harder to resist sexual temptation. Perhaps old habits of personal restraint got lost in the rush to prosperity.

Whatever the explanation, we know that the revolution brought consequences, that when sex became commonplace, it changed the social structures and behavior that Americans had considered normal. We've no way of knowing how many women's lives were messed up between 1968 and 1972, when expected sexual behavior changed so quickly—so that at eighteen a girl was expected to save herself for marriage, but at twenty-two to sleep with a boy on a first date. Rather more women were hurt than conventional wisdom assumes, perhaps.

We know that the taboo against extramarital pregnancies has just about vanished. Not long ago, such pregnancies ended with a shotgun marriage—something which by the mid-1990s seemed both heartless and quaint, a bit like a posse in the Wild West. But shotgun marriages had their uses. As Jencks says, "Shotgun weddings and lifetime marriages caused adults a lot of misery, but they ensured that almost every child had a claim on some adult male's earnings. That is no longer the case."

There are other taboos—at least, there were in the Golden Age. Nobody will ever prove statistically that the sexual revolution led in the 1970s to an increase in divorce, but it probably did. It is surely possible to argue that hedonistic demands for things like a "good sex life" reduced the taboo against divorce. (Your wife always has a headache? Find another one.) We know, now, that children suffered thereby. Andrew Cherlin has said, "In the United States, many marriages that could limp along end because people are bored. I'm not sure that children are harmed in such marriages." But some children are harmed by the divorces that end them.

The sexual revolution, then, shattered some of the assumptions of post-1945 America. It's easy to see why conservatives believe that the decline of the nuclear family must flow from the culture wars. In part, it does. But it's not the whole story. The economy played its part, too.

Andrew Cherlin gives a clue as to why this must be so. Not until the late 1960s did a majority of Americans approve of divorce—the cultural change. Yet by then an unprecedented rise in the divorce rate was already well underway. So something more than a culture war was going on.

The culprit, if that is the right word, is the economy. In the years after 1945 female participation in the economy grew only slowly, if at all. But since the mid-1960s women have been flocking to work. In 1960 about three in ten of married women worked. By 1990 nearly six out of ten did. Single women, too, worked more; in 1960, 44 percent did, in 1994, 67 percent. You need proof? Watch the movies. In the 1950s hardboiled stars like Bette Davis and Lauren Bacall couldn't get decent roles, because everyone wanted to see work-shy bimbos. In the 1990s, even sex symbols like Sharon Stone and Demi Moore play professional women. Melanie Griffith starred in a film (one of the subtle icons of the 1980s) called *Working Girl*. Quite right, too. In 1994 more than 48 percent of those in managerial and professional jobs were women. By the mid-1990s, women made up more than half the enrollment in many top law and medical schools.

The increase in working women is marked for all income groups and all age groups. But it's working women with young children who stand out. In 1950 about 12 percent of such women worked; in 1960 19 percent; in 1970 30 percent; in 1980 about 45 percent and in 1994 about 62 percent. In 1994, indeed, no fewer than 59 percent of women with children less than one year old worked, a rate that had doubled in just fifteen years. As a demographic change, this is amazing. It's safe to say that of all the social changes between the Golden Age and the 1990s, the increase in the number of working women with young children is the most extraordinary.

Why did women flock to, or rather, return to, the workplace? Give Betty Friedan her due; some women must have found a life spent baking cookies horrible. And there are other reasons. Married women are far better educated than they were in the Golden Age. A few years after universities admitted GI Bill male students, they welcomed their younger sisters. In 1970 only 22 percent of working women had attended college; by 1994 57 percent had. By the late 1990s, in any given age group under fifty, women will be better educated than men. They will never be in the workforce in quite the same number as men (some women will always want to look after very young children), but the margin, already small, will continue to shrink.

Women are working not just because they are educated, but also because they need to work. If they had not done so in the 1980s and 1990s, their families would not have been able to maintain their standard of living. And "maintain" is the key word. In the Golden Age, Americans could enjoy abundance with just one wage-earner (a man). By the 1990s, the middle-class dream was, for many Americans, attainable only if both parents worked.

This takes us into delicate territory. There is no subject more at the mercy of political partisanship than family incomes and living standards. Liberals say that everyone has gotten poorer since the mid-1970s; conservatives say that liberals twist the figures.

The headline numbers are as follows: between 1947 and 1973, median family income just about doubled (in 1990 dollars, from about $17,000 per family in 1947 to about $35,000 per family in 1973). Between 1973 and 1993, by contrast, median family income saw virtually no growth at all. But those figures are too crude. It's better to use the annual Green Book of the Ways and Means Committee of the House of Representatives, which measures "adjusted family income." This concept allows for the fact that different-sized families have different costs and allows for the growth of single-parent families since the 1970s. Fail to do that, and you understate family income, since by definition the more families there are, the smaller their share of total income will be. The committee's figures are pretax and do not include the value of non-cash benefits like food stamps, two omissions which roughly cancel each other out. And the figures remove a mistake in calculating the effects of inflation which addled the figures before 1983.

All that detailed stuff to one side, the Green Book shows that between 1973 and the 1990s, adjusted family income rose by a little more than 1 percent a year. That seems acceptable, but the years of the Golden Age were twice as good, which is why they remain golden in the memory. Moreover, such gains as were made after 1970 were skewed toward the rich. Crudely, in the mid-1990s the poorest fifth of all families are no better off than they were in 1973. The next fifth are about 3 percent better off; and the richest fifth are about 36 percent better off. As many critics have argued, these figures need taking with a pinch of salt. In a dynamic economy, people become more or less prosperous all the time, because of their age, because they work hard one year and goof off the next, because Grandma left them a nest egg, whatever. Nonetheless, the differences in the performance between income groups is still striking.

Putting all this together, sluggish growth of family income, skewed distribution of wealth—does this not mean that the American economy has "failed" since 1973? It depends. Growth in family income looks sorry when compared with the Golden Age, but that isn't a fair comparison. The Golden Age was unusually good. That doesn't prove that, for families, the years since have been unusually bad.

Indeed, in one sense the increase in women's work since 1973 testifies to the strength of the American economy. It has been able to create jobs. Between 1970 and 1990 the number of jobs in America increased by nearly 40 million, and the proportion of the population employed grew steadily. Robert Reich, appointed labor secretary by President Clinton, once said that "by the last decade of the twentieth century almost all Americans who wanted to work could find a job." That puts it too strongly—it was not true for all workers in all kinds of places at all times—but there's a kernel of truth there. Since 1973, the unemployment rate has never risen above 8.5 percent and has usually been much lower, though admittedly higher than in the 1950s and 1960s. America's entrepreneurs have built thousands of new firms with millions of new jobs. It can be objected, fairly, that not all of these jobs are great, and that unskilled workers, in particular, do not have the wages, benefits, or security of employment that their fathers enjoyed a generation ago. But we should not take our eyes off the ball. America has been able to generate employment for all; many other advanced economies have not.

And so we turn to the biggest question of all. What's all this done to family life? What's left for the American family, that source of so much of Americans' self-confidence in the years of their ascendancy? There are three big changes, most of them driven at least as much by the economy as by changes in cultural values. The first is the declining appeal of marriage, and the popularity of "delayed" marriage—in short, those who do marry do so later than their parents. Women once married partly for economic security and partly for romantic reasons. Now many women no longer need men economically, which gives them a good reason to wait until their heart says yes, if it ever does. Second, the new economy must partly explain the trend to smaller families and children born later in a marriage. Women who have trained for a career want to see a return on their investment, which means that they work, at least for a time. And the stagnation of family-income growth is a powerful incentive for women to stay working (or return to work after having children).

Third, it also seems likely that the increase in divorce is a function of the new economy. Divorce is often the fault of selfish men, and is hardly ever easy on women. But it is a lot easier on all women now, with or without children, than it was in the Golden Age. We do not need to invent cultural reasons to explain all divorces. There have always been unhappy marriages, but until the 1970s and 1980s it was perfectly sensible to imagine why women should remain trapped in them: they needed their husband's paycheck. The wonderful American job machine has weakened the marital chains.

This analysis, which mixes up economics and culture as a way of explaining the decline of the American family, has deeply ironic consequences. Economic conservatives celebrate the American job machine, while cultural conservatives bemoan the changing family. Sometimes—Dan Quayle has done this—conservatives manage to praise one development while deploring the other. But they are two sides of the same coin. Changes in cultural and sexual mores may have contributed to family breakdown, but in modern America, cultural changes have been blamed for too much. It wasn't just the culture which changed America from the cohesive nation it had been in the Golden Age to something quite different. Underpinning everything was a slowdown in economic growth. That slowdown substituted uncertainty for predictability. At the same time, because of pressure on family income, the new economy also encouraged women to take advantage of opportunities they had never had before. So, yes, the 1960s and 1970s were confusing times, in which the assumptions by which Americans had happily lived were stood on their head. But the confusion which followed the Golden Age was not all bad. For one thing, it liberated qualified women in a way that has improved both their lot and that of a wider American economy and society. Looked at closely, the cultural confusion after the Golden Age may yet be capable of being the seedbed for an American renaissance.

CHAPTER SEVEN

Coming Apart:
The 1980s

Not everyone got rich or happy during the Golden Age, but everyone got richer (and hence probably happier) than they had been in the prewar years. The rising tide of prosperity lifted all boats. Conventional wisdom has it that the 1980s were different. By the end of the decade, the 1980s were dismissed as years of greed, profligacy, and growing inequality. In the 1992 presidential campaign, Bill Clinton's stump speech could have been reduced to the following: "The 1980s. They sucked."

Actually, they didn't. Much went right for the American economy in the decade. Between the end of the recession in 1982 and 1990, America had seven years of strong economic growth. The great American job machine created employment opportunities galore. In 1975, as we have seen, Norman Macrae of *The Economist* had worried that American capitalism had lost its animal instincts, and couldn't think of a single world-class modern American entrepreneur. Ten years later, Americans had shown that they would dominate some of the crucial industries of the next century. In electronics, telecommunications, biotechnology, and entertainment, American entrepreneurs of the 1980s swept all before them.

Nowhere was this more evident than in the vital computer industry. In software, an American company, Microsoft, became a hegemon. In hardware, newcomers like Compaq and Apple had challenged IBM. Then, hardly before they had time to enjoy their success, they were themselves taken on by nimble upstarts like Gateway 2000, which built a world-class high-techology company in, of all unlikely places, North Sioux City, South Dakota. No other country in the world came close to matching America's startling ability to build corporate giants from nothing. And at least as important, many of America's oldest companies showed that they were no slouches. By the mid-1990s, the automobile companies themselves had won markets back from Japanese and European imports. There was every likelihood that the economic juggernaut would keep on rolling. Parents may have despaired of American kids, with their ponytails, their sloppy shirts, and their sloppier language, but hunched over their PCs, American children were much more conversant with the technology of tomorrow than the children of any other country.

Yet for all these successes, it's clear that during the 1980s the "rising tide" of the economy no longer brought equal prosperity to all. And this is why, despite the statistical growth of the 1980s and 1990s, Americans don't find today's conditions to be as good as their memories (their *accurate* memories) of the Golden Age. When every allowance had been made for the partial nature of some statistics, when every partisan attack on Reaganomics had been discounted, the unfortunate truth remained that, during the 1980s, America had become a more unequal society. The author Richard

McKenzie, in a *defense* of conservative economic policies called *What Went Right in the 1980s?*, puts the position fairly. "No one disputes the fact that during the 1970s and 1980s the incomes of many Americans floundered, even declined, nor that the rise in people's incomes was significantly slowed by historical standards (in line with changes in productivity, first slowing to virtually zero in the 1970s and then rising again in the 1980s). Single parents and those with very limited education were especially hard hit. Union workers frequently lost their protected bargaining positions due to growing domestic and international competition. As a consequence, many workers' real incomes sank, forcing their spouses to enter the labor market to maintain or improve their families' economic status." Behind that dry and careful statement, you could hear a nation's fabric start to tear.

Economics provides the numbers for a larger, sociological truth. In the 1980s, the experiences of Americans drifted further and further apart. The real classlessness of the Golden Age, the portability of the suburban experience, the shared thrill of the first TV programs, all withered away. After 1945, regions had become more like each other, and economic opportunity was spread more evenly. More like, but not identical. After thirty years of a "New" South, high school graduation rates in 1990 remained fixed in a pattern that had been set years before. In Vermont 92 percent of students graduated; in Louisiana just 57 percent did. Along the Canadian border was a line of states which routinely graduated more than 80 percent of their high school students. And with awful predictability, the four states with the worst graduation records were in the South.

But in the 1980s, even the limited convergence of regions seemed to end. For the first time this century, the decade saw an increase in regional disparities of average income. Rich states got relatively richer; poor states got relatively poorer. The long period during which the poorest region, the Deep South, nudged ever closer to the national average came to a stop. When the data are broken down into smaller economic units, like local labor markets, the absence of convergence of average incomes in the 1980s is yet more marked.

It is impossible to say whether the end of economic convergence was an aberration. It may have been; by the mid-1990s it seemed that regional convergence was back on track. Still, for those Americans who had thought that all parts of the country offered, more or less, the same potential for a good life, the 1980s were a shock. For some Americans, this was no longer a nation and time of plenty; others had a greater abundance of wealth and goods than anyone else in the planet's history. Americans risked drifting apart.

In some measure, that is because Americans lived in new ways and new places; and the old ways and old places got left behind. Consider all cities which in 1990 had more than 100,000 people. Of the twenty such cities that grew fastest in the 1980s, eleven are in southern California. Of those eleven, three are in Riverside County, to the east of Los Angeles, which is almost pure desert. Rancho Cucamonga, for example, nearly doubled in size from 55,000 to 101,000 in the 1980s. The combined population of the Riverside and San Bernardino metropolitan area grew from 1.1 million in 1970, to 1.5 million in 1980, to more than 2.5 million in 1990—by which time it was bigger than Detroit city and the entire metropolitan areas (city and suburbs) of both St. Louis and Pittsburgh.

As late as the mid-1970s, the Northeast and Midwest combined had more than half America's population. By 1991 they had just 44 percent, and by 2015 they will have less than 40 percent. Between 1980 and 1990—ignoring immigration from abroad—the Northeast had a net out-migration of more than 2.5 million, the Midwest more than 1.7 million. The West had a net in-migration of about 1.1 million and the South of more than 3 million. Immigration to the Sunbelt from abroad just added to the growth. In the 1980s, the total population rose by 9.8 percent. But the population of California rose by 25 percent, of Texas more than 19 percent, and of Florida by nearly 33 percent. Those three states accounted for more than half the population increase in the nation.

Just as movement to the South and West has continued, so has suburbanization. In 1990 more than half of all Americans lived in suburbs. Of the twenty fastest-growing cities of the 1980s, only five were "stand-alone" urban entities; the rest were suburbs of somewhere else. In the 1980s, everywhere became more suburban. Subdivisions paper the plains along the Front Range of the Rockies; malls sit in southern Illinois fields where grain elevators once peered above the corn like churches in Burgundy. Estates with Anglicized names—here a Devonshire, there a Bishopsgate—creep out of Washington, D.C., into the Virginia hunt country. The suburbs that surround New York like a great horse collar from the Jersey beaches to the Connecticut shoreline now have a population greater than that of Belgium.

Americans now do not just live in the suburbs; they work there, too. At the end of a century of development which started when the Singer Sewing Company moved its factory to New Jersey, the suburbs have become the diffuse heart of the American economy. It isn't just offices that have gone to the suburbs, though they have—only economically unsuccessful cities, like New Orleans, now have more office space downtown than in the suburbs. Factories, too, have gone suburban. The space demanded by modern manufacturing methods and inventory control means that firms look for greenfield sites, like the giant Motorola plant stuck on the prairie west of Chicago's O'Hare airport.

Americans do their shopping in the suburbs, as well. The "malling of America" is a cliché, but true. Shopping centers like Tyson's Corner outside Washington (with, according to Joel Garreau of the *Washington Post*, more retail space than downtown Miami) or the Galleria on Houston's west side (with more shops than Cologne) have become symbols of the way we live. In many metropolitan areas, suburbs offer a much better range of shops than do inner cities. Houston's best restaurants are in the Galleria. Fairfax County, Virginia, has cultural facilities which rival those of nearby Washington, D.C. There is no more "city game" than basketball, nor any place more definitively a city than Detroit. Yet the Pistons play in suburban Oakland County, not in the Motor City.

Because they live, work, and shop in the suburbs, Americans are ever more reliant on their cars. At the turn of this century, America's public transport was the envy of the world. Streetcar lines ran for miles from city centers to suburbs, the cars rocking through fields on the way. According to Kenneth Jackson of Columbia University, at the turn of the century Berlin's streetcar system, the biggest in Europe, would have ranked only twenty-second in America. Los Angeles, which the ignorant think was "made" by the motorcar, sprawls the way it does because development followed the lines of the Pacific Electric Railway.

Such transport systems could only work if cities were as they had been in Roman times, with arterial routes running from the periphery to the center. In the 1980s, American cities were post-Roman. Picture a typical suburban family, with two or three wage-earners. Each may work in a different suburb, shop in yet another one, and go to the movies in yet another. That makes planning public transport systems a nightmare, and explains why no other country has so many cars per head as the United States. Anthony Downs of the Brookings Institution notes that between 1975 and 1990 the American population increased by about 16 percent; the number of miles traveled by cars went up by nearly 44 percent.

Everyone now thinks they need a car; in the 1980s, says Downs, vehicle populations increased more than human populations in thirty-six states and the District of Columbia. In 1990 there were more vehicles registered in Idaho than people. In the 1980s the average work trip increased by 27 percent, to nearly eleven miles. Commuting journeys of more than an hour each way became common.

One conclusion from these trends is to say that we are merely seeing a continuation of the very population movements which made America more unified in the years after 1945. Well: yes and no. It's true that by the end of the 1980s the population was more evenly spread across the continent than ever, but it's also true that the 1980s showed that the movement to the Sunbelt and the suburbs did not bring the same blessings to all. Some places were left in shadow. And, with good reason, those who lived in such places didn't like it.

Sunshine is not a panacea. Though the West and the South have long attracted Americans, not all parts of the Sunbelt are affluent. Sunshine can coexist with deep-rooted social problems: witness the 1992 riots in Los Angeles. For every glistening suburban tract in Colorado you can find a trailer park with poor whites and Latinos, with beer cans dumped at random and a few mangy dogs roaming around. For every nice subdivision in southern California, there is housing where immigrant families are squashed together in squalor.

In the South, the 1980s were a reality check. In a 1986 report, a task force of the Southern Growth Policies Board chaired by then-Governor Bill Clinton of Arkansas concluded that the South was only "halfway home"; it still had a long way to go. The report noted uneven economic development in the region. "The sunshine on the sunbelt," it argued, "has proved to be a narrow beam of light, brightening futures along the Atlantic seaboard, and in large cities, but skipping over many small towns and rural areas."

Indeed, when the 1980s were over, Americans could see two "Souths." The population growth of the Atlantic states raced well ahead of the national average, but that of the inland and Gulf states atrophied. The nation as a whole may have grown by nearly 10 percent in the decade, but Alabama, Arkansas, Kentucky, Louisiana, and Mississippi all grew by only 4 percent or less. Throughout the 1980s, the Atlantic South had unemployment rates well below the national average, while the Gulf and inland South had rates well above the average. The South rediscovered rural poverty, not just the obvious degradation of the Delta, but the poverty of small manufacturing towns, with an unskilled workforce and levels of illiteracy stunning for a developed country. The educational standards of those who live in the rural South are far below those who live in southern cities, which are themselves nothing to celebrate. In 1986, it was reported that 80 percent of Kentucky's unemployed workers could not be retrained because they lacked basic literacy skills. In the mid-

1990s you could wander around southern mountain towns where the records on the jukebox haven't changed since Elvis left Tupelo, and wonder where, precisely, the "New" South was to be found.

Just as there is more than one "South," so there is more than one type of "suburb." There are suburbs with no corner shops or downtowns; and there are suburbs with functioning Main Streets. There are suburbs in southern California where commuters leave home at six o'clock for a two-hour drive to work; and there are suburbs like Reston, Virginia, where, amazingly enough, your office and favorite restaurant might both be a five-minute walk from home. There are suburbs with decent bus lines and suburbs with none. There are suburbs where the infrastructure is decaying (Macomb County, Michigan, for one) and others in Florida and the West where fiber optic cables link homes to each other and the wider world. There are majority-black suburbs, like Prince Georges County, Maryland. There are suburbs that are crime-ridden, and gated suburbs which screen out potential troublemakers. There are rich suburbs and poor suburbs. Kenilworth, a north shore suburb of Chicago, is plutocratic; Ford Heights, also in the Chicago suburban ring, is destitute.

It isn't just within the suburbs and the Sunbelt that some places have been left behind. Small towns continue to decline. Although the 1970 census seemed to show an unexpected growth in the rural population, it didn't really happen. Most "rural" growth was in counties that were still classified as if they were in deepest country, but which were really on the outer edge of conurbations. Counties such as Loudoun County, Virginia, or Gwinnett County, Georgia, were considered statistically "rural" long after they had come into the orbit of their proximate cities, Washington and Atlanta. Once it was recognized that such places were really suburbs, the "reruralization" thesis lost its bite. The 1980s saw this trend continue. A study for the National Governors Association found that nonmetropolitan counties next to urban centers grew healthily—in other words, they became suburbs—while counties unadjacent to cities lost population.

"True" rural areas continue to hollow out. Most midwestern states lost rural population in the 1980s. Some rural counties in Kansas, for example, now have populations of 2,000 or so, with just 150 students in their schools—fewer than they had at the turn of the century. By the 1980s, few small towns could retain population and an economic base unless they had one of three things: a tourist attraction (like the old mining towns of the Rockies, reborn as ski resorts); a retirement community (which explains the boom on the Ozark plateau); or a university (like Oxford, Mississippi, or Lawrence, Kansas). Small towns without such amenities are struggling.

Like suburbs and small towns, cities, too, have pockets of deprivation, places that have been left behind. It is quite true that "gentrification" of run-down neighborhoods is now more than twenty years old and that in the 1980s many city centers saw quite substantial growth in employment. But like the supposed revival of small towns, this merely flattered to deceive. Consider Chicago, which is in many ways a more attractive city now than it was in the 1970s. The city has maintained a world-class downtown shopping area: the Miracle Mile along Michigan Avenue. New housing has sprung up on the edge of the central business district. In the mid-1970s, the district north of the Loop and west of Lake Michigan was run-down and derelict. Now, renamed "River North," it is one of the centers of the city's nightlife, stuffed with art galleries and restaurants. In the 1970s, it was feared that Cabrini Green, a notorious slum just a few blocks from the Miracle Mile, would blight the whole area. In fact, Cabrini Green is now an island of deprivation in an area that looks quite prosperous. Chicago was not alone; other city centers had a terrific 1980s. According to John Kasarda of the University of North Carolina, Washington saw a net increase of 49,000 jobs downtown between 1980 and 1988. New York City did even better. On the back of Wall Street's boom, it added 115,000 jobs in financial services before the crash of October 1987. Economically, the 1980s were the best decade that New York had seen since the 1950s.

Yet in the vast majority of cases, those choosing to live in gentrified inner-city neighborhoods are young professionals, who, for a few years, will enjoy an apartment next to a nightclub. When they marry and have children they will up and off to the suburbs. As Kasarda says, when 400 white-collar workers decide to move from the suburbs and live in the Loop, the papers are full of it. When 80,000 Chicagoans move to suburban Du Page County, nobody turns a hair; yet that, roughly, is the scale of things. For every job gained by downtown Washington in the 1980s, a very good decade for the city, ten were created in Washington's suburban ring. America's cities had a little longer in the sun than its small towns, but not by much.

Worrying though the decline of small towns and divisions between city and suburbs may be, by the end of the 1980s the real challenge to American society lay elsewhere. Deserted small towns are depressing places; but they are not murderous ones. Most parts of America's cities and most of its suburbs plainly inhabit the same universe. But some areas in America have now almost lost contact with the established

pattern of the economy. It is in those places that the crisis of
the American spirit lies.

The very poorest county in America is Shannon County,
South Dakota. It has a landscape of sublime beauty; whisper-
ing cottonwoods in the valley bottoms, big skies, badlands
etched on the plains as if the creator had thrown a celestial
bucket of acid on them. And it has social conditions which
would shame many countries in Asia. Shannon County has
an unemployment rate around 50 percent. Many homes have
no inside toilet. Suicide rates are twice the national average,
murder and infant mortality rates three times as high, and
deaths due to alcoholism almost ten times as high. There is
no bank, no clothes shop, no drugstore. In the county's main
town, the closest thing to a restaurant is a small taco stand.

No prizes for guessing the county's nature: it is a reservation for the Oglala Sioux Indians. Foreign visitors to America
are rendered speechless by the reservations, by the absence
of economic activity, by the random violence, the crude
crosses that dot the highways, memorials to death by drunk
driving. On the Hopi reservation in Arizona, famous for its
culture the world over, the steep sides of the mesas are lit-
tered with garbage, wrecked cars and trucks, rotting food, all
tipped mindlessly over the edge.

Not enough people live on the reservations for their fate
to engage America's attention, but the fate of Rust Belt America is another matter. Not long ago, the Northeast cities were
the beating heart of the American dream. Millions of Americans still live close to the cold waters of the Atlantic and the
Great Lakes; not all of us define the good life in terms of
good climate and a decent mountain bike. The strength of
the social and economic fabric of the Rust Belt matters—and
it is fraying.

In the mid-1990s, the Monongahela Valley in western Pennsylvania did not look as bad as Shannon County, but it looked bad enough. All but one of the great steel plants that once lined the river had closed, leaving either sites bulldozed to a pool-table smoothness or great rotting sheds of iron.

In one ten-year stretch from 1979, the region lost 65,000 jobs in steel. Between 1960 and 1990, the combined population of the towns of Braddock, Homestead, Duquesne, and McKeesport fell from about 80,000 to about 55,000. And the numbers tell only a fraction of the story. The towns are mournful, run-down, their shopping centers scruffy. Braddock's famous Carnegie Library closed in 1974; in the late 1980s, Homestead sadly boasted that it was "the odor control capital of the world." Most companies that remain are weak, serving shrinking markets. Those who leave the area are the best qualified; in one survey of sixty-seven emigrants from Duquesne, all but one had been educated beyond high school, and all but eleven were under the age of thirty.

Naturally, the conditions of the Mon Valley, and places like it, breed resentment—those who live there would be unnatural saints if they felt anything else. And because those people deserve better, it's easy to be sentimental about the decline of places like the Mon Valley. Easy—and unwise. Look a little more closely and the mix of success and failure which typified the 1980s comes into sharper focus.

As a share of the national economy, manufacturing has remained constant for forty years, accounting for around 18 percent to 22 percent of output. Total manufacturing employment has remained stable, at about 18 million to 20 million. While millions of jobs have left the Rust Belt, almost all of them have stayed within the United States. The flip side of decay in McKeesport and Duquesne is a boom in Norfolk,

Nebraska, or Plymouth, Utah—both towns far away from the Rust Belt, and both with new steel mills. The Mon Valley, in other words, was not killed by foreign competition. It died because domestic steel firms built more productive plants in new sites. It was productivity, not the Japanese, that destroyed McKeesport.

Besides, the Mon Valley towns are suburbs of Pittsburgh, and not even distant suburbs. Homestead is just a few minutes from the row houses of south Pittsburgh, where Paderewski once raised a Polish army to fight in World War I. In many ways Pittsburgh is a better place to live in than it was in the days of Big Steel. Its air is clean, its shops and restaurants are more cosmopolitan. It is a pointless value judgment to call a city a "success" if it offers well-paying jobs to men who work in blast furnaces, but a "failure" if it offers well-paying jobs to women who work at computer terminals.

Taken as a whole, in fact, greater Pittsburgh did rather well in the 1980s. In mid-decade, its unemployment rate was well above the national average, but by the early 1990s was below it. But the nature of employment changed. Pittsburgh became a center for the health care industry, and its two universities won worldwide reputations for their links with industry. Where once the city was typified by the Jones & Laughlin plant on the banks of the Monongahela, now its hallmark is postmodern office blocks. Though the steel mills have gone, the level of disposable income in Pittsburgh continues to rise, which suggests that there are still some good jobs to be had. This isn't surprising. Skills rise and fall in demand all the time, towns wax and wane. In 1900 America had 374,000 teamsters (real ones, driving teams of animals); now it has almost none. In 1900 a map of Colorado had thriving mining settlements which are now ghost towns known to none but cross-country skiers and mountain bikers.

Yet such an analysis offers cold comfort. In McKeesport, where volunteers at the Mon Valley Unemployed Workers Committee sift through their cases—here a repossession, there a welfare lien on an old man's assets—jobs in the health care business look a world away. When asked how they feel about the "new" Pittsburgh, the men of McKeesport reply, "We feel left out." Why? Surely not because there's something inherently dignified in pouring hot metal into molds (even if there is, steel is never coming back to the Mon Valley). The real point about the decline of the Valley is rather different. When towns die which once lived on unskilled manufacturing, we don't miss the awful jobs that men were once asked to do: what we miss is a sense of cohesion among all social classes. We miss the Golden Age.

In the Golden Age the central economic truth was not a march toward social equality but simply that those years were good for everyone. In the 1980s the American economy grew strongly for seven years, and manufacturing posted productivity gains almost at the sustained level of the Golden Age. But though most American families benefited from the 1980s, income inequality increased. Class divisions became more evident. This wasn't Ronald Reagan's fault. It can be explained by simple economics.

Since the late 1970s America has lived through a time of sustained technological change, which has had two effects on industrial structure. First, technology has created new jobs, millions of them, which require high-level skills. Second, technology has led to productivity gains in manufacturing because of computer-assisted operations, robotics, and the use of advanced materials. At the same time, the economy has become more open to competition from abroad. And there has been an influx of immigrants, many of them with low skills.

You don't need an econometric model to predict the result. America is living through a period of increased supply of unskilled workers, while there is less demand for them—and more for those with higher skills. The predictable result is a shift in relative incomes, a shift which militates against the chances of Mon Valley steelworkers ever being able to enjoy the ever-increasing abundance they thought was their birthright. It is skills and education which lie at the heart of income inequality. Americans with high school educations or less have, broadly, seen limited gains in their standard of living since the mid-1970s; those with college education have done fine. In part—though it sounds heartless to say so—the working classes brought their misfortune on themselves. Scratch a Mon Valley town like Homestead, and you will find a society which, until very recently, prized a good high school football team above decent graduation rates, and which collectively assumed that kids would follow their fathers into the mill. This was fine when millworkers were earning today's equivalent of $20 an hour; by the time the mills had gone, it was a catastrophically shortsighted attitude.

Moreover, this shift of employment toward higher skill levels has coincided with a shift of manufacturing to the suburbs. It is the combination of these trends that has been so devastating to the old towns and cities of the Northeast and Midwest. John Kasarda claims that "Between 1953 and 1986, New York City shed more than 600,000 manufacturing jobs and nearly 200,000 jobs in the retail and wholesale trades, while employment in the city's white-collar service industries expanded by more than 800,000." That is the "spatial" dimension of the new American economy. But there is an educational dimension, too: Kasarda says that "New York City lost only 9,000 jobs between 1953 and 1970 in those industries in which mean jobholder educational levels in 1982 were less than high school completion, but it lost more than one million jobs in these industries between 1970 and 1986. During the latter period, the city added 322,000 jobs in those industries in which mean educational levels exceeded 13 years of schooling." Similar profiles could be constructed for all the great cities of the Northeast and Midwest, for Philadelphia and Boston as much as for St. Louis and Chicago.

This double shift in employment from one location to another, and from one sort of educational qualification to another, has created a growing sense of alienation of classes from each other. Any discussion of class in America is fraught with peril. The legacy of slavery and continued immigration has meant that "class" divisions in America are constantly overlaid and transmuted by race and ethnicity. In the period after 1945, the use of class as a social determinant was considered almost un-American, as if to breathe the phrase "working class" was to deny America's accomplishments. America had a "middle class" and (by the 1980s) an "underclass"; only Europe had something in between.

In fact, for most of America's history, class divisions have been real, deeply felt, and accompanied by a violence rarely seen in Western Europe. The Homestead strike of 1892, the Ludlow massacre in 1914, the judicial murder of Joe Hill in 1915, the vicious company goons that Henry Ford unleashed at the River Rouge plant in 1937—violent class conflict persisted in America almost until the outbreak of World War II.

Everyone knows class divisions are widening once more.

"The numbers of the rich will grow more rapidly in the coming years," says one writer. "Real wages for low-skilled jobs will increase more slowly, if at all. . . . I fear the potential for producing something like a caste society, with the implication of utter social separation. . . . All the forces which I can discern will push American conservatism toward the Latin American model. . . . The Left has been complaining for years that the rich have too much power. They ain't seen nothing yet."

The author is not some bearded, potbellied relic of the 1960s, but Charles Murray, a leading theorist of modern conservatism. Murray is right. Changes in the structure of the American economy, in the family, and social pathologies like crime have borne much more heavily on poor people than the wealthy. Whether or not "the poor pay more," as Engels claimed, they certainly suffer more from crime. In the 1980s, those with incomes below $7,500 were twice as likely to suffer crimes of violence as those who earned more than $50,000, and three times as likely to be robbed.

In fact, there may be no modern society where elites have so lost touch with the lifestyles and aspirations of the working class. (When a president feels the need to buy socks at a supermarket to "stay in touch" with the people—as George Bush did—you know he isn't.) "We have lost our respect," wrote Christopher Lasch, "for honest manual labor." Of course, there are "working-class" TV series, like *Roseanne* and *The Simpsons*. But, tellingly, they are comedies. Few films or novels really capture the grittiness of working-class life, and those that try don't sell very well. In Paul Schrader's magnificent 1978 film *Blue Collar* you could hear, and almost smell, what life was like in a Detroit car factory. The film was a raging success in Europe, but try finding it in an American video store. In London, still one of the world's most livable cities, public housing projects have always been speckled about randomly; even in the most affluent neighborhoods, you can bet there's a project nearby. That's *why* London is so livable. In America, by contrast, projects are huddled together, out of sight of the pampered rich. If you're a prosperous Chicagoan, you have to make quite an effort to see the Robert Taylor Homes.

Some fashionable social mores just exacerbate class divisions. Ray Oldenburg has mourned the decline of "third places"—neither entirely public nor entirely private—which once provided a mixing place for people of all classes. Neighborhood bars once did that (try finding one in most suburbs now); so did Main Streets. The claim that a shopping mall can re-create the jumbled-up sense of social cohesion of Main Street, is, says Oldenburg, to "skate freely on the brink of total nonsense." Visit one of the few remaining working-class bars in any American city, and watch regulars "belly up"; then visit a yuppie health club; spot the difference. It is in these subtle social differences that class distinctions are made flesh, literally. Those who never finished high school are more than twice as likely to be fat as those who have gone to college. In 1970, 35 percent of high school dropouts smoked cigarettes, as did 28 percent of college graduates. By 1993 the number of smokers in the first category was 37 percent, but among the college-educated smoking had become taboo; only 13.5 percent smoked cigarettes.

The very issues and language of "progressive" politics have left working-class Americans in the lurch. In the 1930s, Woody Guthrie, the troubadour of the blue-collars, celebrated the great dams of the Pacific Northwest which brought power to the people. By the 1990s, progressives considered those dams an environmental abomination which ruined the lives not of the working class, thank you, but of *fish*. "The culture wars that have convulsed America since the sixties," wrote Lasch, "are best understood as a form of class warfare, in which an enlightened elite (as it thinks of itself) seeks not so much to impose its values on the majority (a majority perceived as incorrigibly racist, sexist, provincial and xenophobic), much less to persuade the majority by means of rational public debate, as to create parallel or 'alternative' institutions in which it will no longer be necessary to confront the unenlightened at all."

The list of indicia of class division goes on. The "enlightened" take their children out of public schools and place them in private ones. As any dinner party in any moderately affluent American home proves, private education is a growth industry. Between 1970 and 1990, the number of children enrolled in all high schools dropped from 14.6 million to 13.1 million, but the number of children enrolled in non-religious private high schools soared, from 303,000 in 1970 to 768,000 in 1993. In many prosperous American suburbs and in almost all American inner cities, the public high schools no longer provide the sense of common purpose among all social classes which was once their pride. The affluent can move to private communities, gated "neighborhood associations" with their own standards of admission and their own security force. Those with a modicum of cash can practice what Robert Reich terms an "internal secession," leaving those less fortunate to stew in their own juice.

Perhaps the sharpest recent proof of the new importance of class came during the 1993 debate on the North American Free Trade Agreement. The elites—the editorial boards, the think tanks, the academics—were uniformly in favor of

NAFTA. It had all the attributes of the new enlightenment: it was "internationalist"; it could be justified by reference to that new shibboleth, "the global economy." The congressional fight against the treaty, by contrast, was led by David Bonior, a Polish-American Democrat from (where else?) Macomb County. Bonior explicitly opposed the treaty on class grounds. "The work of America," he argued, in a speech on the final day's debate, "is still done by people who pack a lunch, punch a clock, and pour their heart and soul into every paycheck. And we cannot afford to leave them behind." The troops and the money of the anti-NAFTA coalition came from labor unions. Black activists were also overwhelmingly opposed to NAFTA. A rally in August 1993 to celebrate the thirtieth anniversary of Martin Luther King's march on Washington was dominated by anti-NAFTA T-shirts, workshops, and slogans, potent symbols of the new fears of the working class.

NAFTA was ratified; and unions look doomed. Their public image has never recovered from the racketeering scandals of the 1950s and 1960s. The web of laws, state and federal, which confine union operations are too thick to be wished away. And America will never again see factories and mills like those which once dominated Detroit and the Mon Valley, each with thousands of workers, each a breeding ground for class solidarity. But given the economic and social turmoil of the 1980s and 1990s, it would be a brave pundit who guessed that class divisions would not one day become violent. After the 1994 elections, it became briefly fashionable to note the rage and alienation of the "angry white male." That was a nice little tag, but anyone with a passing acquaintance with American history would have called it something different: the return of the working class.

From a distance, foreigners look at the new American class divisions and smile a rather nasty smile. At least some of them actually *like* the fact that the Golden Age and its claims of unbridled American ascendancy have been tarnished. After all those years of being preached the virtues of a classless America, the smile says, we can now see the truth. But this triumphalism turns to horror when foreigners look not at the new working class but at America's largely black underclass, at the crime-ridden ghettos, the crack cocaine epidemic, the level of single-parenthood, the young men with no attachment to the labor force. Foreign observers read of German tourists murdered on the freeway a few minutes from Miami airport; they hear of an old British tourist who got off the Washington Metro at the "wrong stop" (a stop just a few blocks from the White House), cut through an alley, and was shot. They send television crews to film the shiny pants of winos, the crack vials crunching underfoot, the prostitutes who turn a trick for a few dollars. Comfortable Americans think of the underclass, shudder, and decide to stay within the relative safety of the suburbs. They remember Sherman McCoy, hero of Tom Wolfe's novel *The Bonfire of the Vanities*, taking a wrong turn in the South Bronx, and ending in "a vast open terrain. . . . The hills and dales of the Bronx reduced to asphalt, concrete and cinders in a ghastly yellow gloaming."

The growth of the underclass has spawned a rich academic literature. Some theories explain the underclass as a cultural phenomenon, a reaction to the breakdown of accepted patterns of social responsibility. Scholars like Charles Murray of the American Enterprise Institute claim that the underclass is a rational response to welfare policies which reward behavior once labeled deviant, like single-motherhood. Others explain the underclass as a reaction to past and continuing racism in labor and housing markets.

In the late 1980s and early 1990s, the "standard theory" of the underclass concentrated on the double shift in demand for employment. Simply put, this theory holds that after 1970 the economic demand for unskilled black men dried up. Jobs have migrated to the suburbs, but those who need such jobs are in the cities. The old pattern of bus routes which linked neighborhoods to city centers is now economically useless. In some inner-city ghettos, up to three-quarters of households don't have a car. Moreover, the gains of the civil rights movement—the end of segregated housing, new opportunities for qualified blacks in the public sector—contributed to a black middle-class flight from the cities. Old black urban areas lost their natural commercial and social leadership. The ghettos became dominated by low skills and listlessness; oases in reverse.

A decent test of this theory came during Boston's booming 1980s. Three of the area's core industries—electronics, financial services, and real estate—had a great decade. In 1987 unemployment in Boston averaged 2.7 percent—a labor market so tight that economists would describe it as in a state of labor shortage. Unemployment among young black men and unskilled workers declined dramatically. This improvement took place in an economy from which many blue-collar jobs had already left. In very, very tight labor markets, workers can switch jobs—mill hands can become office workers—but Boston in the 1980s was a peculiar place, with a speculative boom which took the average price of a modest single-family home from $78,000 in 1983 to $175,000 in just four years. It's not realistic to base policy on such an aberration. Besides, the tight labor market still left untouched a group of poor people who seem to have lost all connection with employment. Single-parent families continued to grow in number.

This is a worrying conclusion. It seems to show that a booming economy does not eliminate all the social behavior which can transmit poverty from one generation to another. Economic factors and cultural ones interact with each other. In Chicago, recent research suggests that black inner-city workers are disadvantaged in the labor market even when they try as hard as they can to get jobs. Two reasons for this suggest themselves. First, there may still be racial discrimination in labor markets, or at least racial stereotyping which diminishes the chances of black youngsters finding work. Second, even those in the ghettos who want to work may lack the educational or social skills that equip them for employment, at least outside frantic Boston-type booms.

The underclass matters not just because it stunts the lives of those who are a part of it, though, God knows, that is bad enough, but also because it wrecks all sense of social cohesion. And since Americans have come to regard their time of cohesion as normal, they are ill-prepared for tackling the manifold problems of underclass America. A nation risks being split apart when many of its people grow ever more prosperous while others sink into degradation. Worse, comfortable America is frightened of the underclass, and fear eats at a nation's soul.

The fear is partly understandable. In November 1991, Washington, D.C., was introduced to a nineteen-year-old called Henry "Little Man" James. He had already fathered two children by two separate women, and was said to be part of a cocaine-peddling ring whose headquarters were a few blocks from the Capitol. On a winter's night, he and some friends went for a drive; James said he felt like "busting some-one." So he did; he took a potshot at a passing car and snuffed out the life of a thirty-six-year old newlywed woman, just like that. When arrested, the police asked him (on TV) what he was doing the night of the killing. With a diabolical grin, James replied, "I was out maintaining my composure." No doubt about it: James and his ilk are truly frightening.

James's victim was black. Black Americans suffer from crime far more than whites—a black American is about five times more likely to be murdered than a white American. Although there are some pretty grim suburbs around, there is no suburb anywhere in America whose worried parents are asked to tolerate anything like the crackle of gunfire, epidemics of robbery, or drug-induced misery that are the everyday lot of black parents in the poorest part of the in-ner city. But this fact does not breed a sense of comfort on the part of white Americans. It fuels a sense of fear. For many white city dwellers, the sociologist Elijah Anderson has argued, the mere sight of a young black male on the street is enough to summon up fear of crime. And it's not just white Americans who feel that way. In December 1993 Jesse Jackson told a Chicago audience, "There is nothing more painful to me at this stage of my life than to walk down the street and hear footsteps and start thinking about robbery—then look around and see somebody white and feel relieved."

Nations can't long maintain their unity when such fear, and such divisions, run rampant. In the long run, such divi-sions can only be ameliorated when all Americans have the same access to the skills which are now needed in the econ-omy. There is some good news here. In the mid-1990s, black high school graduation rates had become very close to white ones. Sadly, this good news has to be balanced with some bad, and that comes in what has happened to black male educational performance beyond high school.

Black enrollment in colleges and universities increased markedly in the late 1960s and early 1970s. In 1976, precisely the same proportion of black high school graduates signed on for higher education as did white high school graduates—32 percent in both cases. But by 1993, the old divisions had been rediscovered. That year 43 percent of white high school graduates enrolled in colleges, but only 29 percent of black graduates. Between 1976–77 and 1989–90, the number of bachelor's degrees awarded to white students increased from 808,000 to 883,000, about 9 percent. Bachelor's degrees awarded to black students increased from 59,000 to 61,000, or about 3 percent.

Why did black college enrollment fall away after the mid-1970s? One explanation is a shift in patterns of financial assistance from grants to loans. This may have worked to the disadvantage of black students, who tend to come from poorer homes. But this is only part of the story, since the black fallout from higher education is exclusively a male phenomenon. Measured by either college enrollment or degrees conferred, black women have outperformed black men since the late 1970s. In fact, the increase in their participation in higher education has outpaced that of white men.

Between 1976 and 1990, for example, white male enrollment in undergraduate degree programs increased by 3 percent while the number of bachelor's degrees actually awarded fell by 6 percent. At the same time, black male enrollment increased by 2 percent, but the number of bachelor's degrees awarded fell by 8 percent. Black women, by contrast, increased their enrollment by 33 percent, and their number of bachelor's degrees by 15 percent. (White women did better still, increasing undergraduate enrollment by 37 percent and their number of bachelor's degrees by 27 percent.)

This distinction in the performance of black men and black women is perplexing. Black men and black women have received the same information about the labor market; changes in programs of financial assistance should have affected both equally. It is hard to avoid the conclusion that the growth of social pathologies, especially of black single-parenthood, has blighted the prospects of black men much more than black women.

When this truth is placed along the economic reasons for the growth of the underclass, a startling picture emerges. For all the new significance of class in America, perhaps the most troubling of all cleavages is not between classes at all, and not between different ethnic groups, but within the black community. Broadly speaking, two-thirds of America's blacks have seen their economic opportunities rise since the 1970s, but by the 1990s, the remaining one-third was arguably as isolated from the American mainstream as it had been before the civil rights revolution. Though many thoughtlessly symbolize the underclass by a feckless black single mother, this actually stigmatizes an American success story. Through the vicissitudes of economic change, black women have held their own; it is black men—or at least, enough of them to be a problem—who are in danger of slipping out of the mainstream of American life.

So by the mid-1990s, the 1980s had started to come into reasonable focus. There had been substantial economic growth, and a revival of corporate America. Many Americans got even richer than their parents did; they were the children of the people of plenty. Yet, for deep-rooted technological and economic reasons, rather than because of a failure of policy, growth was no longer the nation's essential glue. On the contrary, the lifestyles of regions, classes, and races were drifting further apart.

In post-1945 America, building on the traditions of the New Deal, it would have been natural to look to the federal government to ameliorate these divisions, and indeed, this was done. George Bush, just a few months after a great triumph in the Gulf War of 1990–91, was excoriated because he had no "domestic policies"—nothing to say on health care reform, education, or urban renewal. Bill Clinton did, or seemed to, and that, in a nutshell, was why Clinton and not Bush won the 1992 election.

Yet the federal government could no longer work its magic. Clinton came to office with one and a half hands tied behind his back; popular trust in Washington as a force for national cohesion had all but collapsed. The author Jonathan Rauch reports, for example, that in 1958 75 percent of Americans said they trusted the federal government to "do what's right" but that by 1993 only 20 percent of Americans trusted Washington. Much of the explanation for this collapse of trust lies in the dozen years of political crisis between Dallas and Watergate, years which would have wrecked a political system less securely founded. Part of the explanation must also lie with Ronald Reagan. Reagan's term of office from 1981 to 1989 brought to an end a rare twenty-year period when no president had served two successive terms. Enormously popular throughout almost all his time in office, Reagan had roots in both the Midwest and California; he hitched his star to intellectuals, but at the same time used popular culture to enhance his image. Yet despite his oft-stated admiration for FDR, a central theme of his presidency was to diminish the reputation of government in public esti-mation. Government, as Reagan said at his first inaugural, was part of the problem, not part of the solution. If a popular president thought that, why should anyone else doubt it?

In fact, there were good reasons for being suspicious of Washington, which by the 1980s had become an unlovely place. The numbers employed by the Congress doubled; the money spent on elections soared; political action committees doubled in number in one decade; trade associations moved their headquarters from the heartland to the capital. K Street, that strip of architectural horrors in downtown Wash-ington, became synonymous with lobbyists, lawyers, and public relations firms, ready to dash up to "Gucci Gulch" on Capitol Hill to lobby the members of the House Ways and Means Committee. "Hyperpluralism"—a term coined by Jim Thurber of American University—had come to dominate the capital, so that for every proposed action there was an equal and opposite reaction by those threatened by it. A po-litical system which had had the virtues of stability—and the American system of government is unique in its longevity—had become prey to the vice of immobility. By 1995 Bill Clinton was sounding almost Reaganesque, warning against the tendency of government institutions to "abandon the original purpose for which they were established and, in-stead, to become more concerned about preserving them-selves, their prerogatives, their position, their power. At its worst," said Clinton, "government can act just as a powerful monopoly—unaccountable, abusive of power, and immune to change." Fifty years after FDR's death, in other words, there was a broad consensus that the cohesive role which the federal government had lately played in American life had come to an end. Bob Dole launched his campaign for the presidency in 1995 by brandishing that charter of upmarket opponents of Washington, the Tenth Amendment. "The powers not delegated to the United States by the Constitution," reads the Amendment, "nor prohibited by it to the States, are reserved to the States, respectively, or to the people."

Dole's move was less a break with the recent past than a recognition of reality. For the truth about America in the 1980s and 1990s was not, as George Bush's opponents had argued in 1992, that it had no domestic policies. Precisely the contrary was true. America was brimming with domestic policies: policies on education, housing, welfare, the environment—on everything from the laying of fiber optic cable to the right approach to gypsy moth extermination. But those policies were coming from state and local governments, not Washington: domestic policy had been denationalized.

Arkansas made teachers acountable for their performance; Chicago introduced sweeping systems of self-management in its public housing projects; states across the nation legislated for new approaches to welfare—in 1993, Wisconsin passed a law to withdraw from the federal welfare system altogether. California regulated everything from automobile emissions to the proper fuel for backyard barbecues. In the year before President Clinton unveiled his own abortive plan for health care reform, no fewer than fifteen states had enacted their own reform plans. As Republicans took control of Congress after the 1994 elections, so the movement of domestic policy away from Washington merely gathered pace. Program after program was converted to "block grants," chunks of money for the states to spend as they wished.

In large measure, the denationalization of domestic policy is a return to a pattern of American democracy that predated the New Deal. The Constitution, as generations of students have learned, is a grant of limited, enumerated powers to the federal government. Tocqueville saw the point. States, he argued, were the "ordinary and undefined governments which provide for the daily needs of society," while the federal government was "exceptional and circumscribed."

Granted, the federal government has constantly increased its powers. But it has always had to justify its growth into new areas, either before a suspicious court of public opinion, or before real courts of law. With the exception of the power to wage war, it is hard to think of a single aspect of policy that has not, at one time or another, been claimed as a prerogative by a state. In few other countries would a unit of subnational government have been able to claim that it could write its own code of international tax law; California does so. States have always taken seriously the argument of Justice Louis Brandeis that "it is one of the happy incidents of the federal system that a single courageous State may . . . serve as a laboratory; and try novel social and economic experiments without risk to the country."

Most Americans have missed a profound change in the way they are governed. As late as the 1950s, when state governments were often thought (and often rightly thought) to be corrupt and hidebound, liberals would never have suggested that states should be encouraged to find new powers for themselves. *Brown v. Board of Education* and the other great civil rights cases were a frontal attack on the power of states to make their own domestic policy. But then came a succession of conservative administrations in Washington, and a period of persistently high federal budget deficits. Even if the federal government had had the will to adopt expansive domestic policies, it did not have the wallet to do so. So liberals perforce looked to state and local governments for action. In the 1990s a city planner in the heavily Democratic city of Cleveland said, "In the 1970s I lost all my best people to Washington. In the 1980s I recruited the best people in Washington to come here."

Increasingly, Democratic politicians who aspired to national office were men who had made their mark in state governments. Compare the political histories of John Kennedy, Lyndon Johnson, and Hubert Humphrey, all of whom made their mark as legislators in Washington, with the leaders of a later generation. Jimmy Carter, Michael Dukakis, and Bill Clinton all carved national reputations by staying at home and looking for local solutions, albeit ones with national application, to local problems.

Combined, these trends have led to a veritable explosion of subnational government. Between 1950 and 1990, the federal government payroll expanded from 2.1 million people to 3.1 million. This increase, the stuff of thousands of complaints by conservatives, was dwarfed by developments in state and local governments. In the same period, state governments more than quadrupled in size—they employed a little over 1 milllion in 1950, more than 4.6 million in 1992. Local government employment grew almost as fast; from 3.2 million people in 1950 to 11.1 million in 1992. State and local government payrolls grew most quickly in the 1960s and 1970s, but the 1980s did not exactly see retrenchment; the real expenditure of state governments more than doubled in the decade.

If the commitment to a federal system of government is worth the paper on which it is written, some devolution of power must be desirable. The nation spans a continent. The social conditions of Florida, for example, are vastly different from those of West Virginia. Even states that are contiguous to each other may have developed quite different traditions. Compare Massachusetts, which for long has had an almost Scandinavian social democracy, with the home-grown tax-hating conservatism of neighboring New Hampshire. America's states are too diverse for one size of domestic policy to fit all, and federalism has much of which to be proud. A system of government which enables its subnational units to achieve things as great as the California university system or the Adirondacks State Park in New York is not to be despised.

It's important to note that it isn't just states who "do" domestic policy. So do cities and counties. To an extent, this, too, makes sense. San Francisco, in the years of the AIDS epidemic, has very different public health needs from San Diego; the environmental concerns of a county in the mountains of western Maryland are quite different from a county on the shores of the Chesapeake Bay. And, to be sure, local control of schools has indeed encouraged a mosaic of innovation and experiment: here a school board introduces vouchers, there a district experiments with total immersion in a foreign language for its kids.

The best argument in favor of this new form of domestic policy is the oldest one, that states and cities are indeed laboratories of democracy. Yet there has been little examination of what the claim actually means. It presumably means that laboratories find what works and then disseminate the best practice nationally. Ask how this dissemination is supposed to take place, and those whom we can call "laboratorists" will probably babble on about "networks." A formal and informal system of conferences, associations, interest groups, publications, and the like, they argue, takes good ideas and spreads them across the country.

Does that really happen? Sometimes, no doubt: but even then, the process can be painfully slow. Some outside observers are hard put to see any dissemination of best practice, at any pace. Ask representatives of the insurance industry, which is regulated by the states, if best practice is quickly adopted nationwide and you will receive by way of answer a hollow laugh: what such businessmen actually see is a confusing mess of legislation which increases their costs.

Even state legislators in the forefront of innovation concede, in their more honest moments, the difficulty of forming networks. Bill Clinton himself—the very apotheosis of networking, a past president of the National Governors Association and a man who never saw an innovative idea he didn't think could be tried in Arkansas—has complained how difficult it is to take local success stories and spread their lessons across the country. In the late 1980s, John Kitzhaber, then the chairman of the Oregon State Senate (and now the state's governor), worked on an ambitious plan to extend the numbers eligible for Medicaid while limiting the medical procedures for which the state would pay. He lamented the absence of any interest at the national level in his work, saying that the federal government gave an impression of "towering arrogance." But he also candidly admitted that few other states showed much interest, either.

In fact, the cumulative effect of federal, state, and local governments all anxious to expand their reach may now be counterproductive. Competing federal, state, and local bureaucracies have made America an overgoverned nation. The sense that even in Congress, a body of the national government, votes should be determined by what makes sense for a member's district rather than the national good has bred a politics of the pork barrel. "All politics is local" sounds like a nice slogan; in fact, it is deadly corrupting. Beyond all else, the denationalization of domestic policy ignored a salient truth of modern America: this was a society which needed to be brought together, which needed something to counterbalance the way in which classes, races, and regions were drifting apart. Instead, the denationalization of domestic policy simply exacerbated a worrying trend.

America isn't obviously in crisis—at least, not the kind of crisis which those who have lived in any other industrial society have suffered this century. In and of themselves, none of the new divisions which became manifest in the 1980s were critical. The nation's regions had always had different strengths and weaknesses, social classes had always enjoyed different economic opportunities, while, axiomatically, many black Americans had never shared in the nation's prosperity. The fact that the suburbs of California and the booming towns along the Front Range of the Rockies looked different from the Mon Valley should not have been the stuff of great drama; the division between city and suburb was one which some cities had managed to avoid. Nor were the fractures unique to America. The same economic forces which hurt the American working class were evident in all advanced economies, all of which saw the same premium on skills and education, all of which were forced to worry that many of their people would lose all touch with the world of work. By the mid-1990s, it was not just the U.S. that was faced with an underclass mainly made up of an ethnic minority. In the suburbs of Paris, North Africans were alienated from the French mainstream and flirted with Islamic fundamentalism. In inner-city London, the 1980s saw riots among those of West Indian ancestry, who suffered levels of unemployment persistently higher than those of whites.

So what *was* peculiar to the United States? Two things: First, the federal government, which had recently been a unifying force in the country, had lost its authority. Second, America had no folk memory to help it heal its new divisions. All it had was the memory of the Golden Age, that strange time when divisions were hardly noticeable; and that memory was now of little use. This absence of a road map was doubly troubling. For in addition to the fractures within American society, the country was faced with a quite novel challenge from abroad: an internationalization of its economy and population. This internationalization brought yet more divisions in its wake, and the way in which those divisions might be healed was far from obvious.

CHAPTER EIGHT

Inside the Door:
The 1990s

In the Golden Age America's relationship to the rest of the world had a double aspect. The country was both self-contained and faced an external threat, and these factors combined to reinforce a sense of national unity. By the mid-1990s, this peculiar conjunction, never seen before in America's history, had ended. The global economy had wormed its way into American businesses and their workers' lives; immigration was reaching levels rarely seen before; and, not least, the Soviet Union had gone—poof!—just like that. So it would be pointless to look for an icon of America's international relations on a base of the Strategic Air Command (which, by 1991, didn't even exist) in the cornfields of Indiana. In this respect, too, the heartland had changed. The new heart of America's international relations had moved to places much more scruffy than the clipped lawns of a SAC base. Places like Tijuana, Mexico.

Fifty years ago, Tijuana, at the top of the Baja California peninsula, was a tacky, flyblown town with a population of about 30,000. Americans found the place a useful joke, a

prop for novels and films when someone needed a quick marriage or divorce, a refuge from the law. Angeleno kids went
there to get wasted on tequila and screwed in its cat houses.

By the mid-1990s, that old Tijuana was long gone. Sure, it
was still tatty, but now, with more than a million people
(making it one of the fastest-growing cities on earth) it formed
an uneasy megalopolis with San Diego, manicured haven of
retired naval officers. Tijuana's main street was dotted with
the trademark stores of global capitalism—here a Benetton,
there a Gucci. There were a pair of gleaming skyscrapers
and an international cultural center. Tijuana's businessmen,
dressed in L.A. casual gear, would boast to visitors that they
could live in San Diego if they chose, but, frankly, preferred
life in Mexico. And then they would bore you with tales of
their latest trip to Japan.

In San Diego, conversations typically took a different
turn. You were told about raw sewage drifting up from Mexico; about illegal immigrants who dodged the traffic on the
interstate and then lived off Uncle Sam; about gangs of violent drug runners. You heard that wages in Tijuana's factories
were an eighth those in California, and would suck jobs away
from the American middle class. As Mexico modernized its
economy, those who lived in Tijuana exhibited a confidence
that their proximity to the U.S. gave them a privileged place
in the "global economy," a phrase they used often. In San
Diego, you were just as likely to hear the same phenomenon
described as a threat. By the mid-1990s, those unlikely twin
cities had come to typify a new relationship between America and the rest of the world. "Foreign policy" had become
domesticated, taken out of the hands of striped-pants diplomats and given to businessmen, cops, and immigration officers. The outside world had changed the ways Americans

lived and worked, and altered the very sense of who an "American" was. In the Golden Age, the world had been kept at bay; now, like a giant, pregnant Pacific turtle, it had crept onto America's shores.

In the Golden Age, the external threat from the Soviet Union helped support all kinds of domestic developments within America, from the creation of a massive defense industry to support for scientific education. But the national unity around the Soviet threat could not survive the turmoil of the 1960s and 1970s. Strategically, Vietnam broke the mold. The old certainties of foreign policy could no longer command universal respect. Much, though certainly not all, of the foreign policy establishment still wanted to contain communism wherever it might appear. But for many others, Vietnam showed the folly of containment, which, they thought, was bound to lead to doomed adventurism abroad in places where the U.S. had no business and little interest.

Much later, it became clear that something of the first importance had happened: America's role as the defender of freedom and democracy was no longer a matter of broad agreement, a fixed and unexceptionable part of the landscape. Far from being a source of national unity, America's foreign policy became one more indicator of the ways in which it was falling apart. And then in the late 1980s and 1990s, Soviet power collapsed. With its collapse came the final nail in the coffin of the foreign policy consensus. With the end of the Cold War, the salience that had surrounded America's role in the world since 1945 simply disappeared.

The proof of that came in the New Hampshire primary of 1992, as the New England air turned damp, then cold, and the circus of politics made its quadrennial trip to the Granite State. The primary was anticipated to be of interest only to Democrats. George Bush was an incumbent Republican president whose skillful diplomacy had eased the transition from communism to democracy in Eastern Europe; the economy was recovering from a mild recession. The previous winter Bush had led a multinational coalition to victory over Saddam Hussein, the Iraqi dictator whose invasion of Kuwait had threatened the world's supply of oil. The Gulf War had cost America little blood; just over a hundred Ameicans had died. Yet just one year later, Bush received virtually no political credit for his leadership. Instead, Pat Buchanan, a conservative journalist who had opposed the war, entered the primary and did astonishingly well, winning 37 percent of Republican votes.

Granted, the Bush campaign was feeble, the president himself alternately remote and frenetic, but any idle student of American history might have thought that a triumph over first communism and then an Arab tyrant would have counted for something at the polls. Instead, while New Hampshire was supposed to be in the middle of a deep economic depression, Bush didn't seem to care; Buchanan did. And that was it.

It was hard not to feel sorry for Bush. He had spent his time in the White House doing, and doing well, what every president since 1945 had thought to be their main job: making the world a safer place. But he was snubbed for it, dismissed as a president who was not interested in domestic policy. Bush was "America's foreign minister," sniffed Paul Tsongas, a Democratic candidate for the presidency. (Times had sure changed: Richard Reeves points out that John Kennedy's inaugural address had all of two words on domestic policy.) While some conservatives clung to their internationalism, convinced that America should shape the post–Cold War world, others took the collapse of communism as a signal to retreat behind those two broad oceans which protect America from the world's turmoil.

Liberals displayed no more coherence. From 1992 to 1994, as trouble spots like Haiti, Bosnia, and Somalia erupted into violence, Democrats as much as Republicans found themselves on both sides of an issue. Some liberals who had opposed intervention abroad when it was a proxy for fighting the Soviets—in Central America, for example—had a magical conversion. It was the black political leadership which demanded American intervention in both Somalia and Haiti.

Such an account of the confusion in foreign policy at the end of the Cold War could leave one thinking that Americans agreed on nothing; that this was one more baleful example of a country unable to find a sense of common purpose. Actually, Americans agreed on much. They may have been all over the lot on whether Russia had replaced the Soviet Union as a threat, whether the war in Bosnia impinged on vital American interests, whether it was worth "saving" Haiti, but they knew that with the end of the Cold War, the principal purpose of foreign policy was economic.

Some inkling of the new mood was evident in polling done by the Chicago Council of Foreign Relations in 1990, when the Soviet Union still existed. The council found sharp differences between the foreign policy goals of the "elites" and "the general public." Elites were worried about the spread of nuclear weapons, worldwide arms control, and the global environment. The top three goals of the general public were quite different: protecting the jobs of American workers, protecting the interests of American workers abroad, and securing adequate supplies of energy. No less than 60 percent of the public thought that foreign policy had a major impact on unemployment at home; only 30 percent of the elite group did.

Four years later, when the Times Mirror Center for the People and the Press conducted a similar poll, the picture had subtly changed. In the detail, there were still some differences between elites and the public. But on the big picture they agreed by large majorities: strengthening the domestic economy was a key goal of *foreign* policy. And more of both groups were dissatisfied with how things were going in the United States than they were in the outside world.

The most sensible conclusion to these findings is this: Americans had quite rationally stopped being scared of the threat from the world *outside* their borders. That old source of cohesion had gone with the Cold War. But many of them had become very concerned indeed with a new "threat" posed by the outside world *inside* America's borders. And the reason for that can be summed up in two words: trade and immigration.

Americans whose worldview was forged in the Golden Age weren't prepared for the internationalization of the economy, for a good reason: in the Golden Age the economy wasn't internationalized, but a self-contained whole. Of all the things that happened to America between the 1970s and 1990s, few were so important as the reversal of this fact. The creation of an integrated global economy was one of the goals of American policy-makers at the end of World War II. American policy-makers responded to Soviet power not just by security programs but with economic policies, principal among them the promotion of free trade. The removal of trade barriers, it was argued, would create the conditions for global economic growth. Prosperity would bolster America's allies in Western Europe and Asia, making them less susceptible to the blandishments of communism. Free trade piggy-backed on the Cold War.

The goal of a global economy was achieved, better and faster than Americans had anticipated. The wrecks of Europe and Japan picked themselves off the floor, satisfied their own markets, and then turned to America. New technologies made it easier to transport goods across oceans; tariffs were reduced; barriers to foreign investment were lowered. And so trade grew as never before. Lumping goods and services together, the "tradeable" sector of the economy—the proportion accounted for by either exports or imports—was less than 10 percent in 1960. By the mid-1990s the tradeable sector accounted for around 30 percent of the national economy, and the jargon of international trade—GATT, NAFTA, and trade laws like Super-301—had become a staple of the chattering class.

How popular was free trade in the Golden Age? Not very. The record of the opinion polls is murky; as usual, much depends on the way in which questions were posed. But a balanced view of the polls by Page and Shapiro concludes, "Most Americans like the idea of free trade (and cheap imports) in principle, but over many years large majorities have favored some measure of protection to safeguard American jobs." The larger point, perhaps, is that for most of the Golden Age, free trade was not much of a public concern. The American economy was self-contained: there's no point in being scared of what can't hurt you. And because public opinion was relatively relaxed about free trade, so were professional politicians; at least until the early 1970s, there was a strong bipartisan commitment to the virtues of open markets.

The political consensus was not total. In the late 1960s, as trade surpluses gave way to persistent (though terribly small) deficits, so pressure grew for policy changes, especially from labor unions. In August 1971, as part of a package of measures taken to prop up the dollar, John Connally, Nixon's treasury secretary (and arguably the only man with true protectionist instincts to have held that job in modern times), imposed a temporary 10 percent surcharge on imports. Businessmen, once relaxed about foreign competition (which was easy: there wasn't any), started to lobby congressmen for protection. After the elections of 1974, Congress, which for forty years had developed elaborate mechanisms to head off just such lobbying, "reformed" itself in ways which made it easier for business to seek special favors. And so throughout the 1970s, 1980s, and 1990s, the virtues of free trade have always had to to be argued in the political arena; they can no longer be taken for granted.

Meanwhile, in the supermarkets and Main Streets, America had changed forever. Those who had once bought almost nothing from abroad save bananas now went on a binge of importing. Take cars. Though American car manufacturers have always had a global reach, they achieved it by building plants abroad. Exports of cars made in America have always been trivial. Yet throughout the Golden Age, so were imports; nobody sensible would have traded a huge American car, as big as a living room and just as climate-controlled, for a tinny little box from Europe. As late as 1967, the United States actually ran a trade surplus in cars. But the first oil shock in 1973–74 was a watershed. Americans junked their gas-guzzlers for sprightly Japanese and European models. By 1990 America had a trade deficit in the automotive sector of around $42 billion—about 40 percent of its total deficit in merchandise goods.

From French wines to German machine tools, from Korean computers to Indian textiles, the American consumer went on an import binge. The production of goods became globalized, so Detroit's Big Three subcontracted not to Joe's body shop down in Ypsilanti, but to Yasu's plant in Osaka. Americans imported goods even when they thought they were buying American. Like a virus in a horror movie, imports can creep into a familiar product and transform it into something exotic. In 1990 Robert Reich noted that something which, despite its name, seems as all-American as the General Motors Pontiac Le Mans, was nothing of the sort. It was assembled in Korea, and had bits and pieces from Japan, Germany, Taiwan, Singapore, Britain, Ireland, and Barbados. The Le Mans was the global economy made tangible.

Americans took to exporting almost as much as to importing, with just as dramatic an effect. Millions of Americans now rely on markets an ocean away for their paychecks—a fact of life they would never have dreamed possible during the Golden Age. Take Fort Smith, Arkansas, a blue-collar town on the Arkansas river, almost equidistant from Little Rock and Oklahoma City, the headquarters of Baldor Electric, which is the second largest American-owned maker of motors.

Roland Boreham, now Baldor's chief executive, arrived in Fort Smith from California in the 1960s. Back then, he says, the firm didn't think of itself as a "national" company. In the 1960s, says Boreham, "California was as far away as Taiwan is now." This was quite normal. The American economy was so large that companies could make a good living from regional markets. But in the Golden Age those markets were bound together, and by the late 1960s a firm like Baldor could ship goods along the freeways to anywhere in the country.

Then something unexpected happened. Baldor's competitors had once been familiar American firms like General Electric. From the 1970s, the competitors had German and Japanese names—Siemens and Hitachi. There was no such thing as a protected American market for Baldor's goods. If the firm was to grow, it would have to do so abroad, so in 1978 the firm decided to look for exports. It soon had offices in Munich and Zurich, and by the mid-1990s made 13 percent of its sales abroad.

The lesson of Baldor is that competition at home led to exports abroad. Other companies found themselves exporting because their products went to American customers who themselves had built assembly plants all over the world. Many of such companies were and are quite small. America's exporters are not just the great international companies like Boeing, or the agricultural combines who have been exporting American grain for more than a century. They are, increasingly, small- and medium-sized firms who a few years ago thought a commercial mission out of their state to be the height of adventure. Naturally, many still do, and banks often don't help them change their ways. An executive in a Michigan high-technology company tells of a large bank in Detroit which thinks financing trade with Italy is risky; yet Italy is the industrial world's fifth largest economy.

Nonetheless, the suprising thing is not how few regional and local companies export, but how many now enjoy it. In the corner of northwest Arkansas around Fort Smith and Fayetteville, poorly served by interstates and miles from an international airport, there are scores of firms large and small exporting not just electric motors, but everything from perfume, to live stud cockerels, to parking meters. Don Tyson, the chicken king of America, whose headquarters are in Springdale, Arkansas, now exports 10 percent of his out-put. If Arkansas can live by international trade, so can any-where.

The internationalization of American business extends to the service sector. By the early 1990s, Hollywood's share of foreign markets had reached all-time highs, while the share of the domestic box office taken by foreign films had slumped. In the early 1970s, foreign films had 7 percent to 9 percent of the American box office; by the mid-1990s, they took less than 2 percent of box office receipts. Similarly, swoop down the ski slopes at Breckenridge, Colorado, and you will hear not just Texan, or Yankee, but pure Cockney. Nearly 10 per-cent of Breckenridge's business comes from Britain. The town's international marketing has been so successful that skiers are happy to fly ten hours from London to Denver.

Between 1986 and 1993, Breckenridge exemplified one more facet of the internationalization of America. Its ski area was carved out of land owned by the U.S. Forest Service, but it was operated by a Japanese company. This, too, was new. In the Golden Age foreign direct investment in America was tiny. The French and British had liquidated their old foreign holdings to pay for two great wars; the Japanese had not yet expanded abroad; South Korea and Taiwan were Third World countries, with workers ankle-deep in paddy fields.

Since the 1970s all that has changed. There have been two great waves of foreign investment, one in the late 1970s and early 1980s, and another in the late 1980s. During the second wave, Japanese firms bought Rockefeller Center in New York, great chunks of real estate in Los Angeles and Hawaii, tire companies, film studios, and one of the largest record companies. And they built factories on greenfield sites to make cars, consumer electronics, and advanced high-technology goods. British firms bought brick and minerals companies and hotel chains, and expanded their telecommunications and chemicals holdings. The French bought defense companies; German drug, textile, and car firms built plants in the Carolinas. And all the while, state and city governments stuffed subsidies into the mouths of foreign firms.

This "selling of America" wasn't popular, and led to a backlash against foreign firms. When a subsidiary of Toshiba evaded export controls and sent some high technology to the Soviet Union in 1987, big-muscled congressmen smashed some of the firms' products on the Capitol steps. "Getting tough" with Japan became a national pastime. Yet the scale of such foreign investment in the U.S. is still quite small. The proportion of the workforce employed by foreign firms rose from less than 2 percent in the 1970s to just 5 percent in the early 1990s. (In manufacturing, where foreign investment has been concentrated, the figures are somewhat higher; employment in foreign manufacturing affiliates has risen from about 3.5 percent in the 1970s to a little more than 11 percent in the 1990s.) Though Japanese firms once owned much prestigious property, foreign holdings of American real estate are still tiny; perhaps only 1 percent by value of total ownership of land.

By comparison with the Golden Age, this rash of importing, exporting, and foreign investment was aberrant—that was not how the American economy was supposed to be. But in international terms, America has become normal. In the Golden Age, only American multinationals had the size, technology, and managerial skills to expand wherever they wished. Since the 1970s, other countries have caught up. Still, in the early 1990s, American investment abroad dwarfed foreign investment in the U.S. The share of American manufacturing workers employed by foreign companies is still only about half the figure in Germany and Britain, and a third of the figure in France. It is only by comparison with the Golden Age that the level of foreign investment looks odd. It isn't odd when contrasted with that of other countries. And it isn't odd when compared with that of other eras in American history. Whether it was on the railroads or the ranches, the sinews and muscles of pre-1914 American capitalism were nourished by foreign capital. And so they are again. In this respect, as in many others, we have returned to the past.

Just as trade and investment brought the world to America, so did tourism. The number of tourists arriving from outside North America more than doubled beween 1984 and 1995. Germans and Britons bought condos in Orlando, where they could tan themselves lobster-red and drink cheap beer to their heart's content; well-mannered Japanese couples walked hand in hand round Honolulu and Las Vegas; the daughters of South America's oligarchs, dreaming of underwired bras and an apartment in South Beach, headed for Miami.

In the same vein, American tourists traveled more themselves. Yet most Americans are still not real international animals. In any one year, only about one in forty Americans travels outside North America, a level of contentment with home unique in the world. It is quite common to meet Americans without a passport; anywhere else in the developed world, that is rare. In lots of ways, great and small, the U.S. remains insular. A foreigner proffering traveler's checks denominated in anything but dollars is greeted at American banks as if he were nuts. Policy-makers in Washington are ignorant of other countries' approach to issues. Washingtonians can talk for weeks without ever admitting that America can learn anything from the French on crime control, the Dutch on drugs, or the Germans on education and training. And sometimes the indifference to other countries and cultures takes a nasty turn. In the parking lot of the UAW union hall at Willow Run is a sign warning that foreign cars will be towed. Don't ask if they mean it; they do. During Japan's boom years from 1986 to 1991, hostility to all things Japanese was easy to find, whether in Michael Crichton's bestselling book *Rising Sun* or Chrysler chairman Lee Iacocca's doom-laden complaints about Japanese car companies.

True to form, in 1990, a poll for the Chicago Council of Foreign Relations found a substantial majority of Americans who thought that the main threat to America came from Japan. Yet such hostility is far from uniform—mainly because the internationalization of the economy impacts on different Americans in very different ways. In this respect, the new foreign policy really has driven Americans further apart from each other. It has exacerbated social and economic differences which had other roots.

Economists argue until they are blue in the face that there's nothing praiseworthy about encouraging exports or restricting imports. Report after tedious report says that, in the long run, protecting uncompetitive industries benefits nobody. But to lesser mortals the chronic trade deficits signal that the country has "failed." For working-class Americans, the claim that free trade is good for America's tomorrow gets lost in the pain they have to suffer today. And sometimes that pain is real: try as hard as you can, you will not make a cheaper soft toy in Pekin, Illinois, than in Beijing, China.

Some parts of the country have had a "global" economy for years, and the "threat" of foreign competition doesn't bother them. Others have had little contact with the outside world.

About 23 percent of Washington State's manufacturing employment is involved in the export trade, and about 16 percent of Oregon's. Exports of merchandise account for about 20 percent of Washington's gross state product (the statistical definition of merchandise excludes Microsoft's software— which, if included, would boost the figure much higher); and about 11 percent of Oregon's. Contrast that with two southern states. Just over 9 percent of manufacturing employment in Georgia and Mississippi is export-related, while exports account for less than 4 percent of either state's gross state product.

This suggests that the Pacific Northwest is more cosmopolitan than the South, but the true picture is a bit more complicated. Foreign investment is much more important to Georgia than to Washington or Oregon. When the wave of foreign investment crested in the 1990s, it was southern governors, not western ones, who were scared, because foreign investment has played such a crucial part in modernizing the South's economy. In fact, there are sharply different attitudes to the global economy within any given state or region. Take Hawaii. Just behind Waikiki Beach are stores owned by the great Japanese retailers; any serious American shop has assistants who can speak Japanese; any serious golf course is marketed in Japan. In some of the best hotels in Honolulu you can think that the trade is dominated by lovesick Japanese couples. The Hawaiian tourist industry thrives on all this. But when a Japanese billionaire bought seventy-five homes in Oahu in 1987 and the price of property went through the roof, locals went mad. The mayor of Honolulu sent a blunt message to Japan: "Enough. We don't want you and we don't need you." The same diversity of view holds good in the South. In the bars of small mountain towns, where the men sport ponytails and the women tattoos, it would not be wise to suggest that foreign trade and investment are good for American jobs. But in Greenville, South Carolina, German investors have been a happy part of the local community for more than forty years. In Atlanta every businessman able to hold a mobile telephone brags that the award of the 1996 Olympic Games made the city "world-class."

To capture the many aspects of the "globalization" of the economy, take a closer look at Seattle. The city has always had an international aspect. Before 1900, Japanese immigrants farmed fruit and vegetables in Seattle's hinterland; by 1940, the great Japanese trading houses had offices in the city. After 1945, Seattle became an industrial center on the back of a single company, Boeing, one of the greatest exporters in the world. As Boeing grew, so the Puget Sound region developed a network of subcontractors making everything from airliner seats to avionics, and, through Boeing, became exporters themselves. In the 1980s, Microsoft, a second international giant, settled in Seattle. Just like Boeing, Microsoft depends on international markets for much of its growth; and just like Boeing, it has spawned subcontractors who are similarly "global" in their ambitions. Together, Boeing and Microsoft imbue the corporate culture of the region with a commitment to free trade. When the heads of government from the Pacific Rim countries met for a summit in Seattle in 1993, it was sometimes difficult to tell if Bill Clinton was the host, or Boeing. (The Chinese delegation had little doubt—they were there to talk planes, not politics.) The Washington Council on International Trade, a group of local businesses, likes to use a simple phrase: "Washington is not Michigan."

Yet even in Washington State, whose corporate elite is not

scared of anyone, the limits to internationalization are striking. There are few foreign-owned firms in Seattle, and few foreign banks. Seattle may be equidistant from Japan and Europe by air; but it has few international flights. Those who live in the city didn't mind if a Japanese partnership bought the baseball Mariners (so long as Ken Griffey, Jr., stayed), but rural Washingtonians hated the deal. Washington State may live and die by international trade, but only 40 percent of high school students study a foreign language, and most of them for just two years or less. True, in 1992 Washingtonians favored free trade with Canada and Mexico by a two-to-one margin, but a majority also thought that foreign investment in real estate and manufacturing did more harm than good. Those two great oceans still work their magic; the U.S. still dislikes thinking of itself as but a cog, however big, in an international machine. Even in Seattle, many Americans still like to think they stand alone.

In short, the internationalization of the economy has been "welcomed" in very different ways in different regions and among different social classes. For elite Americans— who learn French, vacation in Italy, talk on the phone at work to colleagues in London and Tokyo—the international economy holds no terrors. On the contrary, it has visibly improved their standard of living; the world of "plenty," confined in the Golden Age to things American, is now a truly global one. Strawberries from New Zealand! Vacation cottages in the Cotswolds! ("No further than California, you know.") But for working-class Americans, the global economy is a threat. It means not only that they have to compete, as they think, with workers earning a fraction of their pay. It means that their plant may not be owned by the local family which first built it, but by a German multinational firm which, they suspect, would close it down in a trice if it could find a cheaper source of labor in Mexico.

Mexico—now there's a symbol of the new America. A great wave of immigration, much of it from south of the border, has transformed the way the country looks, sounds, and smells. After the mid-1960s, the closed borders of the Golden Age were thrown wide open. In fact, the borders all but disappeared. In the late 1980s, you could drive east from downtown Tijuana, across the dry gullies where the Japanese and Koreans had built their electronics plants, to the famous "football field" in Zapata Canyon. On any evening, on the far side of a sagging single-strand rope wire—the border—you would see hundreds of Mexicans hawking tacos and T-shirts, playing soccer, laughingly watching the headlights on the cars of the American immigration service a mile away. As night fell, the Mexicans would fan out into the gullies, and by daylight most would be safely in Los Angeles.

The old, homogeneous, single-language America—the America of the Golden Age—has gone, and it went very quickly. In 1952, there was a slight relaxation of the almost total ban on immigration from Asia, but as late as the early 1960s few immigrants were admitted, and most of them were from Europe. The turning point was the Immigration Act of 1965. The act ended the system of national origin quotas which had governed immigration since the 1920s, and had two consequences. First, it opened a spigot. In 1970 about 9.6 million of those living in America were foreign-born, or 4.7 percent of the total population, the lowest proportion recorded at any decennial census. In the next decade 4.5 million legal immigrants were admitted, and by 1980 the number of foreign-born had risen to a little over 14 million, or 6.2

percent of the total. In 1990 that population had grown to nearly 20 million, or 7.9 percent of the total. Second, the act changed the places from which immigrants came. In the period from 1940 to 1960 more than half of all immigrants had been Europeans. In the 1970s only 17 percent of immigrants were European, while 35 percent came from Asia, and 44 percent from the Americas. In the 1980s about 7.3 million legal immigrants were admitted or, having once been illegal, attained immigrant status. Of this total, only 10 percent were European. Mexico alone provided 1.7 million legal immigrants in the 1980s, a scale of immigration from one country not seen since Italians and Russians streamed through Ellis Island nearly a century before.

By the mid-1990s, foreign accents were everywhere. The busboys, the cleaners, the taxi drivers, the witnesses at the O. J. Simpson trial, they all spoke accented English. In southern Florida, southern California, and along the Rio Grande Valley, a bilingual society was developing. Arrive at Miami airport and you would think the native language was Spanish; cruise a shopping mall in Orange County, California, and you could absorb the luscious aromas of Indochina.

The new immigration has changed some parts of America more than others. In 1960, five of the six states with the highest proportion of foreign-born residents were on the East Coast (the sixth was Hawaii). New York, with 13.6 percent of its population foreign-born, was the most "cosmopolitan" state. As late as 1970, more foreign immigrants settled in the Northeast than anywhere else, heading, like their forefathers, for the fruit stalls and bars of Boston and New York. But between 1985 to 1990 the South received more foreign immigrants than the Northeast, and the West more than twice as many. Though the total population of foreign-born Americans nearly doubled between 1960 and 1990, from nearly 10 million to nearly 20 million, in fourteen states the foreign-born population actually fell. If birth abroad is a decent test of cosmopolitan attitudes, then some states in New England and the Midwest were more "nativist" in 1990 than they had been in 1950 (though not New York, which remains as attractive to immigrants as it has ever been—in 1990 nearly 16 percent of the state's population was foreign-born).

Immigration has altered the Sunbelt beyond recognition. Texas saw its proportion of foreign-born double between 1960 and 1990, while southern California was remade. In 1960 just 8.5 percent of Californians were foreign-born; in 1990 nearly 22 percent. A run-down neighborhood in central Los Angeles had become "Little Korea," while a great swath beyond the old mission church in Olvera Street had become Mexican—just like it used to be 150 years before. Thousands of Central Americans, dispossessed by the wars of the 1980s, had settled in the city, while to the east of downtown, Monterey Park had an Asian majority. In 1990, one in five of all new immigrants to the country intended to settle in just four districts of southern California: Los Angeles–Long Beach, Anaheim–Santa Ana, San Diego, and Riverside–San Bernardino.

Southern California may be immigrant-central, but the new accents, tastes, and smells are everywhere. In Washington and Chicago as much as in Los Angeles, shops in poor neighborhoods are owned by Koreans. In Detroit as much as New York, convenience stores are owned by Arabs or Punjabis. From Minnesota to northern Virginia, Asian immigrants are running for election to school boards. Within the group of those who speak just one language—Spanish—the new immigrants show a great diversity. It is a long way, in more than miles, from Washington Heights at the tip of Manhattan, where Dominican street hawkers sell slices of oranges and merengue blares out from ghetto blasters, to Miami's Calle Ocho, where Cuban exiles eat chicken and rice and deify Ronald Reagan.

For those who doubt that America has changed since the 1970s, the best recent proof, perhaps, came during the 1994 soccer World Cup. From Los Angeles to Dallas, from Washington to New York, throngs of newly arrived Koreans, Mexicans, Irish, Bolivians, Nigerians, and many others packed the stadiums in a month-long multicultural, multiethnic festival of the world's most popular sport. In the America of the Golden Age, soccer had been a mere curiosity, the redoubt of a few old Hungarian refugees tapping a ball to each other in New York's Central Park. By 1994, it had become the game of the new America.

That new America of the World Cup is with us for as far as the eye can see. The familiar, stable ethnic shape of America during the Golden Age has gone, and isn't coming back. In the next century, America will have a face with far more Latino and Asian features than now. In 1996 the Census Bureau projected population to the year 2050 based on the levels of fertility, mortality, and immigration in the early 1990s. In the bureau's "middle" projection, total population rises by 50 percent in sixty years, to reach about 394 million in 2050. Of this total, the non-Hispanic white population is expected to decline from 74 percent of the total in 1995 to 53 percent in 2050. The black population will grow from 32 million to 61 million; or from 12 percent of the total to 16 percent. But the Asian population—a fast-growing ethnic group—will likely grow from 9 million in 1995 to 34 million in 2050; or

from 3 percent of the total to 9 percent. And in the same period, the Latino population will grow from 27 million (10
percent of the total) to 96 million (24 percent). Even if
draconian limits were to be placed on new immigration, this
pattern will not change much. In 1988, the fertility rate of
the foreign-born—the number of children they could be expected to have in their lifetime—was 40 percent higher than
the rate for American-born women. In 2010, the Census Bureau predicts that Asian-Americans will have fertility rates
about the same as white Americans, but 20 percent lower
than that of blacks. Latino Americans will have rates about
12 percent higher than that of black Americans, and nearly
40 percent higher than that of whites.

Inevitably, the scale of immigration in the last twenty
years has brought a backlash. In the mid-1990s, it is common
to read that today's immigrants (and tomorrow's likely immigrants) are somehow "different" from those who had come to
America's shores before. They are, supposedly, poorer, less
skilled, more likely to be a drag on the public purse. They
had arrived in a country in which the institutions of cohesion
and assimiliation had been allowed to atrophy. So they
would beggar the public revenue, drag down the level of
skills, and stay within their own racial and ethnic enclaves. In
short, they would contribute to a progressive and debilitat-
ing fragmentation of the society. By 1993 opinion polls
found more Americans willing to restrict immigration than at
any time since 1945. The next year, voters in the state of California were asked to support Proposition 187, which would
have removed all state benefits—health, welfare, and education—from illegal immigrants and their families. The proposition was endorsed with 60 percent of the vote.

Though the vote on Proposition 187 was decisive, real

debate on the new face of America had been joined a year earlier, during discussion of the North American Free Trade Agreement. NAFTA was a godsend to academics; it encapsulated most of the concerns about the new internationalization of America.

In 1985, Mexico's government had started an economic reform program which opened the country to foreign trade and reduced the size of the public sector. In the summer of 1990, Carlos Salinas de Gortari, then the president of Mexico, announced that he was interested in free trade with the United States. In the spring of 1991 Congress gave Bush's administration negotiating authority, and by the time of the election of 1992 ministers from Canada, the United States, and Mexico had initialed a North American Free Trade Agreement.

But in the two years between the visit of Salinas to Washington and the signing of NAFTA, the political climate had changed beyond measure. There had been a recession—not a particularly deep one, but one which seemed to hurt the middle class hard. Recovery from the recession brought little new job creation. Ross Perot, a Texas billionaire, had campaigned for the presidency in 1992 on the message that the economy had gone to hell, and that America was being ripped off by its trading partners. After the election, he made opposition to NAFTA the centerpiece of his populist appeal; and was joined, to the surprise of no student of the post–Cold War world, by Pat Buchanan.

In 1993, on talk show heaped on town meeting, fear welled up and crystallized into opposition to NAFTA. The fear touched all the changes to the economy since the end of the Golden Age. It was a fear of those whose high-wage, low-skilled jobs seemed threatened by competition from abroad;

a fear that immigration was changing the familiar face of America. At times, it mattered not that almost all worthwhile economists claimed that NAFTA would create more jobs than it would cost; or that there was something odd about America being frightened of an economy a twentieth its size. All that mattered was fear.

It is instructive to think how NAFTA would have been received had it been suggested at the start of the Golden Age. In 1943 Wendell Willkie had argued, "Our present standard of living in America cannot be maintained unless the exchange of goods flows more freely over the whole world. It is inescapably true that to raise the standard of living of any man anywhere in the world is to raise the standard of living by some slight degree of every man everywhere in the world." In the 1950s, NAFTA would have been tacked onto the Cold War, explained as a way to spread prosperity to Latin America and blunt the appeal of socialism. Indeed, John Kennedy's own Latin American program, the Alliance for Progress, had just such coloring. But by the time the real NAFTA debate was joined in 1993, there were no Willkies, with a generosity bred of self-confidence; there was no Kennedy to summon up the specter of communism.

In the worried America of the 1990s, NAFTA took on the form of dramatic ogre. It was debated solely as if it were a matter of domestic policy—it would save or lose so many jobs, it would have such and such an effect on wages. All that mattered was the new fear; the fear of trade, the fear of immigration, the strangeness of a world which was no longer divided into spheres of good and evil. Granted, in November 1993 NAFTA was ratified by Congress—but then came Proposition 187, the fear returned, and in the mind of America Tijuana continued its unlikely transformation from a joke to a threat. Sensible people asked if we could not get over such ugly simplicities. To which, though none dared say so, there was an easy answer: we could, because we had done so before. The new internationalization of America was not new at all. It was a return to the patterns of an older country, a country quite unlike that of the Golden Age, a country when the voice of America was not just English, its habits not yet apple pie and TV. We can't understand today's America unless we remember the totality of the American experience: not just the strange years after 1945.

CHAPTER NINE

The New Country

After the Golden Age each of the factors which made America following 1945 such a strong, self-confident, and unified society atrophied and died. We can regret this, and indeed, it's natural that we should. But at the same time we need to remember that the cultural, economic, and social conditions of America in the Golden Age were unprecedented; if we take those years as a mirror in which to see ourselves we will find our likeness distorted. Yes, America has problems, and it is trite to say so. But these are *problems*, things that can be solved. They are not the end of the world. Americans shouldn't overexaggerate their present discontents, but will always do so if they think that the Golden Age was normal and the years that followed an aberration. Precisely the opposite is the case. The messy, fragmented babel of a place that America is today is what America has usually been. Americans need to get over their sense of loss for a more orderly place, and move forward. There's no point in reliving just one part of the past; as it approaches the next century, the nation needs to do something at which Americans are very bad: remember and learn from the whole of their historical experience, not just a few odd years of it.

The turmoil of the years since the end of the Golden Age has battered Americans' self-confidence, and made them see reality in a worse light than they need to. They worry, for example, that they have lost their ability to develop the community spirit that has got them over crises and disappointments in the past. From the earliest days of the republic, and probably before, a sense of "community" has seemed to be part of the natural endowment. Of all the insights of Tocqueville, none was more genuinely radical than the importance he ascribed to voluntary organizations. "Americans of all ages, all conditions and all dispositions," he wrote, "constantly form associations. They have not only commercial and manufacturing companies, in which all take part, but associations of a thousand other kinds—religious, moral, serious, futile, general or restricted, enormous or diminutive. . . . Wherever, at the head of some new undertaking, you see the government in France, or a man of rank in England, in the United States you will be sure to find an association."

Yet by the 1990s it was common to read that such public-spiritedness was on the wane. Americans, it was thought, had become atomized, less willing to share the burden of community activity. Michel Crozier, an affectionate French critic of America, wrote, "The United States today is no longer the America Tocqueville described. Its voluntary associations have ceased to be the mainstay of a democracy constantly on the move but are now simply a means of self-defense for various interests." The very word "community" had become loaded and unhappy. Often it was used simply to dignify a pressure group engaged in a bit of special pleading ("the arts community" wants this, "the AIDS community" demands that). Even more offensively, the idea of "community" could be used by self-appointed spokesmen to endorse certain forms of behavior: so if you were a member of the "gay community," for example, you had to like the Pet Shop Boys rather than Mozart.

For some, like the academic Robert Bellah and his associates, authors of two influential books whose titles (*Habits of the Heart* and *The Good Society*) neatly encapsulated their concerns, the principal culprit for the decline in community spirit seemed to be the market. "Americans," they wrote, "find themselves under the pressure of market forces to which the only response seems submission. . . . Economic ideology that turns human beings into relentless market maximizers undermines commitment to family, to church, to neighborhood, to school, and to the larger national and global societies." For others, like the Republicans who in 1995 threatened to overturn President Clinton's national service legislation, the source of the problem was precisely the opposite. It was the growth of government—not the market—which had diminished the sense of community, by appropriating the activities which self-governing groups of citizens would once have done for themselves or others less fortunate. Crozier, for his part, thought that modern America had pressed a "passion for law to the edge of madness" and complained that legalism has contributed to "This breakdown of community structures [which] has made America a country full of anxiety." (Anyone who has ever been to a PTA meeting where someone volunteers to paint the school windows knows what he meant—within minutes lawyers will have warned about the dangers of liability.)

In a 1995 essay called "Bowling Alone," Robert Putnam of Harvard University made perhaps the most subtle modern analysis of community and its discontents. Putnam identified the rise in women's employment, the collapse of the nuclear family, and "the technological transformation of leisure"— VCRs and other forms of "home entertainment"—as sources of a decline in what he called "social capital." Americans (and especially American women), in this view, no longer have the time or energy to devote to community-building, while technology has brought entertainment out of the Main Street and into "the family room."

All this makes life sound grim, but it's wrong; or at least, it isn't clearly right. For all the books written on the subject, we cannot really know whether a spirit of community has declined or not, because there is no adequate way of measuring it. Certainly, membership of PTAs declined between the 1950s and 1980s, but so did the number of schoolchildren. The uptick of school enrollments in the 1980s was accompanied—*mirabile dictu*—by a concomitant rise in the membership of PTAs. Women may no longer have as much time to devote to community affairs, but the evidence of Big Brother programs, mentoring, and, not least, fathers' involvement in schools, suggests that men are at least partially filling the gap. Elsewhere, we may simply be counting the wrong things. It's true that older American voluntary groups like the Elks and the Lions are in decline; but who has yet tracked the social significance of one of the most interesting of all 1990s voluntary groups—parent-organized soccer leagues? Take a look at any suburb on any Saturday, and you'll see thousands of kids, from tots to teenagers, kicking balls around. Fifteen years ago, the leagues didn't exist.

In fact, there are reasons to think that America is entering a period when community spirit will be made fresh once more. One such reason has already been touched on: since the birthrate unexpectedly rose throughout the 1980s, the number of children entering school in the 1990s (and beyond) will be larger than most demographers had expected. And nothing so brings a community together as the state of its schools.

Many towns and cities, moreover, have spent the 1990s in a conscious effort to manage their growth. The hope is that they will keep to a size which, with luck, encourages the personal interaction which is the seedbed of community spirit. Growth management, it should be said, is sometimes done for questionable motives—the flip side of community spirit is a suspicion of outsiders. And it is never easy. The cities which have most been able to promote policies which limit urban sprawl often have characteristics which don't travel. (The best example in America of successful growth management is Portland, Oregon—a delightful city, but with geographic and social conditions replicated in not a single other place of its size.) On the other hand, the scale of suburbanization in the 1980s was so vast that developers now have oodles of undeveloped property between the outer suburban ring and city centers. This is where the next developments will be built, flecked in amongst the suburbs, linking them all together. In other words, after the dispersal of homes and employment of the 1980s, we may be about to enter a period of settlement which encourages the consolidation of the American population, and with it, a new sense of community.

In economic life, too, there are signs that a time of turmoil is behind us. The number of Americans employed in manufacturing has now been stable at about 20 million for nearly two decades. The American economy is never again going to be the self-contained monster which it was after 1945. "Decline," though the word is not really an accurate description of the process, was inevitable. The economic hegemony that America had in the Golden Age has gone, and will not come back; America's share of world output is now just about where it was in 1914. The world has shrunk, barriers to trade have been lowered, new technologies have made it easier to transport products across vast distances. Countries which were once wrecks have been transformed into the power-houses they always should have been. With the collapse of communism, the world is starting to rediscover what it was meant to be before Gavrilo Princip started the long night-mare in the summer of 1914 on a street in Sarajevo. For eighty years, the world has been knocked out of its preor-dained course, as Japan and the European countries lacerated themselves in two world wars and two hateful ideologies. Prague was not meant to be half as poor as Vienna, though for fifty years, it was. Had it not been for communism, Russia might have had a modern economy in the 1920s, and been able to challenge Britain and Germany; now it will have one a century later. Japan, had it not been seduced by war, would have been an economic giant in the 1940s, not the 1980s. Had it not been for communism, China's enormous eco-nomic potential would have been a staple of newspapers long before the 1990s.

Many people are frightened about the new economic or-der. They are obsessed with America's declining "competi-tiveness," whatever that is, and worry that the future will somehow belong to others. But we should remember that the global economy is not new at all—recall Keynes's descrip-tion of 1914, of a "social and economic life, the internation-alization of which was nearly complete in practice." Once that trick of memory has been made, it becomes much easier to see how America's return to conditions resembling those which obtained before World War I can be a call to new greatness.

The new world, for one thing, is not yet a single global market. It isn't half as frightening as people fear. As Paul Krugman has said, "The world is not as interdependent as you think." Particularly not if you are an American. America is not Hong Kong, a place of which it really makes sense to say "it lives or dies by trade." Hong Kong is a dot on the landmass of Asia. The United States makes up half a continent. The greater part of the American economy will always consist of Americans producing goods and services for other Americans to buy.

Once again, the great shock has already happened; the period of greatest turmoil is already over. The real change in America's foreign trade occurred between 1960 and 1980, when the value of both imports and exports (in constant prices) more than trebled. It is simply shoddy economics to assume that international trade, or competition from foreign firms, will dominate everyday life. In the future, your children are going to buy their candy at the local store, not fly to Mexico for it. You may buy French bread, but it will be baked by a local baker, not in France. The truck that delivers the bread from baker to store will fill up with gas at a local station; and so on. Of course, some of those bakers, candymakers, and gas stations will be owned by foreign corporations, though far fewer will be than in most other advanced economies. But why should that be a problem? With the exception of those few, exceptional years after 1945, foreign ownership of American assets has been an uncontroversial fact of life. It was foreign capital that, a century ago, built the railroads and broke the prairies, dug the mines and shipped the ore.

What about the working class? Well, it's quite true that many of the low-skilled, high-wage jobs on which the prosperity of America's Golden Age was founded have been lost. It is also true that some of them have been lost because of the competition from low-wage economies. But as the case of the Mon Valley shows, most of those jobs were lost because American firms increased their productivity. In any dynamic economy, some occupations will do well at some times, and some badly. The Bureau of Labor Statistics predicts, for example, that between 1990 and 2005 the number of prison guards will increase by 62 percent and the number of switchboard operators will decline by 23 percent. If that decline happens, it will not be because of foreign competition, but because of increased productivity, which in this case means telephone systems with call-forwarding, voicemail, and the rest.

What matters, as always, is productivity, and the economic growth it brings. American firms will provide their workers and consumers with a higher standard of living if they are more productive in their own country. World trade is growing fast, and "emerging markets" like India and China will soon demand goods presently made in the developed world. American firms will never have those markets to themselves, in the way that American firms could dominate Latin America after 1945, but Americans need not fear that their private companies cannot compete for business. In the 1980s and 1990s it became plain that America's companies did not bear some scar of original sin that would soon consign them to second-class status. On the contrary, in February 1994, the *New York Times* was able to argue that America was "the envy of the industrial world. . . . It is the United States, and not Japan, that is the master of the next generation of commercially important computer and communications technologies and also of leading-edge services from medicine to movie-making."

The wrenching transition of the American economy in the last thirty years came at a price, a price in upheaval, lost dreams, and dying towns, but it also brought with it great benefits. The foreign competition to which America was exposed as the world came to its shores was the best kind of stimulus for new investment and better design. In 1994 American workers had nearly four times as many computers at their disposal as Japanese workers. The messy, mixed-up kids of TV, early sex, and broken marriages turned out to have a natural talent for writing software. The universities which were supposed to be mired in nothing but abstruse debates about political correctness were actually turning out tens of thousands of scientists and technologists, a disproportionate number of them children of those same immigrants whom the nativists would have kept away from America's shores.

The entrepreneurialism—the Yankee ingenuity—which has always been a feature of America spawned new and dynamic companies. Sometimes, the victims of these interlopers were older, sclerotic household names. IBM was humbled not by the Japanese, much less by the Germans, but by younger American companies. Sears dumped its catalogue and closed scores of stores not because some French or Korean firm discovered how to retail goods better, but because a man called Sam Walton from that strange bed of dynamism in the Ozarks did. Deregulation of the telephone system may have confused consumers for a while, but it gave MCI the room to challenge AT&T, and the competition spurred both companies to heights attained by no firm outside America.

Sensible parents despaired of whoever it was who managed to push fifty TV channels (let alone 500) into their living room; but they then realized that the race to put something on all those channels had bred an entertainment industry that had come to dominate the world.

Economically, there is no reason why America should not have a future as bright as its past. The country still has a tremendous endowment of natural resources and human skills. Its economic potential is underpinned by a culture that venerates hard work and risk-taking, and a stable political system. This is a combination presently unmatched elsewhere, and it will remain unmatched for many years to come.

What of the external threat that bound America together in the Golden Age? Easy; it's gone. The Cold War was a unique event in American history. Never before did the United States have the same identifiable "enemy" for more than four decades; never before had the nation so systematically ignored George Washington's injunction against foreign entanglements; never before had another country apparently possessed the power to destroy the United States itself.

Little wonder the Cold War helped to unify America. And little wonder that whatever came after the Cold War, it could never have the same intensity of effect within the hearts of Americans. When the trade deficit ballooned in the 1980s and the Japanese bought Rockefeller Center and downtown Los Angeles, there were those who seemed to think that Japan would one day pass muster as a substitute "threat" for the Soviet Union. The comparison was ludicrous. There is a very real difference between trade wars and real wars. In one, people may temporarily lose their jobs; in the other, people permanently lose their lives. In any event, by the early 1990s the Japanese economic miracle had run out of steam; the great wave of Japanese direct investment abroad had crested. As a unifying "threat" of the kind that the Soviet Union once was, Japan just doesn't cut it.

And for the time being, nor will anywhere else. The old truths about America have reemerged. The two great oceans are still there; the two landward neighbors are still weak or friendly. Only America has the ability to project military power wheresoever it wants: only America has scores of satellites, hundreds of planes so stealthy that other nations cannot detect them, thousands of spies. Only America has a fleet of aircraft carriers able to defend its interests thousands of miles from home. Fifty years after the end of World War II, America is, in geostrategic terms, once again a very, very safe place.

Such safety does not mean that America has become isolationist, cut off by choice from the rest of the world. For other countries, America has never been so important; its unique combination of economic, political, and military power means few international problems can be solved without America's involvement. Just as it was before 1914, America is once again a country with which everyone wants to be friends.

Quite apart from diplomacy, America is more engaged in the world than it has been for many years. The nature of that engagement is economic, cultural, and personal, just as it was before 1914. It no longer depends on the gunboats-and-striped-pants crowd who dominated America's foreign relations after 1945. The global spread of American business, and the presence of foreign competitors in American markets, has made what was once distant seem familiar. In the fall of 1993, the secretary of state found himself discussing the prospects of American oil companies in Kazakhstan, a central Asian country which but two years before had not even existed. The integration of the three North American economies has brought foreign policy home; Mexicans complain about America's brutal taste for capital punishment, while Canadians protest America's culturally ruinous export of country music. Film director Quentin Tarantino, discovered in a video store in Manhattan Beach, California, becomes a cult hero in Europe, while godly young Mormons and Seventh-Day Adventists convert thousands in the barrios of Latin America. And then there is immigration, that huge, transformative aspect of modern America. All of this conspires to bring the world close to home, just as it did before World War I. All this makes America a more "international" place than it has ever been before. It is not an "internationalism" based on the threat and fear of another nation of the kind that once bound America together, which is good; that old internationalism damn near incinerated us all.

For some Americans, the new relationship with the rest of the world runs the risk of fragmentation within America's shores. That fear turns on just one factor: the degree to which the new immigrants come to feel themselves American. Assimilation has never been easy. In 1910, it was no easier for a Polish worker in Pittsburgh to learn English than it is for a Cambodian in Los Angeles today. Nor did assimilation mean that immigrants gave up their own customs and identities; rather, those experiences transformed America. If they hadn't done so, Anglo-Saxon Americans wouldn't eat bagels, and city halls wouldn't be patronage machines.

All the same, assimilation was not a myth. Earlier immigrants managed to take the best of America while retaining a loyalty to their roots. A five-minute walk around Chicago's northwest side, through the Polish neighborhoods, past the Ukrainian churches, shows a mixture of ethnic pride and harmony which is far more rare, worldwide, than Americans realize. There's plenty of evidence that newer immigrants want to pull off the same trick. In Santa Ana, California, a few minutes away from the muscular Protestantism of the Crystal Cathedral ("Tough times never last, tough people do!") stands a typical suburban shopping mall—except that it is called El Toro Bravo, stocks the goods you would expect to find in a small Mexican town, and has a dentist on the premises called Chung Kim. Half a block away is the Orange County Vietnamese Acculturation Center; nearby, a Mexican church and a Korean church share the same building. Messy? Sure: but something of which America can be proud.

So it can of what is happening on a great university campus like Berkeley or an exclusive private high school like Phillips Exeter in New Hampshire. Wander around such places and you will stand amazed at the number of Asian students. Between 1976 and 1990, the number of Asian-Americans enrolled in undergraduate courses increased threefold; for graduate degrees it doubled; and for professional degrees, like law and medicine, it increased more than four times. By 1990, more than half of Asian-American doctorates were in computing, math, and sciences. If you want an indicator of how the America in the next century will be different from that of today, those figures will do.

There are, doubtless, a few communities of recent immigrants from Southeast Asia who marry only each other, who live in poverty, and whose children may well do so, too, but the figures don't lie. Taken as a whole, Asian-Americans are taking the same path to prosperity as Jewish immigrants did 100 years ago. They are investing in education and the sciences, and using family and kinship networks to fund new enterprises. And they are enjoying themselves. In Houston's discos you can see Vietnamese-American kids wearing alligator boots and bolo ties dance to rap music, which is as good an example of the melting pot as any.

Still, that pot needs to be kept warm. Ben Wattenberg of the American Enterprise Institute keeps a close eye on the rate of intermarriage among immigrants, the numbers who marry outside their ethnic groups. It takes time for intermarriage to become common. Among Italian-Americans born before 1920, for example, almost two-thirds married other Italian-Americans; of those born after 1950 only about a fifth did. By the 1980s, about one in three Latinos and Asian-Americans married outside their ethnic groups, which puts them about where Italians were in 1945. The new immigrants could go either way; the crude total of marriages between Latinos and others continues to rise sharply, but the proportion of Latinos marrying outside their ethnic group has actually decreased since the 1980s.

To some, that is a warning sign, confirmation that today's immigrants are "different." But today's immigrants and today's social conditions are not so dissimilar from those of a century ago that the old processes of assimilation can no longer work their magic. To an extent which few appreciate, everything depends on just one group: Mexican-Americans. Immigration from Mexico is unlike that from elsewhere. It is more heavily freighted with a troubled history. "Immigrants" are settling in a territory which Mexico once owned. It is uniquely easy for Mexicans to maintain ties of family and politics with their country of origin, and hence easy to resist the siren calls of American institutions. Mexican-American children can, and do, visit their relatives in Mexico each summer, while Mexican politicians from Baja California raise money in Orange County, California. Mexicans probably have the lowest skills of all the large immigrant groups, and arrive in America poorer than almost any others. In 1993, only 4 percent of Mexican immigrants held bachelor's degrees, compared with 65 percent among immigrants from India. Above all else, the scale of modern immigration from Mexico dwarfs that from anywhere else. Between 1980 and 1993 the number of Mexican-born residents of the U.S. rose from 2.2 million to 4.3 million—from 15.6 percent of the total foreign-born population to 23 percent. In the short term, the North American Free Trade Agreement will almost certainly increase Mexican emigration, since it will lead to unemployment among Mexican farmworkers.

For all these reasons, Mexican-Americans provide the toughest test for the virtues of immigration. If Mexican-Americans behave in the way that other ethnic groups did before them, then most worries about the effect of immigration on America's future can be laid to rest. If, by contrast, Mexican-Americans see themselves as set apart from the American mainstream, then the Balkanization of America becomes a genuine concern.

If one image helped secure the passage of Proposition 187, it was the sight, at a rally the weekend before the vote, of opponents flying Mexican flags. No matter that this was just teenage exuberance; no matter that the flags had probably been left over from the World Cup. For those predisposed to think so, the flags were a symbol that Mexican-Americans had, at best, a dual loyalty.

If so, it's America's own laws that have let them think they can have one. After the "rights-based" politics of the 1960s, immigrants probably do feel less formal pressure to assimilate

261

into mainstream culture. They can demand bilingual education; they can ask for special treatment for cultures and customs. "Contemporary immigrants," writes Peter Skerry of UCLA, in *Mexican Americans: The Ambivalent Minority*, "bring with them more than the bundle of clothes that earlier immigrants brought." They also bring "bundles of rights and entitlements, which may not get exercised by them directly, but which will most certainly get exercised on their behalf by vicarious representatives."

Skerry has shown that Mexican-Americans have developed different institutions in the Rio Grande Valley and in Los Angeles. In Texas, Mexican-Americans have used the traditional, albeit slow, methods of political and social assimilation. Slow—but not unsuccessful. In 1992, Henry Cisneros, one of the Valley's favorite sons (and who had already been mayor of San Antonio), became the secretary of housing and urban development in Washington. In Los Angeles, by contrast, Mexican pressure groups have claimed the appurtenances of an oppressed minority. They have turned not to political parties and the ballot box to advance their claims, but to lawyers and courtrooms. They have used the Voting Rights Act, originally designed to help blacks, to carve out protected territories for their professional politicians.

On its face, this is worrying. However much Mexican-Americans may have suffered at the hands of "Anglo" America, they have not borne anything like the historical injustice visited on blacks. For most of their time in the U.S., most Latinos have thought of themselves as an ethnic immigrant group like any other—attached to their own culture, but keen to share in the common dreams of America. If Latino leaders now claim that they deserve special treatment as a group, two consequences will follow. In fact, one already has.

From Los Angeles to Chicago to New York, Latino use of the Voting Rights Act has led to bitter disputes with blacks. After the Los Angeles riots in 1992, black and Latino groups engaged in battles on construction sites, searching for the "correct" share of work rebuilding the city that each should have. Second, as Proposition 187 made abundantly clear, such a strategy simply alienates "Anglo" society. It pitches ethnic groups against each other in a battle which none can win, but in which America's commitment to a society with shared values is a certain loser.

There's enough here to be convinced that assimilation of Mexican-Americans is a pipe dream. Now look at the other side of the ledger. Whatever the political strategies of their leaders, much anecdotal evidence suggests that Mexican-Americans are, in fact, just like any other group of hyphenated Americans. Some of them eat *mole* sauce every day, some only on holidays; some of them stay close to the church, some drift away; some vote Democrat, some Republican. But there is no need to rely on anecdote. The landmark Latino National Political Survey, released in 1992, provides hard evidence of assimilation. Nearly 80 percent of Mexican-Americans born in Mexico speak more Spanish than English at home, but fewer than 12 percent of those born in the United States do so. More than 90 percent of "Anglo" respondents to the survey expressed a strong "love" for the United States; but so did 84 percent of Mexican-Americans. No fewer than 91 percent of Mexican-Americans thought that citizens and residents of the United States should learn English; 62 percent of them disagreed with the proposition that Latin Americans should be favored by the immigration laws. Naturally, there were differences between Mexican-American attitudes and Anglo ones; on balance, Mexican-

Americans (like most Latinos) take a more positive view of the role of government. But taken as a whole, there is a weight of evidence that this crucial ethnic group sees itself as just one more part of the American mosaic. That is the best possible sign that the future of America can be just as bright as its past.

Immigration does remain a source of concern, but for a distinctive reason: it can be thought threatening by many black Americans. That shades into a bigger issue: in the new America, what are the prospects for the only group of Americans whose ancestors did not come here of their own free will?

The extent to which black Americans are going to share in a common culture with all Americans remains uncertain. Any assessment of the level to which black and nonblack Americans inhabit the same cultural and economic "space" is bound to start with the claim, a correct one, that America has come a long way. Common sense tells us that there is a huge difference between a society which legally protects racial discrimination and one that outlaws it. Three decades of laws mandating equal opportunity in employment, and three decades of slow but steady changes in corporate practice, have made the American workplace more racially integrated than any other on earth. It is inconceivable that a modern American company which craved the respect of its peers would not have, and implement, an equal opportunity policy: this claim could not be made for the generality of Japanese or European companies. Blacks have been elected as governors and senators of states with large white majorities, and served as mayors of cities that are majority white. They have commanded the armed forces and held high cabinet positions. In the 1950s, for any given level of education, black earnings were between 60 percent to 70 percent of white earnings. By the 1990s, to simplify a tale with many unexpected twists and turns, the gap had been significantly reduced, so that on average blacks with the same level of education as whites might expect to earn around 80 percent to 85 percent of white earnings. "Despite America's residual racism," writes the author Shelby Steele, "there is an enormous range of opportunities open to blacks in this society."

Why is that achievement not celebrated more often? Partly because Americans set themselves high standards. "Compared with Europe," writes Andrew Hacker in *Two Nations: Black and White, Separate, Hostile, Unequal,* "the United States has always prided itself on emphasizing equal treatment and social mobility. Given these aims and ideals, the United States carries a greater obligation to achieve amity and equity in relations between the races." Measured against such a standard, it is easy to think that not much has changed. Blacks are still more likely to be poor than whites, suffer worse health, are more likely to be the victims of crime, and generally have life chances significantly less well endowed than those of any other racial group. Racism has not yet been eradicated from the nation. True, black high school graduation rates are now quite close to white ones. True again, the 1980s saw a continuation of the steady growth of the black middle class. In just one decade the proportion of black families whose annual income, in 1991 dollars, was more than $50,000 rose from 21 percent to 32 percent. But the continued explosion of black families headed by a single parent meant that, in the same decade, average black family incomes expressed as a proportion of the national average actually fell.

Moreover, the 1980s and 1990s saw a rebirth of black separatism. From black-only dorms in universities to the growth of black-only suburbs, the message of the recent past appears to be that integration is a chimera, and that a new retreat into racial redoubts will mark the next few decades. Separatism, argues the new conventional wisdom, may be beneficial for blacks. Historically black colleges enroll only about a fifth of all black students but award about a third of all bachelor's degrees granted to blacks. It follows that the dropout rate for black students at such colleges must be very much lower than that seen elsewhere.

But one interesting change has been almost lost in the welter of statistics. Between 1970 and 1990, the number of marriages between blacks and whites roughly quadrupled, increasing from about 2 percent of all marriages where at least one partner was black to about 6.5 percent. This flies in the face of those who can see only a rebirth of separatism. And even if separatism in education and housing did appeal to blacks in the next century, how much damage would this do to America's innate sense of unity? For those who dreamed in the 1960s of a genuinely integrated America, of course, the development of black suburbs and a voluntary resegregation of schools may be sad and disappointing. But the lifestyles and habits of those who live in such suburbs are, in all the ways that count—the way we treat our neighbors, how we worship, the things we buy—essentially indistinguishable from those of their white neighbors. Black Americans, in many ways, are the most "American" of all Americans. By comparison with the rest of the population, they are intensely patriotic, Godfearing, more likely to use the armed forces as a ladder to professional advancement, more skeptical of foreign aid, less likely to travel abroad, less likely to embrace the latest food fad from overseas, and more likely to stick with a native sport like basketball than to form soccer leagues. If the rest of America loved its country as much as black Americans, the nation wouldn't have half the problems it now faces.

This does not mean that there is no threat to American cohesion bound up with the fate of black America. There is; but it has nothing to do with voluntary separatism in education and housing. Majority-black Prince Georges County, Maryland, looks more like neighboring majority-white Montgomery County than Anacostia, the poorest part of Washington, D.C. It is Anacostia that we should worry about, not Prince Georges County. In the 1980s, the sociologist William Julius Wilson calculated that in the poorest neighborhoods of America—those where 40 percent of the population is below the poverty line—65 percent of the population is black. Wilson found that while only 2 percent of poor whites lived in neighborhoods where poverty is tightly concentrated, 21 percent of blacks did.

It is the underclass, mainly black and concentrated in a handful of cities in the Northeast and Midwest, that should concern America. By international standards the United States has achieved a level of racial equality of opportunity, and an integrated workforce, beyond those seen anywhere else. But no other country in the developed world (yet) has anything like the American underclass, with the most tenuous connection to the labor market, with endemic drug-taking and illegitimacy, with frighteningly high crime rates. London, Amsterdam, and Paris have their rough spots, but they do not have anything like the horrors of Detroit, and those Americans who think that they do are living a dangerous self-deception.

Precisely because the economic and legal situation of most blacks has improved so markedly in the last fifty years, it is hard to take seriously the claim that America's race relations are in a state of crisis. The deep and troubling divisions within American society are principally ones of class. It is only because so much of the underclass is black that an issue of class has become presented as one of race. "What is called the race crisis," wrote George Will in 1995, "is a class problem arising from dysfunctional families and destructive behavior."

Taken literally, Will's statement is nonsense. Members of a dysfunctional family are not, by virtue of that fact, consigned to a life of stunted chances—if they were, Ronald Reagan and Bill Clinton would not have become president. Economic opportunity and the lack of it, and an unequal share of the resources that allow individuals to respond to economic change, are the principal factors that produce an underclass. But Will has half a point. It is by now hardly disputable that family breakdown makes everyone's future life harder, especially those of the women and children involved. Richer Americans have resources of wealth and supportive networks which allow them to bear those burdens better than poor Americans. To this extent, family breakdown and the rise of single-parenthood is indeed linked to class: it can keep those already disadvantaged by economic forces stuck at the bottom of the ladder.

That is why Americans desperately need to know if family life, yet another force for cohesion in the Golden Age, can recover its strength. The prognosis is mixed. Some things seem to have changed for good. Sex before marriage is not going to be uninvented. The availability of safe and reliable contraception—ironically, one of the great technological breakthroughs of the Golden Age—has changed patterns of sexual behavior across the developed world. The stigma once assigned to giving birth out of marriage, also, looks to have shrunk to virtually nothing. The taboo against divorce long since disappeared from Americans' mental maps.

Yet in the familiar and, to many, depressing figures on the family, one striking fact has been overlooked. Just as in the economy, the big changes are over. The real shock came in the 1960s and 1970s, in a shift from one type of family formation, one model of "normal" sexual behavior to another. And this shift took place in a remarkably short period of time. But that period is now past. The divorce rate peaked in 1981, half a generation before this book was written. The shift toward smaller families, with the average date of birth of first child much later than it had been, happened nearly twenty years ago (and is, in fact, now reversing itself— women are starting to have children earlier). The great explosion in the proportion of births to unwed mothers happened not in the 1980s and 1990s but in the 1960s and 1970s. Since then, however alarming the number of births out of wedlock may seem, the rate of change has actually been quite modest.

Some of us (most of us?) may not like the new American family life, but it shows signs of finding a new level of stability and predictability. In the 1960s, parents did not know if their teenage children would be sexually active or not, and this created a quite novel cultural tension. That tension has been removed; teenagers have sex, and parents know it. We may find that a society can cope with a certain level of both divorce and illegitimacy, *so long as neither is growing fast.* Of course, we cannot know that for sure; but Americans must be allowed to hope that stability (even of a sort that many deplore) is preferable to the constant turmoil of change.

In like fashion, it is impossible to think that the number of working women with young children will continue to grow. In 1992, for the first time in thirty years, the rate of labor-force participation of such women did not increase. It may very well be that this was an aberration, a lagged consequence of the recession of 1990–91, but don't bet on it. If only because some women will always want to stay at home with young children, there has to be a limit on the number who go to work. Very likely, we have found that limit; we can say with some certainty that no more than about 60 percent of all married women with young children will work outside the home.

This, too, is a sign of a new stability (that word again). In the period immediately after the Golden Age, the economy placed unexpected demands on the family. In the 1950s, men were expected to work and married women, by and large, were not. Then came a violent period in which that assumption was stood on its head. Now most families expect to need two wage-earners. The shock of change from one family structure to another is behind us.

If all this optimism about our present state is valid, what will it do to the real and troubling division in modern America, that between social classes? The rediscovery of social class marks a genuine decline in the state of America since the Golden Age. It can't be wished away by saying it was the inevitable consequence of the rebirth of other countries. It's made no better by saying (though this is true) that pre-1914 America, that period to which we might be looking for lessons, was class-bound, too.

However, if the predictions of a new stability in family life are accurate, they will, in time, affect class divisions. It is reasonable to suppose, in other words, that the contribution family breakdown made to the creation of the underclass will, at the very least, not get any worse. Of course, it is not the modern American way to wait for deep social transformations to weave a benign change in behavior. Americans want action to ameliorate social divisions. In the Golden Age, they looked for such action to another unifying insitution, the federal government. Insofar as they still do, they look in vain. It seems highly unlikely that Washington is going to be as great a force in the next chapter of the republic's history as it was in the Golden Age.

It is axiomatic that many Americans have always distrusted the central government. The country's ethos has, in large part, been individualistic and suspicious of authority. In a nation that spans a continent, the capital is, by definition, distant and remote from people's everyday experiences. America was settled by men and women who forged self-governing communities from the wilderness; when it became a nation, it granted itself a constitution which limited the federal government to certain enumerated powers. First-time visitors to America are invariably struck by a contempt for central government. In Britain and France, people may dislike the airs and graces of the capital, but they do not say "London!" or "Paris!" with that gut-driven grunt of contempt with which Americans say "Washington!" The bombing of the federal building in Oklahoma City in 1995 showed that such contempt can turn murderous. This is a uniquely American phenomenon. In no other advanced economy, not even Margaret Thatcher's Britain, has there ever been the revolt against taxation which is a constant theme of modern American politics. In France, Germany, and Japan, the reaction to economic hardship is to expect "the state" to do more. In the United States, among at least a substantial chunk of the population, similar circumstances provoke a demand for the federal government to "get out of the way."

Seen against such a backdrop, the period that started with the presidential election of 1932 looks aberrational. For the forty years or so that followed, America faced three overlapping crises: the Depression; war, both hot and cold; and the struggle for civil rights. In effect, most Americans, if never all of them, ceded new powers and responsibilities to the federal government to handle the stresses of such crises. And they were extraordinarily grateful when it did. Perhaps nothing in modern American life, not even the shock that followed John Kennedy's assassination, rivals the depth of loss that Americans felt when, in April 1945, the word came from Warm Springs, Georgia, that FDR had died. Even those most critical of the growth of government recognized its appeal. Ronald Reagan burnished his credentials as a New Deal Democrat; Newt Gingrich, elected speaker of the House of Representatives in the Republican landslide of 1994, has written that a "legitimate argument could be made that between the Depression and the civil-rights movement a strong federal government was appropriate."

In the mid-1990s, the American economy was not wracked by depression; the country was not at war; and Americans for twenty years had signaled pretty firmly that they were not prepared to grant the federal government additional powers to advance racial equality. The crises that led to the acceptance of an enhanced role for the federal government, in other words, had disappeared, or been shunted off to other social institutions. Moreover, the very growth of federal government powers during the period of crisis had spawned almost as much ingratitude and suspicion as thankfulness.

But should the federal government have an expansive role only in time of crisis? Does the rhetorical commitment to the virtues of state and local government really make sense? Arguably not. We have already seen that state and local governments have grown much faster in the last twenty years than Washington. Yet it's hard to believe that the general level of competence in such sub-federal governments is higher than that in Washington. Tocqueville said, "Any attentive observer notices that the business of the Union is infinitely better conducted than that of any individual state. The Federal government is more just and moderate in its proceedings. . . . There is more wisdom in its views; its projects are planned further ahead. . . . there is more skill, consistency and firmness in the execution of its measures." Is that all now false?

One thing is true beyond any doubt. As foreign observers constantly point out to incredulous natives, the overlapping responsibilities of federal, state, and local governments have turned America into a bossily bureaucratic place. If, for example, you live in Virginia and work in the District of Columbia, the purchase of a car in Maryland will be accompanied by paperwork of a complexity that would have made a Soviet apparatchik envious. Jurisdictions have different rules on consumer or environmental protection. If one state or local government has an agency, everyone wants one. Everyone needs an "Economic Development Agency" with which to bribe Japanese firms to relocate in their area—a tendency which in 1991 the mayor of Louisville, Kentucky, called "madness." In 1991, after a small savings bank went bust in Washington, D.C., the local newspapers asked how the local office of bank supervision planned to handle the scandal. Few asked the better question, which was what a city of 600,000, headquarters to no fewer than three national agencies of bank supervision, was doing with such an office of its own in the first place.

The bureaucratic load of a denationalized domestic policy, in sum, means that America runs the risk of overgovernment. In *Halfway Home and a Long Way to Go*, the groundbreaking 1986 report of the Commission on the Future of the South, it was noted that South Carolina, then with 3.3 million people, had 46 counties, 265 municipalities, 92 school districts, and over 300 special-purpose districts. If you live in Los Angeles you could vote (and this is a simplified list) for a city council member, a county commissioner, a state assembly member, a state senator, state commissioners of education and insurance, a state comptroller, lieutenant governor, governor, a member of the House of Representatives, two members of the United States Senate, and the president of your country.

Just possibly, if all these good men and women were volunteering a small chunk of their time to public service, ready, like Cincinnatus, to return to the plow at any moment, their responsibilities and activities might be mutually reinforcing. In fact, in modern times such officeholders are almost invariably full-time, political professionals, paid as such, and with their own bloated staff. The chances that these overlapping nomenklaturas organize their duties with efficiency cannot be high. Nor are the prospects for reform. *Halfway Home and a Long Way to Go* said that "States should consider consolidating some local governments. . . . The South cannot respond to [a] challenge with its 19th century pattern of local government developed when the county seat was within one day's horseback ride." Yet ten years later, no single recommendation of the commission had seen so little progress.

All of this suggests that the demonization of Washington

and the deification of state and local governments is unlikely to lead to a more efficient public sector. But, in all truth, that is a second-order concern. America may no longer be in a state of crisis: but it still needs glue. The distance between the underclass in Detroit and the plutocrats of Grosse Pointe is far greater than any European country would tolerate, and utterly beyond the frame of reference of the Japanese. At its limit, the strength of the attachment to local preferences makes a mockery of America's claim to be a single country. To take one example: in July 1992, George Bush vetoed a bill that would have introduced so-called motor-voter rules; Americans would have been able to register to vote when they picked up their driving license or at other routine contacts with state bureaucracies. By and large, Democrats had supported such measures; Republicans opposed them, so Bush's veto did not come out of the blue. Still, his reasons for the veto were striking; he said that the social conditions of the states were so different that a simple rule about the eligibility to vote should not apply to all of them. So Bush made the circumstances in which one could win the right to vote contingent upon the right of states to make their own laws. That is mighty strange behavior for the president of a unified nation-state.

The motor-voter law was eventually passed, and Bush's arguments faded into history. They would, in any event, have been of no account if America was so sure of its unity that something like the motor-voter law could be considered a mere trifle. But America still shows deep-rooted regional distinctions, ones that have persisted even when the ethnic and cultural determinants which first brought them into place have long since mutated.

Consider the votes cast by each county in the 1988 presidential election. From Massachusetts Bay across New England, through the old Northwest and along the Canadian border to Oregon, Washington, and northern California, county after county voted for the Democratic candidate, Michael Dukakis. This northern tier roughly approximates to the path that New Englanders took west in the nineteenth century, into regions whose population was later augmented by foreign immigrants from Northern Europe. In 1988, the descendants of these Americans and North Europeans voted for a man who personified the Yankee virtues of good government, sobriety, mediation, and an aversion to violence. Yet Dukakis was not, in the old-fashioned sense, a Yankee at all, but a member of the first generation born in America to Greek parents. Somehow or other, the cultural distinctiveness of New England—forged by religious divines from England more than 300 years before—both communicated itself to this Greek man and to those who voted for him.

Of the twelve states without a death penalty, all but Hawaii and Alaska are in the Northeast or Midwest. Levels of homicide in the northern tier are typically a third those in the South. Of the ten states that voted against female suffrage between 1919 and 1921, eight were also among the fourteen states that rejected the Equal Rights Amendment in the 1970s. A generation's worth of educational reform has not touched an immutable fact of American life: the states along the Canadian border graduate oodles more children from high school than the states in the South. A generation of foreign investment in the backcountry of the Carolinas has not altered the swagger, braggadocio, and old-fashioned patriotism of the mountain towns. Immigration from Southeast Asia has not changed Texas.

Of course, those differences are often a source of pride: they make America what it is. Yet the history books tell us that they can be stretched too far, in ways that once led to a great civil war, and which in more modern times stunted the lives of black Americans. Some Americans, at least, fear that the ties that bind are being stretched too far again. After the House of Representatives passed a welfare bill in 1995 which converted federal programs to "block grants" to the states, John Lewis, a member of the House who as a young civil rights worker had been beaten nearly to death, said the following. "Those who come from the South or from urban centers have real reservations about giving the money to states. They can talk about Wisconsin, that's one thing. But in Alabama, where I grew up, or in Georgia, we lived through states' rights and we're concerned about it. The glue that holds our country together . . . I think we're starting to pull apart."

It's appropriate to bring this book to a close with such an eloquent warning. Yes, there are great sources of strength in America; yes, there is, in some important economic and social respects, a new stability to our lives after a long period of turmoil. But there is still a lot that divides us, and in some ways, the divisions are growing, not weakening. We should not be Pollyannaish; there is much work to do.

The natural optimist takes John Lewis's words as a warning; the pessimist takes them as a prophecy. Think how a pessimist would consider a drive, in 1996, that started at Los Angeles airport. You hear a babel of languages—Spanish, Korean, Chinese—as you shove your way to the rental car counter. You see Mexicans sweeping the floors, clipping the lawns. It's a near certainty that some of them are illegal immigrants, and, for these purposes, you are allowed to grumble inwardly that your tax dollars are paying for their health care and their children's education.

Then you set off north on I-405 toward Santa Monica, through a jumbled landscape whose features are softened by smog. Your eyes sting. After a few miles you turn right towards downtown Los Angeles on I-10. To the north, through the smog, you can make out the hills above Malibu from which the Santa Ana winds whip fires to the ocean. You think about the mindless arrogance of man, choosing to build a heaving metropolis in a place that God treats as a playground. You drive on. To your left, you see the line of the Hollywood Hills, the houses perched on stilts, the unrepentant habitat of the showbiz moguls who, uninvited, shove mindless dreck into your living room. To your right, you can sense the devastation of South-Central Los Angeles, still scarred after the worst riots of the century. You reach the city center, its towers owned by devious Japanese banks. Then it's on through mile after mile of subdivision dropped onto pristine desert, until, after a couple of hours, you come to Palm Springs, a silly pleasure palace, expensive, thoughtless.

This is the pessimistic way to drive to Palm Springs—the way most of the American intelligentsia drives there. Now drive along exactly the same route—this time, as an optimist. Start by remembering that those Mexicans, Koreans, and Chinese in the airport are there for a reason: measured by its attraction to those who can choose where they live, Los Angeles is the world's and the century's most successful city. Ask one of those Mexican women what she intends to do when her hard shift is finished, and she may say that, in the small hours of the morning, she's off to learn English at a language school. Her children, she will tell you with pride, are both at

Long Beach State; and they come home for a family supper each night. Drive north on I-405, past the old McDonnell Douglas plant in Santa Monica, the epitome of the wartime boom which transformed the California economy. Approach the measured curves of the junction with I-10 and remember that in 1971 Reyner Banham, architect and critic, wrote that "the intersection is a work of art, both as a pattern on the map, as a monument against the sky, and as a kinetic experience as one sweeps through it." This is our Louvre, our Colosseum.

Look left, to the houses in the hills of the men and women who created an entertainment industry that has swept the world. From Penang to Paris, popular culture is shaped by a combination of breathtaking risk, technological genius, and a sense of what mankind finds amusing; the brew was patented somewhere north of Sunset. Look right, to the single greatest concentration of manufacturing industry in the Western Hemisphere; spot the new, aggressive firms started by Indian software engineers, by Korean biologists. Sweep past the downtown towers for which the foolish Japanese paid ten times more than their real value. Drive past the east side, where what is probably the most prosperous Spanish-surnamed population on the globe has made its home; drive past Monterey Park, majority Chinese and bursting with talent. Drive past CalTech, where Nobel laureates seem to grow as easily as palms, and remember that any other country in the world would kill for a university half so good. Drive by the subdivisions in San Bernardino and Riverside counties where ordinary working-class people live in comfort still rare anywhere else. Drive by the state university campus where they send their children, so well financed by generous taxpayers that their tuition is almost free. Arrive in Palm

Springs, where the San Jacinto Mountains rise to pierce a cobalt sky, and watch thousands of ordinary people enjoy themselves in the kind of comfort that their grandparents would have thought the stuff of dreams.

Why do we kid ourselves that America is going to hell in a handbasket when it plainly isn't? Why is a glass that is half-full (at least) so often described as half-empty (at best)?

The forces of cohesion that so shaped the Golden Age are not what they were, and some of them, like the ability of the federal government to ameliorate social conditions, will be stunted for a long time, in a way that may prove dangerous. But America is not falling apart. Its new immigrants want to become Americans, while most of its black inhabitants have lives far closer to those of their white counterparts than all but the most optimistic would have imagined in 1945. Drive from LAX to Palm Springs and you will see that immigrants, blacks, and whites display the same addiction to consumer goods, the same veneration of the TV, fire up the grill on the same weekend in May, junk their suits for sweatshirts at the same rate, value the virtues of good-neighborliness in the same way, salute the same flag, take the same Pledge of Allegiance, honor the same president, weep at the same Vietnam Memorial, cheer the same Michael Jordan. That may sound like a commonplace list; it is not a trivial one.

In some respects, indeed, the new America is already taking shape. A period of traumatic change in family life is ending. A vibrant corporate sector and an expanding world economy can provide the economic growth and shared prosperity which once brought a nation together. This is not a bad prognosis for any nation.

At least, it wouldn't be if America could remember more of

its history than those strange, wonderful years after World War II. It cannot duplicate those years; trying to do so is like trying to catch hold of a dream. An older America was once divided by race, class, gender, and region. It overcame those divisions, and made itself into a nation that saved the world. "America," Woodrow Wilson once wrote, "is now sauntering through her resources and through the mazes of her politics with an easy nonchalance; but presently there will come a time when she will be surprised to find herself grown old,— a country crowded, strained, perplexed,—when she will be obliged to pull herself together, adopt a new regimen of life, husband her resources, concentrate her strength, steady her methods, sober her views, restrict her vagaries, trust her best, not her average members." All of that, and more, Americans once did. They should be getting ready to do it again.

Epilogue

Nearly twenty-two years after my first night in Great Neck, I find myself writing this book in my house in a suburb of Washington. It is early spring. The trees have not yet grown their full canopy; later, they will crowd out other shades of color in a thick layer of green that can be heavy and oppressive. The dogwoods are out, which means that the light flicks from white surfaces, to pink, to green, and to nothing but air—the landscape still has an uncolonized space which will be gone by July. The azaleas are just breaking out of bud; in a week or so, they will be gaudy and meretricious, but now they look quite dainty. Washington springs are unsurpassingly beautiful.

This house was built in 1940, when the economy was just starting to show signs of recovery from the Depression, but before war made materials hard to come by. It is two blocks into Maryland, in a subdivision built just before the war but which, to all purposes, might have been built just after it. These houses were the first to stretch metropolitan Washington across what locals call "The District Line" into what was once a country town called Bethesda. They are, as one of my neighbors says, "two-children houses"; you can accommodate a third kid, even a fourth, but you may have to build on the yard or forgo the garage.

Ah, the garage. Now *there's* a clue for social historians. Plenty of the houses are quite modest, but almost all of them were built with garages attached. Their builders knew that those who bought the houses both had and needed cars (in fact, and annoyingly, the subdivision doesn't have sidewalks). The houses have master bedrooms with bathrooms en suite; quite a luxury in 1940.

Who bought these new houses? Almost certainly, many of them were first owned by those who flocked to Washington during the war, when employment in the federal city was exploding. In his memoir of Washington during World War II, David Brinkley reckons that in the year after Pearl Harbor 70,000 new jobs were created; temporary office buildings covered the Mall, lining each side of the Reflecting Pool. Later, the area would house those who worked at the National Institutes of Health, established in 1948, and in the federal agencies that survived and prospered at the war's end: the State Department, the CIA, and, above all, the Pentagon. My own house was owned by a West Point graduate who, after VE Day, became the secretary of the Allied Control Commission in Berlin, and spent most of the rest of his working life in the Department of Defense. You want to know who remade the cracked vessel of the world? The people who lived on my street did.

These were family houses; and the children went to an elementary school built by the Works Progress Administration, a fine New Deal institution, in 1939. The school is a small gem of a building, sturdy but with fine detailing, two bay windows framing a front porch like a pair of spectacles. Those who settled here could walk to Baptist, Presbyterian, and Catholic churches nearby.

The people who bought these houses knew they were living in extraordinary times. In 1952 *The Partisan Review*, a small New York magazine, ran a symposium among intellectuals on the subject "Our Country and Our Culture." The *Review's* editors made no secret of their own position. "American intellectuals," they argued, "now regard America and its institutions in a new way. Until little more than a decade ago, America was commonly thought to be hostile to art and culture. Since then the tide has begun to turn, and many writers and intellectuals now feel closer to their country and their culture."

With a few splendid exceptions those who contributed to the symposium agreed. Many of the replies shared common themes. First, it was useless for Americans to look to Europe for spiritual or moral guidance. Europe had given the world fascism and Stalinism; European art and culture had supped at the table of two devils; the politics of the old European democracies had been spineless in the face of clear and pressing danger. Second, in the 1930s at home, and in the 1940s overseas, America had stepped up to the plate and swung mightily. America, said Arthur Schlesinger, Jr., had demonstrated a brilliant political exuberance in the 1930s; it had "risen to the crisis" magnificently. Third, American democracy had turned out to be something more than a sham. It actually worked; it changed governments and held them to account. It protected individual liberties, or at least, it did so better than was done anywhere else. There was, thought the intellectuals, no gaping hole between the theoretical aspirations of American democracy and its practice. Fourth, America was a land of abundance for all. The sociologist Max Lerner said that "We are farther on the road to reducing poverty to a very marginal phase of our life than any other social system in history."

Above all, contributors to the symposium thought that America had risen to a position of unexpected prominence in the family of nations. Reinhold Niebuhr, the Protestant theologian, said that "without apprenticeship, America has suddenly become the most powerful nation on earth." Lionel Trilling said that he and his contemporaries had "become aware of the virtual uniqueness of American security and well-being." As Niebuhr hinted, many of the writers were worried about this preeminence; they found it possible to express no more than guarded optimism about America. Still, that optimism was remarkable: these were people who would once have swapped a mansion in Connecticut for a garret off the Boulevard St.-Michel, who had once thought that the Depression was the death rattle of capitalism. If this gang of skeptics could admit that, on the whole, America was not such a bad place after all, consider what less sophisticated folk must have thought. In fact, we know that in the postwar years Americans were damn pleased with themselves. As they should have been; America was a strikingly successful place. It could fight and win wars; it could create a great peacetime economy. It could promise the implausible—say, to put a man on the moon in ten years—and then go and do it. It could build mighty rockets and roads; its popular culture swept the world. It responded to challenges, like *Sputnik*. It could make heroes.

But this heroic time obscured as much as it illuminated. The Golden Age was no Utopia. It wasn't much fun for ambitious, intelligent women; the position of blacks was still a national disgrace; blacklists and witch-hunts besmirched America's reputation for tolerance. And at the same time, the very forces that, in a large sense, brought the nation together, in smaller ways tore it apart. As Barry Levinson showed in his 1990 film *Avalon*, the nuclear family could be much more heartless than the old extended family of immigrants. Prosperity itself turned out to be unexpectedly difficult to handle, as the historian David Potter wrote in *People of Plenty*, his brilliantly prophetic work of 1954. The abundance of American life, suggested Potter, created unrealizable expectations. In times of plenty, people dream that social distinctions will vanish. But they never do; and this breeds an inevitable disillusion, all the more painful because sights have been set so high.

Still, that was in the unknowable future. For the time being, all one needed to do was wallow enjoyably in the plenty. Without thinking where it came from; which was a mistake. Outside North America, there has only been one modern society which ever gave its working class such prosperity, so many opportunities, such peace, such freedom from the ravages of war. Not Germany, twice defeated this century; not France, twice invaded. Not Japan, both defeated and, until very recently, feudal in its social distinctions. Not Britain, where a rigid class structure has limited the life chances of its people. The only analogy is with Australia, whose people at the beginning of this century actually had a higher standard of living than that of Americans. Of course, the analogy is not perfect; to take only the most obvious difference, one country has a small population, one a vast one. But both countries have been protected by mighty oceans from the horrors of war on their own territory; both are blessed with an endowment of natural riches; both were built by immigrants.

Yet there's one great difference—a difference of the spirit. From the time of the Pilgrims, America has seen its good fortune as a gift from a beneficent Providence. Australians do not claim so high an honor; they know that they are rich by chance. They call their nation "The Lucky Country" and are wise to do so, for luck runs out and the fear that it may do so keeps people on their toes. But the gift of Providence, or so its recipients may think, need never end. So long as one deserves to receive it, it just keeps on coming. And that's one of America's problems.

Much of Americans' contemporary modern mood of unhappiness stems from their failure to understand how damn lucky they once were. We once knew that. A constant theme of the essays in "Our Country and Our Culture" is the unexpected, sometimes frightening newness of it all. Schlesinger and Trilling, Potter and Lerner knew and said that the times were not normal. This sense of the oddity of the postwar years has been lost. They were (as Australians would have said, had they been asked) a fluke, a giant stroke of luck. The inability to see that, and hence to find a realistic way both of remembering the past and of measuring the present, turned out to be a failure of collective perspective which would prove devastating.

If Americans could only get over that failure, they would see themselves in a much better light than they usually manage. There are still plenty of churches in my neighborhood, and they are still full. But today we also have a Buddhist temple within walking distance, and when the school has an "International Day" its hall is filled with the smell of spices from everywhere between Lebanon and Thailand. My children have friends whose parents were born in India, China, Guatemala, Mexico, France, Turkey, Britain, Spain, and other countries too numerous to list. The babysitters of my children have come from Britain, France, the Philippines, and Bolivia; the children themselves have relatives spread over five continents. Their paternal grandmother never flew in an airplane, but each of my kids had flown 30,000 miles before they were two years old. They trade stories with their friends about the places far away they will visit in the summer.

For all their worldly wisdom, these children have roots in their American neighborhood. The neighborhood, of course, is different from what it was fifty years ago, and it's not perfect (we don't have a neighborhood bar), but it has many of the hallmarks of a true community. The kids play with each other in the street, trick-or-treat in great wolfpacks, swim together in the neighborhood pool. The county government has just given our community association a hall at the local park; two doors away, one father runs that great, unexplored symbol of modern community life, the local soccer team. National politics doesn't seem to have much of a following here, though many of my neighbors work for the federal government; during the supposedly epochal congressional elections of 1994, there was hardly a poster to be seen. Community politics is another matter; the school has 300 students, and at the first PTA meeting of the year, no fewer than 400 parents showed up.

Alexis de Tocqueville, were he to come back to earth and visit our street, would recognize American democracy immediately. We cannot be an entirely self-governing community and would not want to be; my neighbors fly the Stars and Stripes because they know, without being told, that they belong to a great nation—that the essentials of their identity are held in common with Americans everywhere.

I think—in fact, I know—that my neighbors are proud of their country. Two aunts of mine—aged seventy-eight and eighty-eight—made their first visit to the United States last year. On the last night of their trip I asked them what most struck them about Americans. They replied, as I knew they would, by saying, "They love their country." Everywhere they went, they noticed a patriotism, a pride in being American. Like everything else, patriotism can be perverted by bigots; but it doesn't have to be. My neighbors live a quiet patriotism every day, and make the lives of their community the better for it.

I don't need to be told that I'm fortunate, that not everyone can live in a quiet, leafy suburb like this. I know I don't like my children to listen to the evening news—to hear that in one day four people were murdered in Washington, one of them a fourteen-year-old boy on his bicycle. I know that if such tidings were transmitted in London or Paris, in Sydney or Tokyo, they would be a signal that society had broken down. I know that in America we have become so inured to violence that we shrug off such grim statistics, and wish that we didn't.

But I know, also, that the United States still offers a life of abundance and fulfillment beyond the dreams of most people on the globe; that its government grants a greater degree of freedom to its people than almost any other; and that its economy still displays an astonishing ingenuity of the sort that will serve it well in the future. Americans are still, as David Potter wrote, a "people of plenty." Plenty of everything: Bill Bennett, author of *The Book of Virtues* once told me (and I now tell others), "Whatever it is, America has more of it. More good, more bad; more good sense, more craziness; more beauty; more ugliness." It's a big country.

If all this is true, what explains the sullen mood of so many in modern America? Why, to repeat a question I posed when we traveled the road to Palm Springs, is this half-full glass so often thought to be half-empty? This book has tried to suggest one answer: Americans have forgotten their history. Mesmerized by the years after 1945, they lost sight of an older country that was very like the country they now inhabit. Perplexed by the sudden loss of national and social cohesion, they misread the normal for the peculiar, and the aberrational for the commonplace. They need, desperately, to break through the barrier of the Golden Age and recapture the society they once had, and now have once more.

There is a second reason for America's discontent. Americans have not only forgotten history, they have misread geography. Battered by the changes that have come upon them since the 1960s, they have assumed, too often, that other countries have either been spared such horrors or have been able to cope with them better. This is not the case. The economies of Western Europe and Japan are just as troubled by the forces of technology and economics that have challenged their businesses; Europeans, at least, are beginning to wonder whether they can see the miserable birth of an underclass within their cities, whether their societies can cope with millions of immigrants with different customs and religions. Americans have never quite grasped that they do not experience triumphs and tragedies alone, but that rather, for the past 200 years, they have often experienced them first.

For America, the key question for the future is whether its institutions, from the presidency to neighborhood soccer teams, can cope with the second coming of a messy, fragmented society. It should be able to, for America (and this, too, Americans forget) is an old country, whose essentials have been long fixed. Say, for the sake of argument, that modern America began to take recognizable shape not at the time of the Founding Fathers but after the Civil War. The case for exceptional American stability holds. When Lee surrendered to Grant at Appomattox Court House, France and Russia were ruled by emperors; Germany did not exist as a unified country, Italy barely so; in Japan, the Meiji Restoration was still three years away; it was not until 1867 that Britain would extend the franchise in such a way that it was acceptable (just) to speak of it as a democracy. In the intervening years since the Civil War, every one of those six other powers has suffered wars far more calamitous than anything fate has visited on the United States—to say nothing of sundry revolutions, dictatorships, or catastrophic economic turmoil. America has been very lucky and its luck has not run out. It is in that long run of past luck that America should be able to find the resources to cope with the challenges of tomorrow.

America after 1945 went on a wild ride, as if its potential knew no horizons. That was the message of the cars on the Willow Run Expressway, of Hilton Head and IBM, of John Kennedy and the countless millions who saw a new life in the suburbs. The ride took America not into the future but back in time. As F. Scott Fitzgerald wrote at the close of the *The Great Gatsby*, Americans were "borne back ceaselessly into the past." In that past, America had met many dragons, and slayed most of them. It now meets them once more. The task of the old country is to learn how it coped when it was younger.

SOURCE NOTES

I have always thought that source notes belonged in academic texts (which this isn't) rather than in books of general interest (which I hope this is). On the other hand, readers are entitled to know where an author gets his or her ideas, and also what further reading on the subject might be enjoyable. What I've tried to do in these notes is to write a sort of bibliographic essay. So I haven't tried to provide a source for every fact, and haven't even thought of doing an exhaustive bibliography. But I have tried to indicate the books and articles which were most important to me or which I enjoyed most (and, hence, which I think others would enjoy, too). Wherever appropriate, I've noted where I relied on my own reporting.

Prologue

The story of my arrival in Great Neck appeared, in shorter form, in *Newsweek*, July 10, 1995. Pete Hamill's liner notes are to *Blood on the Tracks*, by Bob Dylan, 1974.

Chapter One

America: What Went Wrong?, by Donald L. Barlett and James B. Steele (Kansas City: Andrews & McMeel, 1992), based on a series of articles in the *Philadelphia Inquirer*, was the literary apogee of "declinism" and had an effect on the rhetoric of the 1992 presidential election. For David Potter's prescient analysis of post-1945 America, see *People of Plenty* (Chicago:

University of Chicago Press, 1954). I saw the billboard at Tulsa in 1992. A shorter version of the story of Willow Run and the road to Ann Arbor appeared in *The Economist*, October 26, 1991. Sources for this version are my own reporting from visits in 1991 and 1993, and the archives of newspapers in Ypsilanti and Detroit—especially the *Detroit Free Press*—from 1941 onward. See also *Willow Run*, by Lowell Juilliard Carr (New York: Harper & Brothers, 1952); *Highways to Heaven*, by Christopher Finch (New York: HarperCollins, 1992); and *The Fords: An American Epic*, by Peter Collier and David Horowitz (New York: Summit Books, 1987). Michigan's wartime role is based on interviews in Ann Arbor and Detroit, on the discussion in *Highways to Heaven*, by Finch, op. cit., and on *Detroit Is My Own Home Town*, by Malcolm Bingay (New York: Bobbs-Merrill, 1946).

Chapter Two

The story of Victoria, Kansas, is based on my own reporting. For John Adams and the Constitutional Convention, see, among many other works, *Miracle at Philadelphia*, by Catherine Drinker Bowen (Boston: Little, Brown, 1966), and *E Pluribus Unum*, by Forrest Macdonald (Indianapolis: Liberty Fund, 1979). The role of universities in the development of America is discussed in *The Americans: The Colonial Experience*, by Daniel Boorstin (New York: Random House, 1958). The history of universities in Kansas is based on my own reporting in 1992; see also *The University of Kansas*, by Clifford Stephen Griffin (Lawrence: University Press of Kansas, 1974).

The roots of America's deep-rooted economic vitality are familiar to anyone who has read *Democracy in America*, by Alexis de Tocqueville. I also used *Enterprise*, by Stuart Bruchey (Cambridge: Harvard University Press, 1990). Bruchey's marvelous one-volume economic history of America was a key reference source for me throughout the time I worked on this book. Bruchey introduced me to the sensation with which Britain viewed Cyrus McCormick's mechanical reapers at the Great Exhibition in 1851 (and which prompted a commission of inquiry into American industry by the British government). The tale of *The Champion of the Seas* is well known to those, like me, who grew up in Liverpool. See also *The Tyranny of Distance*, by Geoffrey Blainey (Melbourne: Melbourne University Press, 1966), a classic short history of Australia. But the best way to assess the vitality of American capitalism in the last century is not through statistics but through the eyes of an observant novelist: compare the passages on Lowell, Massachusetts, in Charles Dickens's *American Notes* with the fictional Lancashire milltown of "Coketown" (usually assumed to be Preston) in *Hard Times*.

"The Origins of American Industrial Success," by Gavin Wright, *American Economic Review* 80:651 (1990), details the strength of the American economy at the turn of the century. For the feel of Lowell, Massachusetts, then and now, I relied on my own reporting, supplemented by that of my *Newsweek* colleague Martha Brant. The Monongahela Valley of western Pennsylvania crops up throughout this book; I made regular trips there from 1986 to 1995. I found documents dealing with the 1919 steel strike and with life in the valley in the 1930s among the publications of the Steel Industry Heritage Corporation in Homestead, Pennsylvania. And my *Newsweek* colleague Howard Fineman, a Pittsburgh native, shared memories of the region in the 1950s.

For America on the edge of World War I, I used, among other works, *The Progressive Era*, edited by Lewis L. Gould (Syracuse, N.Y.: Syracuse University Press, 1974), the relevant chapters of *The Populist Persuasion*, by Michael Kazin (New York: Basic Books, 1995); *Pivotal Decades*, by John M. Cooper (New York: Norton, 1990); *Victorian America*, by Thomas J. Schlereth (New York: HarperCollins, 1991), and books and articles cited therein; and I reread *USA* by John Dos Passos (New York: Modern Library, 1937). John Maynard Keynes in *The Economic Consequences of the Peace* (1919; reprint, New York: Viking Penguin, 1988) described why one shouldn't be frightened of the international economy. For a more modern view, see *Head to Head*, by Lester Thurow (New York: William Morrow, 1992). On foreign direct investment flows, see *The Emergence of Multinational Enterprise*, by Mira Wilkins (Cambridge: Harvard University Press, 1970) as well as Professor Wilkins's contribution to a special issue, on foreign investment, of the *Annals of the American Political Science Society*, July 1991. Of the many biographies of Herbert Hoover, I relied most on *An Uncommon Man*, by Richard Norton Smith (New York: Simon & Schuster, 1984). For America at the end of World War II, see *By the Bomb's Early Light*, by Paul Boyer (Chapel Hill: University of North Carolina Press, 1994); *A Democracy at War*, by William O'Neill (New York: Free Press, 1993); *V Was for Victory*, by John Morton Blum (New York: Harcourt, Brace, 1976), and works cited therein; and the wonderful *Manhattan, '45*, by Jan Morris (New York: Oxford University Press, 1987). For a view on the horrors of cohesion, see David Caute's history of McCarthyism, *The Great Fear* (New York: Simon & Schuster, 1979).

Chapter Three

The description of Birmingham and the Vulcan statue is from my own reporting. See also *The Mind of the South*, by W. J. Cash (New York: Knopf, 1941). There is an enormously rich literature on southern economic history. I relied heavily on *Old South, New South*, by Gavin Wright (New York: Basic Books, 1986), and broadly follow Wright's interpretation of the data. See also, among many other works, *The Selling of the South*, by James Cobb (Baton Rouge: Louisiana State University Press, 1982); *Industrialization and Southern Society*, by James Cobb (Lexington: University Press of Kentucky, 1984); and *Standing at the Crossroads*, by Pete Daniel (New York: Hill & Wang, 1986). I used *An Economic History of the South*, by Emory Hawk (1934; reprint, Westport, Conn.: Greenville Press, 1973) to assess the state of industry in the South before World War II. Many of the details of economic convergence are to be found in Richard Easterlin, "Regional Economic Trends," in *The Reinterpretation of American Economic History*, edited by Robert Fogel and Stanley Engerman (New York: Harper & Row, 1972). Convergence can also be traced through the relevant tables of *Historical Statistics of the United States, Colonial Times to 1970* (Washington, D.C.: U.S. Government Printing Office, 1975), which is also essential for understanding the way in which immigration affected—or, rather, didn't—the southern economy.

I owe a great deal to discussions, over the years, with the staff of the Southern Growth Policies Board of Raleigh, North Carolina, who have given me scores of working papers on aspects of the modern southern economy. Jesse White, erstwhile director of the SGPB, first alerted me both to the story of the "buffalo hunt" for non-local investment and to the peculiar role of universities in southern economic history, and hence to the comparison in the text between MIT, CalTech, and Georgia Tech. And for views of the vocation of southern universities that are decidedly non-economic, see *Lanterns on the Levee*, by William Alexander Percy (New York: Knopf, 1941)—which Julia Reed, daughter of the Delta, told me was indispensable—as well as *Look Homeward, Angel*, by Thomas Wolfe (New York: Scribner's, 1929).

The essential data set for race relations in the South at the time of World War II is *An American Dilemma*, by Gunnar Myrdal (New York: Harper, 1944). For the struggle for civil rights, I used, in particular, *The Strange Career of Jim Crow*, by C. Vann Woodward (New York: Oxford University Press, 1957), and *Parting the Waters*, by Taylor Branch (New York: Simon & Schuster, 1988). The role of the judges of the Fifth Circuit is discussed in *Unlikely Heroes*, by Jack Bass (New York: Simon & Schuster, 1981). *The Most Southern Place on Earth*, by James Cobb (New York: Oxford University Press, 1992), brings the story of the Delta almost up to the present day. For the southern agrarians and the Nashville movement, see the works on economic history cited earlier. Wright, in *Old South, New South*, op. cit., quotes (as have others) from *Southerners*, by Marshall Frady (New York: New American Library, 1980), on the dangers of losing southern exceptionalism. The work of John Shelton Reed suggests that the South, in fact, remains a place apart. See his *The Enduring South* (Lexington, Mass.: Lexington Books, 1971), *Southerners* (Chapel Hill: University of North Carolina Press, 1983), and *Whistling Dixie* (Columbia: University of Missouri Press, 1992). I am grateful to Professor Reed for discussing southern exceptionalism with me, as well as for saying, "Oh, you mean there is one?" when I asked him to discuss "the New South."

The New Urban America, by Carl Abbott (Chapel Hill: University of North Carolina Press, 1981), is the source for the division of the country into core and outliers. Professor Abbott generously gave me extensive interviews on the new demography of the country. I am also grateful to John Kasarda of the University of North Carolina for helping me with modern demographics and for giving me an invaluable set of articles and working papers from the Center for Competitiveness and Employment Growth at the University of North Carolina. Professor Kasarda's "Jobs, Migration, and Emerging Urban Mismatches," in *Urban Change and Poverty*, edited by Michael McGeary and Lawrence Lynn, Jr. (Washington, D.C.: National Academy Press, 1988), gives an overview of the spatial mismatch thesis. I supplemented the academics' work with my own reporting on demographic change, especially in Chicago, Kansas, and Colorado. The classic modern history of American suburbs is *Crabgrass Frontier*, by Kenneth Jackson (New York: Oxford University Press, 1985). *The Levittowners*, by Herbert Gans (New York: Pantheon, 1967), is simply indispensable. See also, of course, *The Organization Man*, by W. H. Whyte (New York: Simon & Schuster, 1957), and *The Lonely Crowd*, by David Riesman, et al. (New Haven: Yale University Press, 1950).

For critiques of Golden Age suburban family life, see *The Feminine Mystique*, by Betty Friedan (New York: Norton, 1963), and *The City in History*, by Lewis Mumford (New York: Harcourt, Brace & World, 1961). Also see *The Way We Never Were*, by Stephanie Coontz (New York: Basic Books, 1992)—a superb synthesis and sourcebook on the revisionist case against the idea of postwar family harmony, even if I disagree in part with its conclusions. See also *The Changing Lives of American Women*, by Steven McLaughlin, et al. (Chapel Hill: University of North Carolina Press, 1988)—Dr. McLaughlin was a fount of information for me on patterns of family formation, and much else. Also see *Homeward Bound: American Families in the Cold War*, by Elaine Tyler May (New York: Basic Books, 1988). There is a substantial literature on the reinforcing stereotypes of TV and "real" families—see, for example, *Prime Time Families*, by Ella Taylor (Berkeley: University of California Press, 1989); *Recasting America: Culture and Politics in the Cold War*, edited by Lary May (Chicago: University of Chicago

Press, 1989); and *Television and Behavior* (Rockville, Md.: U.S. Department of Health and Human Services, 1982).

I've never found a book or article that treated immigration in the 1950s even adequately. But *Southern California: An Island on the Land,* by Carey McWilliams (New York: Duell, Sloan & Pearce, 1946), and *Los Angeles,* by Harry Carr (New York: D. Appleton–Century, 1935), touch on an early immigration "problem" in southern California. See also *Strangers from Distant Shores,* by Ronald Takaki (New York: Oxford University Press, 1989).

Greg Bailey told me the story of his childhood as a SAC brat. See his "Farewell to SAC," in *The Bulletin of the Atomic Scientists,* June 1992. The literature on the origins of the Cold War is, by now, notoriously immense. Michael Mandelbaum guided me through its trails. The interpretation here follows *A Preponderance of Power* by Melvyn P. Leffler (Stanford: Stanford University Press, 1992). I also enjoyed reading *The Cold War,* by Martin Walker (New York: Henry Holt, 1994); *The Wise Men,* by Walter Isaacson and Evan Thomas (New York: Simon & Schuster, 1986); *The Devil We Knew,* by H. W. Brands (New York: Oxford University Press, 1993); *The End of the Cold War,* edited by Michael Hogan (New York: Cambridge University Press, 1992)—a terrific collection of essays—and, of course, *Present at the Creation,* by Dean Acheson, (New York: Norton, 1969). Data on attitudes to Russia come from *The Rational Public: Fifty Years of Trends in Americans' Policy Preferences,* by Benjamin Page and Robert Shapiro (Chicago: University of Chicago Press, 1992)—one of the handful of books on which I relied most. On McCarthyism, see *The Great Fear,* by David Caute, op. cit., and the relevant chapters of *The Proud Decades,* by John Patrick Diggins (New York: Norton, 1991). The characterization of John Kennedy's priorities follows *President Kennedy,* by Richard Reeves (New York: Simon & Schuster, 1993). Charles Moskos shared with me his thoughts on the importance of the draft for social cohesion. See also his "From Citizens' Army to Social Laboratory," *Wilson Quarterly,* 17:83 (Winter 1993), and *The Peacetime Army* by Marvin Fletcher (Westport, Conn.: Greenwood Press, 1988). Also see *To Raise an Army,* by John Whiteclay Chambers (New York: Free Press, 1987). The quote from *Time* magazine on the all-American nature of World War II is to be found in *V Was for Victory,* by John Morton Blum, op. cit.

Chapter Four

I took my cues on the intellectual history of the commerce clause from *Novus Ordo Seclorum,* by Forrest McDonald (Lawrence: University Press of Kansas, 1985). See also the chapter by Frank Freidel in *Quarrels That Have*

Shaped the Constitution, edited by John A. Garraty (New York: Harper & Row, 1987; the relevant chapters of *The Court and the Constitution,* by Archibald Cox (Boston: Little, Brown, 1987); and *Economic Liberties and the Constitution,* by James A. Dorn and Henry G. Manne (Fairfax, Va.: Cato Institute, 1987). For an assessment of the wartime experience with planning, see "The New Deal and the Idea of the State," by Alan Brinkley, in *The Rise and Fall of the New Deal Order,* edited by Steve Fraser and Gary Gerstle (Princeton: Princeton University Press, 1989), as well as Professor Brinkley's more recent work *The End of Reform* (New York: Knopf, 1995). I spent some time delving in Alvin Hansen's voluminous works, especially *Economic Policy and Full Employment* (New York: McGraw-Hill, 1947), *The American Economy* (New York: McGraw-Hill, 1957), and *The Postwar American Economy* (New York: Norton, 1964). On the significance of the growth of road transport, I used *Highways to Heaven,* by Christopher Finch, op. cit.; *Freeways,* by Lawrence Halprin (New York: Reinhold, 1966); *Open Road,* by Phil Patton (New York: Simon & Schuster, 1986); and *American Highways 1776–1976* (Washington, D.C.: U.S. Federal Highway Administration, 1976). For the story of Hilton Head, I relied on my own reporting, especially a long discussion with Charles Fraser. The classic account of the importance of the air-conditioner is "The End of the Long Hot Summer," by Raymond Arsenault, *Journal of Southern History* 597 (1984). See also *The Right Stuff,* by Tom Wolfe (New York: Farrar, Straus, & Giroux, 1979).

For the origins of America's postwar international economic policy, see *The Myth of America's Decline,* by Henry Nau (New York: Oxford University Press, 1990). For the history of IBM, see *Big Blue,* by Richard Thomas DeLamarter (New York: Dodd, Mead, 1986); *Big Blues,* by Paul Carroll (New York: Crown, 1993); and *IBM: Colossus in Transition,* by Robert Sobel (New York: Times Books, 1981). For the Monongahela Valley, I supplemented my own reporting with *And the Wolf Finally Came,* by John P. Hoerr (Pittsburgh: University of Pittsburgh Press, 1988), and *Homestead,* by William Serrin (New York: Times Books, 1992)—both of them passionate books which do that remarkable slice of America proud. The discussion of postwar growth has its roots in three books: *The Age of Diminished Expectations,* by Paul Krugman (Cambridge: MIT Press, 1990); *Productivity and American Leadership,* by William J. Baumol, et al. (Cambridge: MIT Press, 1989); and *Policies for Long-Run Economic Growth* (Kansas City: Federal Reserve Bank of Kansas City, 1993)—a superb collection of papers which proves that if you take a bunch of economists and stick them in Jackson Hole, Wyoming, they will talk nothing but sense. Of the many economists with whom I discussed growth theory, I am grateful in particular to David Hale, Norman Robertson, Clive Crook, and Dale Jorgenson.

The history of the University of California is based on reporting and interviews conducted by Emma Oxford. For the significance of the GI Bill, I am grateful for an interview with Dale Jorgenson; see "Investment in Education and U.S. Economic Growth," by Jorgenson and Barbara M. Fraumeni, *Scandinavian Journal of Economics* S51 (1992). For a broader review of post-1945 education policy, see *The Troubled Crusade*, by Diane Ravitch (New York: Basic Books, 1983).

Chapter Five

On the 1960s, see *The Sixties: Years of Hope, Days of Rage*, by Todd Gitlin (New York: Bantam Books, 1987), the best, if (openly) subjective, account of the period. Also see Jim Miller, "Democracy Is in the Streets" (New York: Simon & Schuster, 1987), which E. J. Dionne rightly calls "the best discussion, anywhere, of the meaning of the Port Huron Statement and the ideology of the New Left." See also the relevant chapters of Dionne's own *Why Americans Hate Politics* (New York: Simon & Schuster, 1991) and *Berkeley at War*, by W. J. Rorabaugh (New York: Oxford University Press, 1989). I discussed the New Left with Gitlin, to whom I am most grateful. I've wandered around the museum in the Dallas Book Depository, and I found Don DeLillo's quote about post-Dallas randomness and chaos in the *Seattle Post-Intelligencer*, June 26, 1991. *The Power Elite*, by C. Wright Mills (New York: Oxford University Press, 1970), is required reading for the roots of the New Left. So, for that matter, is *On the Road*, by Jack Kerouac (New York: Viking, 1957); and see *Desolate Angel: Jack Kerouac, the Beat Generation and America*, by Dennis McNally (New York: Random House, 1979), and *Seeds of the Sixties*, by Andrew Jamison and Ron Eyerman (Berkeley: University of California Press, 1994).

For survey evidence on race relations, see *The Rational Public*, by Page and Shapiro, op. cit. For Macomb County (which I've trudged around myself, over the years) and the rise of the Reagan Democrats, I used successive editions of *The Almanac of American Politics*, by Michael Barone and Grant Ujifusa (Washington, D.C.: National Journal); *The Emerging Republican Majority*, by Kevin Phillips (New York: Anchor Books, 1970); and *Chain Reaction*, by Tom and Mary Edsall (New York: Norton, 1991). *Middle Class Dreams*, by Stanley Greenberg (New York: Times Books, 1995), was published after I'd written this chapter, but is now plainly essential reading for the "Macomb" thesis. For Kennedy's racial politics, see *President Kennedy*, by Reeves, op. cit. *The Devil We Knew*, by Brands, op. cit., includes a marvelous account of attitudes to Vietnam. For attitudes to anti-war protestors, see *The Sixties*, by Gitlin, op. cit., and "The Limits of the New Left," by Christopher Jencks, originally published in *The New Re-*

public, October 21, 1967, and reprinted in *The New Republic Reader*, edited by Dorothy Wickenden (New York: Basic Books, 1994). Norman Macrae's brilliant and typically iconoclastic survey of America was published in *The Economist*, October 25, 1975. For Watergate as a historical phenomenon, I found nothing to beat *The Wars of Watergate*, by Stanley Kutler (New York: Random House, 1990).

Why Americans Hate Politics, by Dionne, op. cit., is good on the range of political beliefs in the 1960s. For the economic manifestation of that range, see *Conversations with Economists*, by Arjo Klamer (Totowa, N.J.: Rowan & Allanheld, 1984). Also see "The Problem of Social Cost," by Ronald H. Coase, *Journal of Law and Economics* 3:1 (1960); "Rational Expectations and the Theory of Price Movement," by John Muth, *Econometrica* 29:315 (1961); and "The Role of Monetary Policy," by Milton Friedman, *American Economic Review* 58:1 (1968). And on the slowdown of growth, see *Productivity and American Leadership*, by Baumol et al., op. cit.; *The Age of Diminished Expectations*, by Krugman, op. cit. (this is the source of the quote from Herman Kahn)—and, especially, the papers collected in *Policies for Long-Run Economic Growth*, op. cit. (source of the quoted papers by Michael Darby, Kumiharu Shigehara, and Bradford de Long and Lawrence Summers). For an overview of the story, see also *The World Economy in the 20th Century*, by Angus Maddison (Paris: OECD Development Centre, 1989).

Chapter Six

For Daniel Bell's critique of the hedonistic aspects of American capitalism, see *The End of Ideology* (Cambridge: Harvard University Press, 1988). The story of the 1992 Republican convention at Houston is based on my own reporting; see *The Economist*, August 22, 1992. On the secularism of Michael Dukakis, see *Under God*, by Garry Wills (New York: Simon & Schuster, 1990). I relied on Andrew Cherlin, *Marriage, Divorce and Remarriage*, revised edition (Cambridge: Harvard University Press, 1992), for much of my data on the state of the contemporary family; see also Cherlin's remarks in *The Economist*, December 26, 1992. The quotes from Christopher Jencks on the ways in which cultural and economic matters coalesced with such baleful consequences are from his "Deadly Neighborhoods," in *The New Republic*, June 13, 1988, a review of *The Truly Disadvantaged*, by William Julius Wilson (Chicago: University of Chicago Press, 1988); see also Jencks's collection of essays, *Rethinking Social Policy* (Cambridge: Harvard University Press, 1992). The story of an Amsterdam long ago and far away is based on my own reporting; the Kinsey report was first published in 1948. For the Battelle study of sex lives, see "The Sexual Behavior of Men in the United States," by John O. G. Billy, et al., *Family Planning Perspectives* 25:52 (1993). The relative conservatism of American sexual careers is revealed in Freya Sonenstein, "Sexual Activity Among Adolescent Males in the United States," *Family Planning Perspectives* 32:162 (1992). For the best data set on family finances, see the annual Green Book—or *Background Material and Data on Programs Within the Jurisdiction of the Committee of Ways and Means. The Work of Nations*, by Robert Reich (New York: Knopf, 1991), was an early version of the thesis, by now commonplace, that America's problem was not the level of employment but the type of employment.

Chapter Seven

Three books that make the case for the 1980s as a decade of success are *The Seven Fat Years*, by Robert L. Bartley (New York: Free Press, 1992); *The Growth Experiment*, by Lawrence Lindsey (New York: Basic Books, 1990); and *What Went Right in the 1980s?* by Richard McKenzie (San Francisco: Pacific Research Institute for Public Policy, 1993). Thanks to John Kasarda for data on the fastest-growing cities of the 1980s—see "The Implications of Demographic and Job Shifts for Future Real Estate Performance," by Stephen Appold and John Kasarda, Center for Competitiveness and Employment Growth, University of North Carolina, 1991—and to Cindy Pieropan, of the Planning Department of the city of Boulder, Colorado, for helping me put them in context; see also *Edge City*, by Joel Garreau (New York: Doubleday, 1992). For the history of streetcars, see *Crabgrass Frontier*, by Kenneth Jackson, op. cit., and for life with the internal combustion engine, *Stuck in Traffic*, by Anthony Downs (Washington, D.C.: Brookings, 1992).

One of the most persuasive, shortest, and best-written analyses of the South in the 1980s is *Halfway Home and a Long Way to Go*, by the Southern Growth Policies Board (Raleigh, 1986). The description of Shannon County, South Dakota, comes from reporting by myself and Elizabeth Jelliffe; see *The Economist*, December 19, 1992. The account of the Monongahela Valley in the 1980s is from my own reporting; for John Kasarda on demographic change and New York, see "America's Changing Real Estate Markets," Working Paper, Center for Competitiveness and Employment Growth, University of North Carolina, 1989. *The Truly Disadvantaged*, by William Julius Wilson, op. cit., is a detailed treatment of the "employment shift" thesis of urban decay. Charles Murray's dire warning is to be found in *The National Review*, July 8, 1991. *The Revolt of the Elites and the Betrayal of Democracy*, by Christopher Lasch (New York: Norton, 1995), is a meditation on modern class conflict; see also *The Great Good Place*, by Ray Oldenburg (New York: Paragon House, 1989). For an examination of the effect on local labor markets of a sustained boom, see "Employment and Earnings of Disadvantaged Young Men in a Labor Shortage Economy," by Richard B. Freeman, and "Gains from Growth? The Impact of Full Employment and Poverty in Boston," by Paul Osterman; and for explanations of the continuing low labor market participation of poor black Americans, see "We'd Love to Hire Them but . . . ," by Joleen Kirschenman and Kathryn M. Neckerman, all in *The Urban Underclass*, edited by Christopher Jencks and Paul E. Peterson (Washington, D.C.: Brookings, 1991). I reported the story of Henry "Little Man" James in *The Economist*, December 7, 1991. See also *Streetwise*, by Elijah Anderson (Chicago: University of Chicago Press, 1990), and, for Jesse Jackson's thoughts on crime, *Newsweek*, January 4, 1994. On Washington's ailments, see *Demosclerosis*, by Jonathan Rauch (New York: Random House, 1994). Clinton's comments on the unaccountability of government can be found in *Newsweek*, April 10, 1995, foreshadowing his State of the Union address in 1996. A shorter version of the argument that we have seen a denationalization of domestic policy was in *The Economist*, October 26, 1991; thanks especially to Oregon governor John Kitzhaber; Vera Katz, now mayor of Portland, Oregon; David Harrison and Paul Sommers, of the Northwest Policy Center, Seattle, Washington; Hunter Morrison, director of planning for Cleveland, Ohio; and Jerry Abramson, mayor of Louisville, Kentucky, all of whom helped me sharpen up the argument. *Laboratories of Democracy*, by David Osborne (Boston: Harvard Business School Press, 1988), adumbrates on the well-known aphorism of Louis Brandeis.

Chapter Eight

The passages on Tijuana and the 1992 presidential primary in New Hampshire are from my own reporting. For attitudes to foreign affairs, see *American Public Opinion and U.S. Foreign Policy 1991*, by the Chicago Council on Foreign Relations, an exercise repeated in 1995; *America's Place in the World*, by the Times Mirror Center for the People and the Press (1993); and *The Rational Public*, by Page and Shapiro, op. cit. On the development of trade policy, see *The Myth of America's Decline*, by Henry Nau, op. cit., and *American Trade Politics*, second edition, by I. M. Destler (Washington, D.C.: Institute for International Economics, 1986). On the story of the Le Mans car, see *The Work of Nations*, by Reich, op. cit. The best short source on foreign direct investment is *Foreign Direct Investment in the United States*, second edition, by Edward Graham and Paul Krugman (Washington, D.C.: Institute for International Economics, 1991). The passages on Hawaii, Fort Smith, and Breckenridge are from my own reporting; thanks to Roland Boreham, of Baldor Electric, who patiently explained how a firm in a small regional town came to see that its future lay in the global economy. The section on Seattle and the economy of the Pacific Northwest is based on a series of interviews between 1991 and 1994 with policy-makers and academics in Oregon and Washington State. Those interviews shaped my discussion of many subjects in this book, from the internationalization of the economy, to the unplanned and uncoordinated explosion of subnational government, to the potential and limits of "growth management." I am grateful especially to Carl Abbott, David Harrison, and Paul Sommers; and to Robert Kapp, lately of the Washington Council on International Trade. The background to NAFTA is based on my own work in Mexico during regular visits from 1986 onward, and is brilliantly described in *Continental Shift*, by William Orme, Jr. (Washington, D.C.: The Washington Post Company, 1993). For a sense of how NAFTA might have been heralded in an earlier age, see *One World*, by Wendell Willkie (New York: Limited Editions Club, 1944)—a wonderful book which has stood the test of time.

Chapter Nine

The Trouble with America, by Michel Crozier (Berkeley: University of California Press, 1984), is a wry and affectionate—but disappointed—view of modern America by a perceptive foreign observer. The modern literature on social obligation and communitarianism is getting out of hand. For a thoughtful analysis of the roles of state and market, see *Whose Keeper?*, by Alan Wolfe (Berkeley: University of California Press, 1989). See also *Habits of the Heart*, by Robert Bellah, et al. (Berkeley: University of California Press, 1985), and *The Good Society*, by the same authors (New York: Knopf, 1991). Much of the literature on social capital owes its origins to, of all unlikely things, a study of modern Italy: *Making Democracy Work*, by Robert Putnam (Princeton: Princeton University Press, 1993). Putnam's "Bowling Alone: America's Declining Social Capital," *Journal of Democracy* 6:65 (1995), must be one of the most overquoted academic articles of modern times. For a trenchant discussion of Putnam's thesis, see Fareed Zakaria's review of *Trust*, by Francis Fukuyama (New York: Free Press, 1995), in the *New York Times*, August 13, 1995.

The quote from Paul Krugman on the limits to the global economy comes from his "Competitiveness: A Dangerous Obsession," *Foreign Affairs* 73 (March/April 1994). The passage on the ethnic makeup of Orange County, California, is from my own reporting. On the vexed question of intermarriage, see *The First Universal Nation*, by Ben Wattenberg (New York: Free Press, 1991). Two very different books on Latinos seem to me to be among the most important works on America published in the

1990s. First, *Mexican-Americans: The Ambivalent Minority*, by Peter Skerry (New York: Free Press, 1993), which combines rigorous fieldwork with sophisticated analysis and is a model of its kind—everyone interested in the future of this country should read it. Second: *Latino Voices* by Rodolfo de la Garza, et al. (Boulder, Colo.: Westview Press, 1992), which, by the simple device of quantitative surveys, manages to explode most of the arrant nonsense written about Latinos and their likely influence on American social and political norms. See also my own small tribute to de la Garza's work: "Columbus's Children," in *The Economist*, December 26, 1993. The quote from Andrew Hacker is from his *Two Nations: Black and White, Separate, Hostile, Unequal* (New York: Scribner's, 1992), and the one from Shelby Steele is from *The Content of Our Character* (New York: St. Martin's, 1990).

For the concentration of black poverty, see *The Truly Disadvantaged*, by William Julius Wilson, op. cit., and Wilson's concluding paper, "Public Policy Research and the Truly Disadvantaged," in the collection *The Urban Underclass*, edited by Jencks and Peterson, op. cit. George Will's view of class and race can be found in *Newsweek*, June 26, 1995. For Newt Gingrich's views on the occasional desirability of a strong federal government, see *Newsweek*, April 10, 1995. The nature of the overlapping responsibilities of local governments is discussed in *Halfway Home and a Long Way to Go*, Southern Growth Policies Board, op. cit.; thanks to Jesse White for pointing out that ten years after that report, local government remained unreformed. The discussion of enduring regional distinctions owes much to *Albion's Seed*, by David Hackett Fischer (New York: Oxford University Press, 1989). John Lewis's warnings on the risks of America coming apart were reported in the *Washington Post* March 25, 1995. I would never have dreamed of driving to Palm Springs "optimistically" without having read, long before I ever went there, *Los Angeles*, by Reyner Banham (London: Allen Lane, 1971). The long quote from Woodrow Wilson (which, more than any other single source, inspired the theme of this book) comes from his review of Bryce's *The American Commonwealth* in the *Political Science Quarterly*, March 1889. I found the quote in *The Cycles of American History*, by Arthur M. Schlesinger, Jr. (Boston: Houghton Mifflin, 1986).

Epilogue

For the capital during World War II, when my neighborhood was settled, see *Washington Goes to War*, by David Brinkley (New York: Knopf, 1988). The symposium "Our Country and Our Culture" was published in *The Partisan Review* 19:3–5 (1952). For the curse of unrealizable expectations, see *People of Plenty*, by David Potter, op. cit. The comparison between America and Australia grew out of conversations in Sydney with my cousin John McCririck. The tale of my two aunts' visit to America has been told before, in *Newsweek*, July 10, 1995. And I was unable to find an ending to the book better than that with which I concluded my article in *The Economist*, October 26, 1991.

INDEX